# GOOD GIRLS of CALIFORNIA

## A Red-Light History of the Golden State

Jan MacKell Collins

TWODOT®

GUILFORD, CONNECTICUT
HELENA, MONTANA

**A · TWODOT® · BOOK**

An imprint and registered trademark of The Rowman & Littlefield Publishing Group, Inc.
4501 Forbes Blvd., Ste. 200
Lanham, MD 20706
www.rowman.com

Distributed by NATIONAL BOOK NETWORK

British Library Cataloguing in Publication Information available

Library of Congress Control Number: 2020950632
ISBN 978-1-4930-5096-3 (paperback)
ISBN 978-1-4930-5097-0 (e-book)

♾™ The paper used in this publication meets the minimum requirements of American National Standard for Information Sciences—Permanence of Paper for Printed Library Materials, ANSI/NISO Z39.48-1992.

# CONTENTS

———•••———

# Contents

# ACKNOWLEDGMENTS

Having grown up in Southern California, I have been infatuated with the red-light ladies of the Golden State for quite some time. One of my fondest memories was the discovery of an image from the 1900s of a girl seated on a table in a skimpy outfit. This was in the 1970s at an antiques store in Julian. The young lady's cheerful, almost laughing face intrigued me. I think I paid a whole dollar for the picture, which I still have today. In my naiveté back then, I assumed she was a happy-go-lucky Coca-Cola girl or some such. But as I learned more about historical prostitution as a teenager, I came to see that I was quite wrong.

When my editor, Erin Turner, talked with me of writing a book about California's red-light history, I was elated. I have always loved California's intriguing history, from the days of the ranchos, to my 1960s childhood in Pasadena, to my beach-going days in San Diego, Laguna Beach, and Dana Point. Even when I visit today, certain sights and smells bring memories of my time there flooding back. Researching this book has been quite satisfying. It has reminded me of the ice plant and ivy-enveloped overpasses along the freeways. And the front yards and honeysuckle-filled back alleys of my childhood. I recall the sweet, musty smell of the house my godmother, Irene Smith, lived in. Irene was quite the party girl of yesteryear. Her first job was selling encyclopedias from her car with a girlfriend. After caring for her ailing mother in San Diego, she went to work at the Hotel del Coronado as a waitress. She married twice—first to a gambler and, after he died, to my godfather, Parker. She wound up a cheerful, sweet, and fun little old lady from Pasadena. My mother and I always wondered if Irene was a good time girl herself, but having no proof of that, I am satisfied with thanking her for encouraging me and inspiring me in my writing.

Other memories manifest from our backyard in San Diego, which connected to that of my oldest friend, Lanette Wray. Together, Lanette and I played out dozens of pretend scenarios in our yards and on her back porch, and they were often historic in nature. We faithfully watched *Little House on the Prairie*, spooked around the haunted Whaley House of Old Town, and immersed ourselves in history much more than other girls our age. Our own family histories intrigued us too, and it is little wonder that we both continue to love history today. I don't think I would have fallen so in love with stories of the past if it hadn't been for Lanette.

Of course, I have my parents to thank too. My family's vacations always revolved around visiting historic places, driving down dusty back roads and scouting out ghost towns. When we first visited Bodie in 1973, I simply fell in love with the history of the place and especially Rosa May, the legendary harlot whom so many love reading and writing about today. It has been some decades since I left California, but each time I visit I discover something new about the shady ladies of the West Coast. Most recently, my husband and I spent some time in Trinidad, just south of the Oregon border, where I learned about a good time girl known only as Cockeyed Florence. And, I am indebted to Joshua Lindsey and his gang at Emerald Forest RV & Cabins for allowing me to entertain them with stories and take time off work to do radio interviews at Humboldt State University's KHSU.

On a more scholarly level, I want to thank Lynn Zelem, my new production editor who has carefully gone over my manuscript. Another thank you goes to Bill Holland, former mayor of Powers, Oregon, for lending me B. A. Botkin's *A Treasury of Western Folklore*. This sweet treasure of a book contained some great stories about California's early years. Also,

## ACKNOWLEDGMENTS

Professor Jay Moynahan was, as usual, invaluable, and provided me with materials on Sacramento, San Francisco, San Luis Obispo, San Diego, the gold camps, and so many other places. His research is simply stellar. Thank you too to author Sherry Monahan whose awesome new book, *California Madams*, came out just in time to provide some needed clues as I began my research. Thanks also to Adam Conover, who invited me to be his guest on his show *Adam Ruins Everything*, when it was filmed at the historic Paramount Ranch in Santa Monica—which tragically burned in 2018. Thank you too to Nancy Degnan, who believes in me as both a friend and business partner. My "weird stuff-o-meter" went into the red when I found out she lived in a former brothel on Sunset Boulevard in Los Angeles, and I feel lucky that such unseen forces always seem to keep me in tune with my good time girls.

# INTRODUCTION

---◆●◆---

## *California: The Golden State*

California has a long and varied history. From its beginnings as the home of Native American tribes to explorations by European and Spanish explorers from about 1542 to 1821, the Golden State had long been subject to "divide and conquer" behavior. Especially after 1770, when a series of missions were erected up and down the coast, the lives of residents and newcomers alike were changed forever. Nobody could foresee, however, that the United States would wage a war with Mexico for control of California in 1846, or that the state's famous gold rush of 1848 would bring Anglo men by the tens of thousands along with an entirely new way of life.

A most interesting (and underappreciated) side chapter to the development of California was the prostitution industry, which would have a profound influence on the state as well. To the good time girls of the industry, the money made off pioneer men would quickly soar to profits never dreamed of by ordinary folk. For nearly two hundred years, soiled doves have wiled and beguiled their way through the bureaucratic red tape of governments, a bevy of would-be pimps, and even competitors from their own sex to survive in a man's world. The power and determination of these women is exemplary, even as they lived, and are often remembered for, their shameful lives.

As early as 1835, merchant seaman Richard Henry Dana Jr. made a precarious trip to the Pacific coast aboard the *Pilgrim*. During his year in California, Dana made copious notes about the women he encountered. They were described by him as dressed in European-style frocks bearing short sleeves, with "corsets not being in use." Their shoes were of kid leather or satin, and jewelry adorned their fingers, wrists, necks, and ears. Many of them were Spanish maidens whose way of dress, according to Dana, was "sometimes their ruin." This was not so much because the ladies were prostitutes, but because "if their husbands do not dress them well enough, they will soon receive presents from others." Indeed, Dana observed that parents wished for their daughters to marry well. But wives from any social status were subject to the attentions of other men at that early date. Men knew that the way to a woman's heart was through finery, and the better a woman was dressed, the less likely she was to be seduced by the others.[1]

Dana also commented that he had witnessed "an Indian to bring his wife, to whom he was lawfully married in the church, down to the beach and carry her back again, dividing the money which she had got from sailors."[2] The idea of renting one's wife to a sailor in exchange for money did not seem to bother the natives, as most tribes did not regard offering women for sex as naughty. Rather, the custom of trading, lending, and gifting the intimate favors of both wives and daughters was merely a friendly means of establishing good business relationships. To Mexican officials, however, doing so was offensive. Those women who were caught prostituting their bodies were whipped by the alcalde (the reigning magistrate) and put to menial work—unless they were able to buy the authorities off.[3]

When Sir James Douglas of Hudson's Bay Company arrived in California in 1840, he was told "that the ladies in California are not in general very refined or delicate in their conversation" and also that "even the most respectable classes prostitute their wives for hire, that is, they wink at the familiarity of a wealthy neighbor who pays handsomely for his entertainment." Douglas was inclined to agree with the tradition, noting that the "infamous practice was introduced from Mexico, where it is almost general."[4] But he also no doubt realized that prostitutes, not respectable wives, would keep the mostly single men of California content. In time, especially in the larger cities, red-light ladies were a boon to the economy. The women paid for rent or mortgages, property taxes, monthly license fees, court fines, and donations to charity. Dressmakers, furniture dealers, landlords, liquor dealers, music stores, pharmacies, physicians, police, theater managers, and others in the industry such as madams, pimps, and procurers—all of these and more made money from ladies of the red light.

California was annexed by the United States in 1847. The annexation came just in time, for only a year later, the California gold rush began. Prior to the rush, California's population was guessed to be between ten thousand and fourteen thousand. By 1849, the population had increased to one hundred thousand. California became a state in 1850. Five years later, the California legislature would declare that "keeping or residing in a house of ill fame was a misdemeanor." But California was a big state, and it was growing, fast. In an amazingly short amount of time, lawmen would become far too busy with other lawbreakers to pay much attention to women who sold their wares of their own volition.[5]

Especially in San Francisco, women were arriving in droves by 1850. Not all the women coming to California intended to become sex workers; rather, the female "gold diggers" were hoping to strike it rich by marrying prosperous gold miners or businessmen. When their endeavors proved unsuccessful, the women took cool advantage of being a rare sight among the gold camps and the growing cities and sold their favors instead. Other women, however, did come to California with the sole intention of getting rich as entertainers and prostitutes. In a time and place where women were so scarce, charging outrageous prices for services became a common practice. The ladies were there to make money, and they did so with a vengeance.

Not all women and would-be working girls arrived in California on their own free will. Some were enslaved Chinese girls who were sold to brothel keepers at public auctions. But a good many more were American women hell-bent on making good money, as well as French women who brought with them enviable fashion and style. It was the French ladies, too, who eventually earned the highest pay at certain brothels but also dealt cards for gambling houses. One man recalled Madame Ferrard, a twenty-one dealer who was "pretty as a picture." The man "began betting just to get near her and hear her talk" and remembered, "I lost seventy dollars and she did not notice me any more than the rest of the crowd." The gentleman may have lost his money, but he did not lose the girl; the two eventually married.[6]

Shady ladies also were present in the "Central Diggings" of California as early as 1850. "Vice and crime, I believe abounds more in this country than any other civilized state on the globe," noted newcomer Hiram Ferris. "Gambling of every sort, drinking and hoaring [sic] are common in every city, town and village in California."[7] Others commented on vice and its female participants as well. Of the naughty ladies she saw in 1851, Mrs. D. B. Bates wrote, "Well may it call a blush to the cheek of our own sex when I assert that the immoral predominated as far as the female portion of the community were concerned." Mrs. Bates was the author of *Incidents of Land and Water*, a book about her time in California. She was particularly focused on a harlot she called Lillie Lee. Lillie's mother had arrived in California with a goal to find a suitable home for herself and her daughter. Instead, Lillie ran off to the goldfields with a gambler. "Better, far better, had she immured herself and child in the catacombs of Rome than thus to have launched their frail bark upon the golden wave of a California sea," lectured Bates.[8]

But Lillie's mother perhaps surprised Mrs. Bates when she, "armed with a Colt revolver," went after her daughter and the gambler. In looking for Lillie, the mother visited several houses of prostitution where she saw "elegantly attired women within whose natures long since had expired the last flickering spark of feminine modesty." At last the woman found the couple shacked up at a house. When she knocked on the door and the gambler answered, Lillie's mother pointed the gun at his chest. Lucky for him, Lillie was able to stop her mother from pulling the trigger. The gambler soothed the mother with the promise to marry Lillie. Unfortunately, however, the man was already married. Where the mother went from there remains unknown, but Lillie herself went "down, down, down." Mrs. Bates described her as appearing "in a splendid Turkish costume which admirably displayed her tiny little foot encased in richly embroidered satin slippers." On other occasions, Lillie rode her horse around town "habited in a closely fitting riding dress of black velvet, ornamented with a hundred and fifty gold buttons, a hat from which depended magnificent sable plumes, and over her face, a short white lace veil of the richest texture . . . the fire of passion flashing from the depths of her dark, lustrous eyes. She took all captive. Gold and diamonds were showered upon her." The point of Mrs. Bates's lecture about the perils of Lillie Lee may have been lost on her readers, for the girl seems to have gone off on a most successful career. Only her mother, in the end, suffered heartbreak and loss.[9]

Women like Lillie Lee who made good money were able to outfit themselves in the fanciest of silks and lace. Their manner and dress influenced even respectable women, who also desired to emulate the latest styles. How could they not? French prostitutes often arrived in America wearing the latest fashions from Paris, accoutrements that were mighty scarce in California. And, the income generated by all prostitutes was better than other women and even some men. Soiled doves could therefore afford to order expensive dresses from the few catalogs available or through local merchants, or even from local seamstresses who were instructed to recreate high-dollar, fashionable gowns. The 1855 *Annals of California* noted that "In Eastern cities the prostitute tried to imitate in manner and dress the fashionable respected ladies . . . in San Francisco the rule was reversed—the latter copying the former."[10]

Indeed, dignity, envy, and desire for beauty could not prevent wives and honest women from being upstaged by the local harlots. The women knew that if they could not keep up with the prostitutes, at least where fashion was concerned, their husbands might be inclined to wander into the arms of some strumpet or another. Writer J. Ross Browne noted in his article for *Harper's New Monthly Magazine* in 1865 that the "Spaniards are flush, and like sailors, spend their money on the fair sex with a prodigal hand. Señoritas from San Jose know where their charms can be appreciated, and stage-loads of them arrive in season to partake of the festivities. The late Superintendent undertook to place an embargo upon this branch of commerce, but did not succeed. Enterprising females would come in spite of rules and regulations."[11]

Browne was correct; Anglo women were arriving in larger numbers by 1877. With them, and the men they served, came more gambling, more drinking, and more violence. At the mining camp of Darwin, Jack McGinnis found one of his lady friends, prostitute Nancy Williams, murdered in her home in September. Nancy was in her late forties by the time she arrived in Darwin and was considered an "old fairy." Little was known about her except that she had plied her trade throughout the West, lately at the mining camp of Panamint, before moving to Darwin. She was given the euphemistic nicknames "Aunt Nancy" and also "Featherlegs." In Darwin, Nancy owned a "boardinghouse" next to the Headquarters Saloon. On September 12, McGinnis came to see her around 4 a.m. and found her house in disarray.

It took the lighting of several matches to find Nancy herself, and McGinnis was aghast at what he saw. Nancy was lying facedown on the floor, blood on her face. The man fled in search of help. Two other men, Isaac Giles and Constable William Welch, returned with him. A person unknown had hit the woman three times on the left side of her head and once on the back of her skull. Oddly, two oyster cans filled with nearly six hundred dollars of Nancy's hard-earned savings were untouched—largely because they consisted of company scrip, bank orders, and silver, which was no longer acceptable tender in Darwin. Following a funeral procession attended by much of the town and several fellow prostitutes, Nancy was buried in the local cemetery.[12]

In spite of her tragic end, Nancy Williams had been well-liked around Darwin. The town's newspaper, *Coso Mining News*, complimented her as "being one of the kindest and most liberal of women" who gave "from her purse to all public enterprises." A reward of $1,200 was immediately offered for the capture of her murderer. But no evidence to convict came forward until 1953, when a previously unpublished account of the affair was printed in the *Pony Express Courier*. In it, one Oliver Roberts claimed he knew all about the murder and that Jack McGinnis had done it. The motive was money; when McGinnis saw that Nancy's savings were worthless in Darwin, he beat her to death. Roberts had plenty of information to back up his claim, but none of it was documented. Also, Roberts's memories of the event were quite different from those generated by the coroner, witnesses, and newspapers of the time. Roberts tried to reveal all when his memoirs were published in 1931, but the editor had chosen not to use the account because it could not be substantiated. By the time the tale was finally told in 1953, there was nobody left who could verify the truth.[13]

By 1880, the influx of both people and businesses in California had stabilized the economy to a great degree. The average wages for a prostitute in the western United States were now twenty-five cents to a dollar per customer for ten minutes of the lady's time. California's naughty girls now sometimes moved to other states in their quest for work—or at least to hide their true professions from their families. In 1880, nineteen-year-old Mary Healey, a California native, was recorded by the census as working at the palatial brothel of Annie Hamilton in Prescott, Arizona. With her was an eight-month-old son, Henry. What became of the child remains unknown, but ten years later the *San Francisco Call* published the only known news article about Mary. "An Insane Woman's Suicide," read the headline of the short story, which continued, "Stockton, April 4—Mary Healey, aged 28 years, drowned herself near Acampo, in this county, Thursday afternoon. She was idiotic and unable to care for herself. She deliberately walked into a lake fifteen feet deep. Her body was found a few hours later."[14]

Mary Healey was just one of many shady ladies to travel from and back to California. By the time of her death, San Diego, Los Angeles, San Francisco, and other large cities had long-established, sizable demimondes where thousands of women plied their trade. The 1900 census recorded approximately 729 women with such occupations as dance-hall girl, house of ill fame, mistress, prostitute, saloonkeeper, sporting woman, and even whore—but there were surely many more than that, and notably, many of the ladies were identified as Chinese. In a day when laws were becoming more stringent, women of the night were becoming more and more inclined to tell the census taker they were working at respectable jobs, lest their true occupations come to the attention of authorities.

Although some cities had established their own laws against the prostitution industry by the turn of 1900, California governor Hiram Johnson finally took matters into his own hands in 1913. On April 7, California passed the Red Light Abatement Act, wherein red-light houses across the state were to be closed, with fines and jail for those who violated the new statute. The act was the brainchild of Johnson, who had adapted a similar law targeting the liquor industry in Iowa. Not only would houses of prostitution become illegal, but the authorities would have the power to "remove 'fixtures and movable property' from such buildings," prohibit the property owners from using their buildings for "any use for one year unless court releases same upon bond of owner," set fees "for the removal of fixtures and property, and require that the owner of the property pay the fees," and allow the sale of the said removed fixtures and property "to settle the removal costs."[15]

The official vote for the Red Light Abatement Act was set for the November 3, 1914 election. Arguments for the abatement noted that similar, successful laws had already been passed in nine other states, as well as the District of Columbia. "The owner who rents property for legitimate purposes has nothing to fear from this law," read the ballot. "It simply requires that owners shall know as much about the use of their property as their neighbors know. The owner who rents property for purposes of prostitution has much to fear." But opponents of the act rightfully expressed concern that any owners "of a flat building, rooming house, apartment house or hotel, or even an office building, may become the innocent victim of these sections, and unless the owners thereof establish a censor of morals in their buildings, they will soon become the innocent victims of enthusiastic reformers. But one act of prostitution, assignation or lewdness in any building is sufficient to cause the building to be abated."[16]

Other fears expressed included the assumption that prostitutes would move into other buildings, owned by other landlords, and continue their business there—thereby making more and more buildings subject to abatement. Property damage to such places also was a great concern because it could result in an impaired value of the property. "The property owner and his respectable tenant will pay the price of this act of the legislature," warned the argument, "but, irrespective of that, the prostitute will go merrily on, plying her trade as she has plied it from the beginning, and a citizen will always be doubtful as to the character of the person in the house next door."[17]

None of those for or against the act had anything to offer in the way of rehabilitation or finding respectable jobs for prostitutes, but certainly the concern must have been there. While male brothel owners might certainly find other business endeavors and remain successful, prostitutes would be relegated to menial, low-paying jobs. Many of them would remain unemployed if their prospective employers became aware of their shady pasts. Single and widowed women, and mothers especially, would suffer under impoverished conditions—which was the biggest reason most of them became prostitutes in the first place. Perhaps this underlying truth was why the vote barely passed with only 53 percent casting their ballot in favor of the abatement.

The Red Light Abatement Act, combined with military efforts to close down the industry during World War I, was the end of frontier prostitution as many knew it. As in other places, however, a whole new slew of good time girls would make their debuts in the years following and keep California as lively as it had ever been. By 1923, the infamous Sally Stanford, madam and future mayor of Sausalito, remembered that San Francisco's Tenderloin "was teeming with prosperity."[18] Farther south, Hollywood's budding film industry would see its share of starlets who landed themselves on the proverbial "casting couch" in their efforts to become famous. A whole new generation of good time girls began anew, leaving a history of harlotry all over California that is still talked about today.

# CHAPTER 1

———◦•◦———

## Gilded Girls: The Courtesans of California's Mining Camps

The mining and logging camps scattered throughout California were numerous and diverse. Gold remained the highest mineral on the prospector's list, but there were other interests as well, mainly silver and even borax. Beginning in the 1840s, gold discoveries brought a slew of settlers from all over the world. Instant wealth was on the mind of many a miner as prospectors scrambled for their share of the gold. They came by ship or in wagons, afoot, or on horseback across the barren and hot deserts between California and the rest of the United States. Over time, anything from small camps to blooming metropolises could be found along the coast, in the deserts, or high in the mountains.

In 1848, gold was discovered at Sutter's Mill on the present site of Sacramento, which was first called Coloma. Stories vary about who first came across the gold; one story credits mill owner John Sutter and his carpenter, James Marshall, who tried to keep the find a secret. It wasn't hard to do, since the area had but few Anglo settlers anyway. When general store owner Sam Brannan got wind of the discovery, however, he filled a small bottle with the stuff and proceeded to budding San Francisco. There, he rode down Montgomery Street calling out, "Gold, gold from the American River!" The rush was on.[1]

Sutter, who stood to become quite wealthy, began calling his mill Sutter's Fort. The infant camp was a logical stopping place, since new arrivals could gather information and supplies there. But Sutter, and many others, would be fairly trampled in the wake of thousands of prospectors who swarmed into California looking to get rich. In time, additional gold discoveries would be made east, north, and south from Sacramento. On the northern coast and inland, places like Crescent City, French Gulch, Happy Camp, Orleans, Redding, Shasta, Weed, Whiskeytown, and many others sprang up. One camp, Douglas City, was initially occupied by Native Americans—until Pierson B. Reading discovered gold along the Trinity River. The settlement was quickly overrun, an event that did not please the inhabitants. During a skirmish with settlers, an entire village was killed with the exception of two small girls and a boy. The latter child managed to hide, raised himself, and became known as "Indian Bob." One of the girls, christened Ellen Clifford, was raised by whites and eventually moved to Weaverville. The other child was taken in by an Anglo woman and later sold to a teamster for forty-five dollars.

Naturally, the majority of the first Anglo settlers in California's goldfields were men, and most of them were in dire need of female companionship. One prospector remembered that he "went to minin'" in what he called "the Amador" (possibly the creek of the same name in today's Amador County). At "first they wasn't a woman in a hundred miles," he noted. "And when one did come in one day on a wagon, the men all run to look at her as if she was a show. Better she'da stayed away, an' twenty more like her that come in when the diggings [sic] began to pan out rich. I believe every woman was the cause o' fifty fights an' one or two deaths." The miner further commented that it angered him to see the men fight, because "they knowed [sic] jest what they was—men that had mothers an' sisters back in the States, an' some of 'em sweethearts an' wives." The women who appeared, he said, "was mostly Mexican women, an' some Chilayanos an' South Spainers; an' somehow it was a sort o' comfort to me that there was hardly ever an American woman among the lot."[2]

The man did not comment about the enslaving of Native American girls nor the sex trafficking of young women from Mexico, South America, and the Pacific Islands. No commentary was given either about the Chinese women and children who would be imported from their native lands to serve as prostitute slaves. But while these poor girls were traded and sold like chattel, Anglo men also began yearning to see their own countrywomen. Advertising for mail-order brides was soon appearing in eastern newspapers. One paper in Valparaiso, Indiana, read, "Wanted. Two hundred girls, white, poor, and of irreproachable conduct, not altogether destitute of grace and beauty, to be shipped to CALIFORNIA, and to be there honorably married to the thousands of North Americans and other foreigners who have made their fortunes in the mines, and desire to get married." The advertisement went on to give more particulars, requesting priests to accompany the girls, or their fathers, who would receive half-price passage. Only one trunk per person was allowed, and no advance money was required—but it was made clear that the ships "will not receive any other class of passengers" and would remain in San Francisco for two months.[3]

The virtuous women who would surely answer such advertisements and come west were soon countered with a handful of Anglo floozies, who traveled any way they could to California's gold camps. Placerville, established in 1848, was just one of these places. In January 1849, five men attempted to rob a Mexican gambler and were arrested. There being no jail in which to hold the robbers, a jury of twelve men was selected and ordered the thieves "to receive each thirty-nine lashes." Next, it was discovered that three of the men—two Frenchmen and a "Chileno"— had participated in another robbery and attempted murder elsewhere. A second trial was held, during which the three men were unable to stand up, let alone speak in their own defense, due to the lashes applied to them from the other trial. The men were found guilty and hanged by an angry mob of drunken miners. Thereafter, Placerville was nicknamed "Hangtown." Placerville also had its own little ditty about the wayward women who settled there:

*Hangtown gals are plump and rosy,*
*Hair in ringlets mighty cosy [sic];*
*Painted cheeks and gassy bonnets,*
*Touch them and they'll sting like hornets.*[4]

*Placerville's famous Hangman's Tree is commemorated on a building today.* Jon B. Lovelace Collection of California Photographs, Carol M. Highsmith's American Project, Library of Congress

More and more prospectors came to California as news of the gold rush continued spreading. Stories were told of nuggets being found when a man simply pulled up his tent stake or while cleaning out a cooking pot. The precious metal, it seemed, was literally everywhere. Hundreds of mining camps, most of them temporary, sprang up to house thousands of people. More often than not, these same places would shrink down to nothing once the gold supply was depleted. One such place, Columbia, was founded in 1850. The population was twenty thousand people one year and only five hundred citizens the next.

One of the best-known tales of Columbia occurred during its heyday in 1855. Former prostitute Martha Carlos had retired from her profession and married John Barclay or Barkley in the fall. The newlyweds opened a saloon together. All was bliss until one John Huron Smith came into the saloon, drunk, and demanded to be served. When Martha refused, Smith gave her a "hard shove." Smith's timing could not have been worse, for the insult was witnessed by Barclay as he entered the room. The incensed husband shot Smith dead. Barclay was immediately tried for murder, the crowd siding with the drunken Smith rather than a man who had married a fallen woman. A short time later, Barclay was hanged from a water flume for defending his wife.[5] The widowed Martha was forced to return to her profession as a prostitute and was employed as such at nearby Sonora in 1860.

By the time of John Barclay's untimely death, most of California's gold camps sported a red-light district, or at least some fancy girls. Mokelumne Hill, founded in 1848, became a rough settlement with shootings, wild women, and Chinese sex slaves. When the Hotel de France (now known as Hotel Legèr) was built, the structure served as a courthouse, gambling den, post office, and saloon. Allegedly, a tunnel ran under the hotel that led to a brothel across the street. Later, another building was constructed expressly for keeping enslaved Chinagirls who were regularly auctioned off to men.

There were more: At Coulterville, founded in 1850, a saloon and fandango hall was in place within a year. Whiskeytown also was founded in 1850 after two barrels of whiskey being lugged into the new camp fell off a cliff, along with the mule carrying them. It took two years for the first white woman to make an appearance in Whiskeytown, but by the latter part of the decade a man known as Bon Mix was running a saloon and dance hall. The women working for him were deemed "young ladies of probable virtue," but real women of the night were available in a "small row of cribs" at the edge of town.[6] All of these places, and more, featured a raw, frontier lawlessness that left newcomers from the East aghast. Only the short-lived mining camp of Quartzburg, in Mariposa County, was able to quell the gaggle of murderers, harlots, and gamblers who quickly invaded the camp. The "peaceful element," according to one source, managed to eject all of them from the budding town. Many of those thrown out of Quartzburg simply moved down the road a bit to another camp, Hornitos.[7]

By 1851, shady ladies were rampant in California's gold camps. Shortly after Sonora was founded by a group of Mexicans, American prospectors moved in and were soon followed by "the lowest elements" of white men. Gambling houses, opium dens, and bordellos were soon added to Sonora's growing businesses.[8] Given the number of wayward women infiltrating such places, it is not surprising that the only legal hanging of a woman in California was a prostitute at Downieville on July 5, 1851. Her name was Josefa "Juanita" Loaiza-Segvia, and she was a just-retired prostitute who lived with a man identified only as Jose. The night before her death, one Frederick Alexander Augustus "Jack" Cannon was well into his cups when he stumbled and accidentally fell through the door of Juanita's house. Cannon's two friends picked him up, and the three went on home without incident.

The next morning, Cannon and a friend made the fatal error of stopping by Juanita's home to offer a more sincere apology.[9] Juanita, described as "23 years old and a very beautiful petite woman" with "long black flowing hair" and a "hot blooded personality" answered the door, along with Jose. As Cannon spoke to the couple, Juanita suddenly lost her temper and stabbed the man with a "large bowie knife." The weapon pierced his heart and killed him instantly. The townspeople's reaction was immediate. A mob formed, held a quick trial, and sentenced Juanita to hang. She met her fate at a bridge over the Yuba River. Legend states that Juanita "threw her hat to a friend and said, 'Adios, señores,'" before placing the noose around her neck herself. Then her hands were tied as a white handkerchief was knotted around her eyes. A pistol was fired, and Juanita "dropped three feet to her death."[10] Another source claims a physician who verified that Juanita was pregnant tried to save her, but was "compelled to leave the district" for attempting to do so. Whether he was the same man who was "dragged bodily from the platform of the scaffold and literally kicked out of town" is unknown.[11]

One of the more famous visitors to the California gold camps in 1851 was Louise Clapp, better known as the writer Dame Shirley. Louise arrived at the budding town of Rich Bar and took up quarters at a former brothel which was then known as the Empire Hotel. The lady gave a lively description of the hotel, which still exhibited shades of its bawdy past. "The Empire is the only two-story building in town," she noted, with "two or three glass windows" and built of "planks of the roughest possible description." Inside was a virtual Ali Baba's cave for such a primitive town. The first floor contained a barroom "with that eternal crimson calico which flushes the whole social life of the Golden State with its everlasting red, in the center of a fluted mass of which gleams a really elegant mirror, set off by a background of decanters, cigar-vases, and jars of fruit; the whole forming a *tout ensemble* of dazzling splendor."

Upstairs, "on each side of a narrow entry, are four eight-by-ten bedrooms, the floors of which are covered by straw matting." Each was furnished with "little tables covered with oilcloth, and bedsteads so heavy that nothing short of a giant's strength could move them. Indeed I am convinced that they were built, piece by piece, on the spot where they now stand." Louise further wrote that the "entire building is lined with purple calico, alternately with a delicate blue, and the effect is really quite pretty." It did not escape Louise that the place was built by gamblers and cost eight thousand dollars to be used as a brothel by "unfortunates." By the time she arrived, however, the harlots had moved on and there were only four other women living in Rich Bar.[12]

Rich Bar was smack-dab in the middle of today's Plumas National Forest, but by 1852 good time girls were finding quarters all over the state. They were not always welcome. At Cold Springs, William H. Hampton recalled that some people "tore down a house of ill fame and destroyed all of its effects." At Shasta in October of 1855, Frank Golden was found guilty of running a house of prostitution and fined $410 dollars or forty days in jail. The man chose the latter punishment. A day later, prostitutes Luisa Howard and Matilda Maranda also were fined $250 and $300, respectively. Matilda apparently ran her own bordello; the story about her arrest in the October 10 issue of the *Shasta Courier* was accompanied by an advertisement for the sale of her place, Trinity House, "cheap and for cash."[13]

In Inyo County, silver was discovered by Mexican miners at Cerro Gordo in 1865. Within a short time numerous mines appeared, and by 1868 folks were flocking to the new town. Among them were Anglo capitalists from San Francisco, who formed the Union Mining Company and quickly bought up all the claims they could. By 1870, "several saloons and two houses of prostitution" were available to entertain the miners, a group which consisted of white men but also Mexicans who stayed on as wage labor.[14] One of the town's most prominent and wealthy madams was Lola Travis, a veteran of gold rush California since about 1850. Lola's given name was Delores Treviso. She was a native of Mexico and was only thirteen years old when she first appeared in the census at the camp of Sonora with her two younger brothers, whom Lola supported by working in a fandango hall. By 1853 she had given birth to the first of three children, who came along in quick succession. Long after the father of her children died, Lola and her family (which now included her mother) moved to Lone Pine in 1867. Lola had made enough money not just to support her family, but also to buy a lot on which to build her first saloon. She became a respected member of the community, known for running a clean business and using her profits to feed her mother, brothers, and children—the latter of whom were housed away from the saloon and attended school.

Unfortunately, Lola was not the best mother. One source says she was "harsh, unforgiving and sometimes violent, often hitting" her children hard enough to leave a scar. Such was the price to pay for a mother who was the sole support of her brood. Lola invested her money in other places such as Sageland, where she met saloon owner George Snow. The man would later move to Cerro Gordo; Lola followed after the birth of another child. In 1871, Lola was able to buy out Snow's saloon property and other lots. Soon, a "string of cribs" were lined up behind a fandango hall owned by Lola. At the other end of the street was her only competitor, Petera Romero aka "Mrs. Moore." Petera ran a place known as "Waterfall's" or the "Waterfall."[15]

Fights, shoot-outs, and other violence were common at Lola's. From the rough residents of Cerro Gordo, the lady really could expect no less. These incidents, as well as her wealth, her habit of fancy dress, and being "adorned with gold jewelry," made Lola well-known throughout the entire region. Everyone knew about "Lola's Place," and plenty of bad men and women visited there. Newspapers were rife with shootings there, but Lola was helpless to do much about it. She did, however, donate to the building of a new jail in Cerro Gordo. Petera Romero also donated to the effort, but both women stubbornly refused to abide by a new law in 1872 which forbade opening on Sundays. Lola, Petera, and two other saloon owners were taken to court and fined between ten and fifteen dollars each. Lola was already a familiar face around the county courthouse at Independence, which she visited regularly to assure her property taxes and business licenses were up to date. Besides breaking the new law in 1872, Lola had one other issue: She had kept her house and saloon in Lone Pine, which fell during a large earthquake in March. Lola rebuilt, and some of her family members eventually moved there to live.[16]

In 1875 Lola expanded her business again, this time to the budding camp of Darwin. As before, her new brothel did well but also suffered from occasional violence. In about 1877, a customer named Felipe Perades showed up but was turned away because Lola was busy with another man. The infuriated Perades accused the madam of only liking "gringo sons of bitches" and threatened her with a knife. He was ousted from the house but lingered outside. When he saw Lola's shadow against a window curtain, he lunged at it with his stiletto—and missed. Lola returned the gesture by opening her door and shooting the man in the hip. He died a day later. Lola was taken to trial but acquitted of murder. Even the *Coso Mining News* supported the lady's claim of self-defense.[17]

Darwin and Cerro Gordo eventually began failing due to a decline in mineral production. Then in 1880, Waterfall's (which had become a residence) caught fire. The ensuing blaze burned many businesses, including Lola's dance hall and home. Her losses increased even more when a thief broke into her Lone Pine home and stole her jewelry. Lola wisely took a husband, Refugio Moreno, who was nearly twenty years younger than she and soon opened a saloon in Lone Pine. Theirs was wedded bliss for about three years, until Lola left her husband in 1883 and set out for Mojave. Most of Lola's old properties were now worthless, but with almost all her children grown, she had a chance to start over. Another fire, however, burned her out. The willful woman moved again, this time to Tehachapi where she met railroad supervisor Thomas Cronin. The two married in Los Angeles in 1889 and settled into ranching life in Cummings Valley. Unfortunately for Cronin, Lola was as abusive to her new husband as she had been to her children. Once, she even "picked him up bodily and set him down on the hot surface of her cook stove." For reasons known only to himself, Cronin stayed with her. By his doing so, Lola gained status as a respectable man's wife, and the couple took up mining in about 1900. Cronin formed the San Antonio Mining and Mill Company. Eleven years later the Cronins moved to Bakersfield. Lola died in 1912. Her obituary glossed over the fact that she was once a prominent madam but her great grandchildren keep her story alive today.[18] Most of Cerro Gordo's residents, including the wicked ladies, also moved on after 1880 when mineral production declined—until 1911, when zinc ores resulted in another boom. In the 1970s the rebuilt Waterfall still stood as a former "gilded house of pleasure" in Cerro Gordo.[19]

Fortunately for the good time girls, the desert camps of California remained relatively free of interference from decent citizens. Maybe it was just too darn hot: Panamint City, founded in 1873 at the edge of Death Valley, was surrounded by desert and barren of trees. If it weren't for the rich minerals unearthed there, the prospectors might have chosen a more accessible place, for the rocky terrain offered very few flat spots on which to build. Madam Lola Travis was the first woman to buy property there. Other prostitutes included Nancy Williams and Minnie Wells, the latter of whom opened a dance hall. Panamint's Little Chief Street was soon dubbed "Maiden Lane." The brothels fit in quite nicely with a barrage of saloons up on Main Street. Panamint City quickly became known as a "bad and wicked" town, to the extent that Wells Fargo declined to open a branch office there.[20]

Reigning madams of Panamint also included Martha Camp, who arrived in November of 1874 and whose girls initially came from Virginia

City, Nevada. Her first property on Maiden Lane connected with the Oriental saloon owned by Dave Naegle. Martha was in for a profitable winter; the *Anaheim Gazette* reported that there were "700 men, 10 women and six inches of snow in Panamint and lively times are expected."[21] Among Martha's new clients was Jim Bruce, a temperamental man who was occupied promoting the town. On March 22, 1875, Martha was at her place as Bruce, another man identified as Ed Barstow, and several others engaged in conversation. Sometime after midnight, Barstow and the others left. Bruce stayed behind to spend the rest of the night with Martha.

The madam later recalled how Barstow returned and "asked me to open the door. I replied that I was in bed. He said: 'If you don't open the door, I will kick it in.'" Barstow also demanded to see Bruce. When Martha finally opened the door, she saw that Barstow "had a six-shooter in his hand, and remarked: 'I've got the long legged son of a bitch at last.'" Martha did her best to keep the man from her bedroom door, but he got in anyway. Bruce had been in bed when Martha last saw him, and Barstow managed to blow out the lamp before a shoot-out commenced. Martha believed Barstow was the first to fire a shot, but "did not see [Bruce] until he told me to light the lamp." Barstow was suffering from a fatal gunshot and was duly carried to Bruce's house. Before he died, Barstow "exonerated Bruce of any responsibility and asked that no charges be pressed against him." Bruce was duly acquitted.[22]

In July of 1876, a mass of wicked thunderstorms descended on the entire Panamint area. The local mill blew its whistle to warn of an impending flood, but before anyone could do much the "waters descended from the towering walls about Panamint in a thundering deluge; a wave variously estimated at from five to seven feet high swept down Main Street headed for the canyon below." Much of the town washed away, including the brothels of Maiden Lane.[23] Martha Camp relocated to Darwin, which quickly "developed into a lusty young giant with all the trappings, the saloons, red light houses and roisterous goings-on characteristic of those days." When that town also failed, she left for Bodie in 1879.[24]

Martha Camp was not the only memorable good time girl of the desert. In 1893, a woman known as "Mexican Nell" made her way from Black Mountain near San Francisco to Goler Gulch, a booming mining town some one hundred miles east of Bakersfield. Nell was described as "a curvaceous dark-eyed woman" with a "volcanic" temperament. The lady was a welcome site to the men at Goler Gulch and was "willing to relieve the camp of its tedium and the boys of their [gold] dust." Nell and her girls favored hanging out at Nugent's, a saloon featuring live music and plenty of miners.[25]

Mexican Nell and others like her constituted one of the last generations of gold-camp girls to wander among California's mining towns. By the time gold was discovered at Rand Camp in 1895, California's mining population was a bit more subdued. Eventually rechristened Randsburg, the boomtown soon had the usual influx of gamblers, saloon men, and shady ladies. But the red-light district and its accompanying vices preferred to remain happily rowdy versus violent and dangerous. Furthermore, Randsburg harlots appear to have been welcome to intersperse their business houses among the other legitimate professional buildings of the day. One source talks of "the fluzy [sic] barn" that was located in the heart of the business district.[26]

In December of 1901, a newcomer to Randsburg visited a local dentist to have his tooth pulled. The dentist soon realized his patient had smallpox. The illness spread throughout town, and by the end of Christmas over two hundred people had been relegated to the "Pest House," a large tent acting as a quarantine area. Some of the first patients at the Pest House were prostitutes. When the head physician discovered the ladies were servicing clients from the tent, he procured some respectable men with shotguns to stand guard at the entrance. Those prostitutes who did not catch the dreaded pox took care of the sick at the Pest House—including the respectable women who disliked them.

One patient who refused to enter the Pest House at all was Madam Fay. One day Fay summoned a Dr. MacDonald to her brothel. The doctor found her lying in bed in her room with the curtains drawn. The madam told him she had accidentally applied croton oil, a foul-smelling oil used as a laxative, to her face. Dr. MacDonald examined Fay's swollen red features and gave her something to relieve the pain. Sometime later, Madam Fay saw MacDonald on the street and revealed she actually had been afflicted with smallpox but did not want to be quarantined at the Pest House. Fay thought her little joke was quite funny, but history does not record whether MacDonald felt the same way.

The real scourge of the town, at least according to the respectable element, was "French Marguerite" Roberts. Born in France, Marguerite was a widow with a young son when she first appeared in Randsburg circa 1896. The boy, August, was sent off to school in Bakersfield as Marguerite opened a saloon. Nothing else was known of her until January 11, 1903, when she was running a "bagnio" called the Oasis. That night, Lewis Handi or Hanley of San Francisco appeared at the Oasis. Handi wanted to see one of Marguerite's girls, Ollie Blake, whose real name was Kitty Palmer. They were old friends, he explained. What Marguerite didn't know was that Handi was there to convince Kitty to leave and "abandon her life of shame." The girl was packing her trunk when Marguerite got wind of what was going on. The angry madam sent her bouncer, Michael Suzzallo, upstairs to "interfere." Handi shot Suzzallo twice, once in the windpipe and again in the knee.[27] A few weeks later Suzzallo died. Handi was charged with murder.

An alternate version of this tale claims Ollie had come to town for a job at a honky-tonk, with no knowledge of what it entailed. Upon discovering her mistake, she "stayed behind locked doors" as sympathetic miners sent for her brother. It was he who posed as a customer and gained entrance to the young woman's room. The madam's bouncer was identified as "Big Mitch," and after he was shot, the madam insisted that the killer be put on trial. When the girl's brother was acquitted, the madam vowed to kill Judge Wynne, the defense lawyer in the case.[28]

However the story of Ollie really happened, Marguerite was still running a saloon in June when the building burned during a fire. Her all-new parlor house was well-known by 1905, probably because she openly operated very near to Rinaldi's Market. Mothers, resentful at having to usher their children past Marguerite's door, eventually filed complaints and demanded a segregated red-light district. A letter to the local government in one newspaper charged that "the said Marguerite keeps and runs a dance hall in the very center of the business section of our town; that it is so situated that ourselves and our children are compelled to pass and repass this abominable brothel every time we go to the post office, the drugstore, the meat market, and the Wells Fargo Company office."[29]

The complainants also claimed "that we are continually being insulted by the inmates of this brothel, who are common prostitutes." The article ended by asking "in the name of high heaven and common decency that your honorable body will revoke the saloon license of said Marguerite, and that the other place be licensed to run on the principal streets of our town." The letter ended with a dire warning: "A fire is liable to start during a drunken orgy any night," the writer said, "and once started would quickly wipe out the whole lower half of town, businesses, homes, rooming houses, hotel, and on these windy nights it is hard to tell where it would stop. Under the law our officers have the power to enter all places of unsavory reputation frequented by women and arrest and punish as vagrants everyone found therein." Those people fighting against Marguerite were perhaps justified, but the madam had "accumulated much money, owning the theatre and some other buildings [in Randsburg], besides money in the bank." Marguerite's wealth gave her power, and she knew it. Once again, Judge Wynne was the subject of the woman's wrath after he charged her for some crime—probably running a bawdy house. In court, Marguerite seized a bottle of ink and hurled it at the man. Wynne ducked, but the bottle hit the wall behind him and splattered him with ink.[30]

The tirade continued against Marguerite for two more years, during which petitions, letters, and court cases were filed against her. But the woman had many friends, who defended her as much as possible. Yet her death on April 6, 1907, largely went unnoticed by the papers. San Luis Obispo's *Morning Tribune* on April 23 merely mentioned that "Marguerite Roberts died at her home last Tuesday." Only the *Bakersfield Californian* elaborated further, stating that Marguerite died from some sort of lung trouble "with no hope of recovery" and that she had recently inherited a large sum of money following the death of her father. The article at least expressed some sentiment toward the lady, ending with, "We fervently say, 'Requiescat in peace.'" Marguerite was interred in the Rand District Cemetery at Johannesburg. Whoever tended to her estate took pains to erect a sizable tombstone for her, headed with the one word which surely made the respectable ladies pause in their scorn for the woman. It read, simply, "Mother."[31]

The last known rip-roaring mining camp of the California desert, located in San Bernardino County, was named for miner Pete Osdick in 1919. Osdick liked having a town named for him. When W. Hampton Williams discovered California Rand Silver Mine in 1922 and wanted the town named Hampton, both he and Osdick applied for a post office under their desired names. Osdick won. The town prospered for about a decade—not just because of the silver mine, but also because the town continued to offer both ladies and liquor even after national prohibition in 1920. In this remote desert spot were some thirty saloons with colorful names like the Annex, Irene's, Little Eva's, the Monkey House, the Northern, the Owl, the Pacific, the Red Onion, and the Silver Dollar.

And, of course, most of these illicit places featured gambling and good time girls. They said that the post office was about the only public building in town where one couldn't get a drink. "Where every night is Saturday night," read one advertisement, "and every Saturday night is 4th of July."[32]

The red-light ladies of Osdick were "considered good looking, clean and good company," and favored using one short nickname. Writer Cecile Page Vargo named a few of them: "Jerry" from the Silver Dollar; "Kathy," a tall red-head; the neatly dressed "Lois"; "Tex" from the Owl; and "Rose," one of several women of the same name who was singled out for her habit of stealing the wallets of her customers. Two Native American girls were identified as "Indian May" and "Cokie Joe." One madam, "Red Mountain Hattie," was known to treat her employees like family and exercised the utmost discretion when selecting their clients. She was also well-liked by others; once, after rolling her car near Lancaster, she was able to secure repairs at Picker Brothers Garage simply by flashing her diamond ring and telling the mechanics who she was.[33]

Osdick's wild women, barkeeps, and their visitors seemed beyond the long arm of the law, mostly because the law cared little to try and clean up the town. On those rare occasions when a raid was pending, the guilty parties were tipped off long before police arrived. Bar fights did sometimes escalate into shootings. Once, a harlot known as "Arkansaw" admonished a miner for refusing to buy her a drink. The man, it seemed, was in the habit of treating other girls to a drink and had recently returned from Los Angeles. When Arkansaw gave him "a hard time" for refusing to pay for her drink, he replied, "I don't have to treat you whores any longer; I've got my own woman now." Another man overheard him and demanded that he apologize. When he didn't, he was shot.[34]

By 1929, Osdick was also known as "Sin City," "Inn City," "Never Inn," and several other colorful nicknames. But if there were any more disputes as to the town's rightful name, the post office stepped in and designated the final name as Red Mountain. It was a useless effort, since the price of silver fell during the infamous stock market crash just before the Great Depression of 1929. About one hundred people remain in town today, but Red Mountain's red-light ladies are long gone.[35]

# CHAPTER 2

———•◦•———

## Bodie: Where Bad Girls Came to Stay and Play

The booming and brawling mining camp of Bodie (elevation 8,400 feet) owed its existence to gold discoveries beginning in 1857 at the early camp of Dogtown, located just east of the Sierra Nevada mountain range. In July 1859, a German New Yorker named William or Waterman S. Bodey would discover gold at the foot of a bluff some twelve miles from Dogtown. The bluff, the resulting camp, and the surrounding mining district were named Bodie—the difference in spelling being attributed to an early business sign which spelled Bodey's name incorrectly. It mattered little at the time, for Bodey would perish in a snowstorm the following winter without ever seeing his namesake town.

Bodie got off to a slow start. A passerby in 1864 noted only about twenty wood-frame buildings in the budding town. There must have been at least one saloon by August of 1865, when J. Ross Browne of *Harper's New Monthly Magazine* arrived to write an article about Bodie and was almost immediately enticed to sample "a slug of snake medicine."[1] But it was not until about 1877 that Bodie's mines took off with vigor. The rush was on when the Bunker Hill Mine suffered a cave-in, revealing a "fabulously rich ore chamber." Miners were soon scrambling over the mountains to try their luck.[2] Within a year the population was guessed to be about seven thousand people. Chinese laborers hauled in lumber to sell as building began en masse. Public buildings, including the first school, were erected. Nobody seemed to mind much that Bodie's winters could be harsh, with whipping winds and snow sometimes piling up tens of feet. Temperatures often dipped below freezing, sometimes as early as September. In these frosty conditions, mining could slow dramatically or even cease until warmer weather returned. One miner lamented that during the winter months, there often was "nothing to do but hang around the saloons."[3] To the saloon owners and bawdy girls of Bodie, the complaint was music to their ears.

Lust for riches combined with boredom often amounted to violence in Bodie. One of the first gunfights of record occurred in January of 1878, between John Bresnan and James Blair. Bresnan was killed, and Blair died nearly a month later following an operation on his badly injured arm. Bodie's wicked reputation seemed to grow like wildfire, spurred by exaggerated stories published by various newspapers. When a man was severely injured in a knife fight in December, one newspaper demanded to know, "Why can't a man get along in Bodie without fighting?" The *Weekly Bodie Standard's* answer was tongue-in-cheek. "It must be the altitude," the paper responded. "There is some irresistible power in Bodie which impels us to cut and shoot each other."[4]

One of Bodie's first good time girls of note was Martha Camp, lately of the California camps of Panamint City and Darwin. In 1867, she was in Virginia City, Nevada, when she identified a French immigrant named Jean Marie A. Villain, aka John Millian, as the man she saw sneaking around on the floor of her room in the dead of night. Millian was later convicted of the murder of Virginia City's favorite harlot, Julia Bulette. Within a year of her arrival in Bodie circa 1879, Martha made the *Bodie Daily Standard* after she ousted a rowdy customer from her place by chasing him up the street with a gun and firing five shots at him. Although she does not appear in the 1880 census, one source states that Martha remained in Bodie until about 1885. Then she moved to San Francisco (where she charged a man with threatening her and smashing her windows) and Oakland (where she was described as "hardened to the core.") In the latter place, Martha also made the papers in 1888 when she was accused of holding the trunk of one of her employees until the girl paid her bills. As the year came to a close, a raid netted Martha and several others. Tired of her profession, the lady gave up and quietly disappeared.[5]

Another of the best-known wild women of Bodie was Madame Moustache, known in a kinder time as Simone Jules and Eleanora or Eleanore Dumont. The lady was among the West's best-known female blackjack players, but also dabbled in the dance-hall and brothel business. Most sources agree that Eleanora first surfaced in North America at the Kootenai [sic] mines in British Columbia. There, she spent her savings to construct "a large building to be used as a gambling and dance hall." But the mining camp dwindled so fast that there was little time to recover. Eleanora abandoned her new business and moved to West Side camp in Montana, where she prospered. When she heard that the two men who had built her place in British Columbia also were there, she sought them out, and paid them.[6]

It was at San Francisco's Barbary Coast in about 1849 that Eleanora broke into her career as a cardplayer. Although she initially worked as a dance-hall girl, she soon found her way to the newly opened Bella Union gambling hall. The place was perfect for Eleanora, who first ran the roulette table before graduating to *vingt-et-un*, the French name for "twenty-one" and better known today as blackjack. Not only was Eleanora "strikingly beautiful" with "enormous black eyes and ebon hair," but she always bought a round of drinks with her winning hands—which were many.[7] Other descriptions of her claimed she was so dark that she was sometimes mistaken for "a hundred percent Creole" and was thought to have hailed from New Orleans.[8]

San Francisco was just the beginning for Eleanora. When she left town in about 1854, her next stop was Nevada City, some sixty miles northeast of Sacramento. It was there that she was able to make enough money to open her own gambling house, with a dozen tables running round the clock. The lady easily "gained the reputation of dealing honestly, was always smilingly polite, and the miners liked her—even held her in considerable respect."[9] Although she romanced various men over time, Eleanora found them cumbersome as a whole and preferred to keep her profits for herself.

It was no doubt easier to travel alone, which the lady did with the ease of a gypsy. Her alleged whereabouts throughout her career blend together in a wonderful mix of truth and hearsay, and if stories of her whirlwind trips around the West are all true, the lady must have worn out her traveling trunks with alarming frequency. In Montana, she purchased a saloon and gambling hall in Bannack that came with a brothel. In Virginia City, she worked at Rocky Thomas's dance hall during the winter of 1864–65. Although she was a "chief attraction," Eleanora "had no intimates, no one friend, yet every miner in the camp bowed before her shrine in humble and respectful adoration and lost his gold in ecstasy at her table for the chance of one personal fleeting glance from her eyes or one word from her lips." Writers enjoyed describing her gorgeous features in great detail, using phrases like "abundant purple-black hair," a complexion "of the clearest olive," beautiful "scarlet lips parted slightly to show two rows of pearly teeth," and piercing eyes of "darkest green." Yet on her "short upper lip there was the faintest tinge of down," earning her the unkind moniker of "Madame Moustache," a name she no doubt despised. Being dubbed Madame Moustache seems to have made Eleanora even tougher than she already was. Once, when a hapless bandit "laid his hand upon the beautiful naked shoulder disclosed by her low-cut bodice," the woman stabbed him in the throat with "a long stiletto, rose, and pointing disdainfully at the thing upon the floor, said to an attendant, 'Remove that carcass.'"[10]

Eventually, Eleanora moved on again—to Boise City, Idaho; Cheyenne, Wyoming; Carson City, Nevada; and back to California, where she is said to have opened a very posh parlor house in San Francisco. A year or so later she was back in Montana. Then, in 1877, a reporter for the *Daily News* in Gold Hill, Nevada, chanced to spy her playing cards in Deadwood, South Dakota. He described her as "a plump little French lady, perhaps forty years of age, but splendidly preserved," and noted that she "has bright black eyes and a musical voice, and there is something attractive about her as she looks up with a little smile and says, 'You will play, M'sieur?'" The writer had heard that Eleanora was "very rich," but kept to herself. "Always alone, always the same polite, smiling little woman," he wrote, "always making money." The writer might have been kind in his descriptions of Eleanora because he was infatuated with the lady gambler. But Eleanora was indeed growing older and drinking too much. Eventually, her skills at cards began to visibly slip. As time went on and her wealth dissipated, she began "making up" her face and wore only "cheap tinsel jewelry."[11]

In May of 1878, Eleanora decided to give Bodie a try. The town must have put some wind back in her sails, as the *Bodie Weekly Standard* reported that she appeared "as young as ever, and those who knew her ever so many years ago would instantly recognize her now." For over a year, Eleanora flourished at the Magnolia Saloon. Gradually however, the cards turned against her. On September 8, 1879, she "borrowed $300 of a friend and with her own funds opened a faro bank. It only lasted a few hours."[12] Without a word, Eleanora rose from the table and wandered outside. Nothing more was heard of her until a sheepherder found "the dead body of a woman lying about one hundred yards from the Bridgeport road, a mile from town. Her head rested on a stone, and the appearance of the body indicated that death was the result of natural causes."[13] It was Eleanora, with a bottle of morphine mixed with claret wine lying next to her. There was a note, too, directing "for the disposition of her effects" and stating that "she was tired of life." Eleanora's death was ruled a suicide.[14]

Eleanora left no money for a burial, but the town of Bodie didn't let her down. "To the goodhearted women of the town must we accord praise," the *Bodie Morning News* commented, "for their accustomed kindness in doing all in their power to prepare the unfortunate woman's body for burial."[15] The lady gambler was laid to rest in Bodie's cemetery on the hill above town. "It is said that of the hundreds of funerals held in the mining camp," wrote former *Bridgeport Chronicle-Union* editor George Montrose some years later, "that of 'Madame Moustache' was the largest. The gamblers of the place buried her with all honors, and carriages were brought from Carson City, a distance of 120 miles, especially to be used in the funeral cortege."[16] Eleanora's obituary circulated all over the West. "Those who remember the madam will agree that she commanded a degree of respect very rarely accorded to one of her class, respect due to traits of character," observed the *Butte Daily Miner* in Montana.[17] Another of her obituaries reminded the public to "let her many good qualities invoke leniency in criticizing her failings."[18] Lamented another, "Her life was as square a game as was ever dealt. The world played against her with all sorts of combinations, but she generally beat it. . . . Poor Madame Mustache."[19]

The gentleness with which Madame Moustache's death was handled was forgotten by 1880 as Bodie's wild side further came to fruition. One report recounted that in the previous two weeks, "men have been seriously beaten over the head with six shooters, one has been shot, one stabbed to death, one man and one woman have been knifed, one woman's skull crushed with a club, and she may die tonight. For these seven crimes—for these five lives jeopardized and two taken—two arrests have been made." The next year, Bodie would see its first, and only, lynching.[20] Who were the female victims in these instances, and how did they come to harm? Some of them very well might have been the good time girls working out of several brothels in the red-light district. Maiden Lane and Virgin Alley offered anything from crib girls in one- and two-room cabins to the "elegant high grade salon." The ladies gladly accepted gold nuggets as payment for their services.[21]

Stories over the years have claimed Bodie's red-light district was quite large. Newspaper articles of the time do not verify the assertion one way or another, although stories of bawdy women did occasionally surface. The *Sacramento Daily Record*, for instance, reported in April of 1880 that one Samuel Black was shot and wounded by Jesse Pierce, who had assaulted "a hurdy named Kittie Welles."[22] The 1880 census documents only nineteen prostitutes on Bonanza Street in June, just down the road from the city jail.

### Good Time Girls of Bodie, 1880

| Name | Birthdate | Birthplace | Marital Status |
|---|---|---|---|
| Emma Berry | 1854 | California | single |
| Nellie Booth | 1860 | California | single |
| Katie Carroll | 1859 | Canada | single |
| Agnes Carter | 1856 | California | single |
| Hattie Cass | 1847 | Massachusetts | single |
| Ella Folson | 1860 | Wisconsin | single |
| Flora Franks | 1850 | Prussia | single |
| Mabel Hill | 1854 | California | single |
| Carrie Hoole | 1854 | Iowa | married |
| Lillie Lee | 1852 | Ohio | single |
| Louise Marshall | 1856 | France | single |
| Carrie Martin | 1848 | Canada | single |
| Mary Merscom | 1853 | France | single |
| Emma Morris | 1860 | Wisconsin | single |
| Abbie Pearce | 1847 | New York | widowed/divorced |
| Flora Steel | 1858 | California | single |
| Addie Travers | 1852 | Massachusetts | single |
| Mollie Willis | 1842 | England | married |
| Ida Woods | 1846 | Nevada | single |

All the women were listed as housekeepers except Agnes Carter, who told the census taker she was a hairdresser. And only one of the ladies is traceable even as her identity remains questionable. She was prostitute Flora Franks, who appeared in the 1870 census at San Francisco. Frisco's city directories for 1879, 1880, and 1882 list a Flora Franks as residing at the International Hotel, employed as an actress at the bawdy Bella Union theater. Was the Ms. Franks of San Francisco one and the same as the woman identified in Bodie? The truth may never be known.

What is known is that in 1881, a local pastor called Bodie "a sea of sin, lashed by the tempests of lust and passion."[23] But the town—just like nearby Aurora and numerous other mining camps and towns—suddenly began to fade as quickly as it had grown. As folks moved away, one newspaper commented that the town had become rather quiet; it had been a week since anyone was killed. When a number of mines closed in 1882, it was Bodie's undoing. The population quickly downsized considerably.

In spite of the slowdown, wayward women did continue to make their way to Bodie on occasion. One of them was Lottie Johl, née Charlotte J. Wilson. Born in 1853 in Iowa to George and Nancy Wilson, Lottie married Newton Robert Calhoun in about 1869. The couple had one child, Mattie Mary, later that year or in early 1870. But married life didn't seem to suit Lottie, who divorced Calhoun and left Mattie with her parents. Although most historians claim Lottie moved to Bodie and worked as a dance-hall girl or prostitute circa 1880, she is not documented again until she married a German butcher named Ely Johl in Esmeralda, Nevada, on July 4, 1881. The couple then moved to Bodie, where they lived in a five-room house on Main Street. Lottie carefully selected beautiful furnishings for her new home, and the newlyweds sent out invitations for a housewarming party.

Enter Annie Donnelly, the wife of Johl's partner Charles. Annie knew about Lottie's sordid past and had tried to break up her marriage to Johl and maliciously spread rumors about Lottie all over town. On the night of the party, the Johls waited expectantly for their guests. Nobody came.

Lottie Johl had been put in her place and would be marked as a scarlet woman for the rest of her days. The damaged dove turned to painting to heal her wounds. Annie Donnelly also painted, and it is not unlikely that she was the reason nobody cared to admire, display, or sell Lottie's paintings.

Ely Johl did not take the public shunning of his wife lightly. When a masquerade ball was scheduled at the Miner's Union Hall, Johl sent to San Francisco for the nicest dress he could afford. Author Ella Cain described it as "white satin, all covered with seed pearls and diamonds (just imitations of course), but sparkling like the real thing." Lottie donned her mask and attended without her husband so nobody would know who she was. To her delight, she won the contest for the most beautiful costume. But when Lottie took off her mask, the other guests were not only surprised, but outraged. Lottie's dance partner, said to be a former customer, walked off the dance floor in a huff. Two other men then walked up and whispered something in the woman's ear, causing

*Lottie and Ely Johl's home on Main Street is still a major attraction at Bodie State Park.*
Photo by Daniel Mayer, Wikimedia Commons.

her to run "from the ball in tears." As far as anyone knows, Lottie never attended another social function.[24]

In November of 1899, Lottie suffered some illness and was given a prescription by her doctor. Later that evening, she went into convulsions. The doctor was called to the house but could do nothing to save her, and she was dead by morning. As rumors flew that the former soiled dove had committed suicide, Ely Johl demanded an autopsy. Lottie had died from ingesting poison, which she had been prescribed by mistake. Her doctor does not appear to have been held responsible.

The last battle fought for Lottie's reputation was over her final resting place. Those who considered her a fallen woman judged that she did not merit burial in the cemetery with other respectable people. An angry Ely reminded everyone that his beloved wife had been faithful to him and was a wonderful woman besides. The townspeople finally made a compromise: Johl could bury his wife inside the cemetery— but as close to the fence as possible. The devoted husband ordered an ornate iron fence for the grave. The following Memorial Day, he had a canopy erected over it and decorated it in red, white, and blue bunting with flags and flowers. At the head of the grave he placed a colored portrait of his wife. Over time, Johl's annual Memorial Day decorations drew people to Lottie's grave. Johl continued the tradition until he left Bodie. He was living in Texas when he died in 1914, but his body was returned to Bodie for burial. Although his grave is not marked, Lottie's burial spot and her home with Ely remain popular attractions for visitors to Bodie, and one of her paintings hangs in the museum there.

The June 1900 census records 1,073 residents in Bodie. Of those, 457 were women. But the populace had changed dramatically in the town, which was now home to a number of Paiute natives, as well as an exceedingly large Chinatown. Certainly, there were still some good time girls living in town, but they were not as easy to track as in the days when most of them lived on Bonanza Street. In truth, only one prostitute is identifiable at all: Rosa May, the legendary harlot whose story is ingrained in Bodie's history. But even Rosa's occupation as that of an innocent seamstress is deceiving. Guy McInnis, who was a teenager around the turn of 1900, did later remember that "the red light women would phone" Cecil Burkhams's grocery store and place their orders for delivery. Likewise, Richie Conway was just a child when his father occasionally took him into some of the saloons of Bodie. Conway remembered seeing prostitutes in these places; some of them would pick him up, set him on the bar, and beckon the bartender to "Give him a drink, give him a drink."[25]

Bodie's ladies of the evening became even more elusive when the town began wrestling with temperance issues beginning in 1906. As part of the movement, Bodie barkeepers were required to buy quarterly liquor licenses beginning in 1907—but for a mere dollar apiece. Furthermore, women of any kind were now forbidden from going into saloons. Still, at least a handful of ladies lingered in town. When Emil Billeb arrived in Bodie in 1908, he remembered at least four women: Big Bonanza, Big Nell, Bull Con Josey, and Rosa May. Anna McKenzie, who was born in Bodie in 1896, remembered that in later years the girls of the line would phone their grocery lists in to the local store. According to Anna, the "red light girls kept to themselves and were well ordered." Whenever a miner died, Anna said the ladies would "take up a collection and offer the money anonymously to the miner's family."[26]

Some of the women to which Anna was referring might have appeared in the 1910 census. The document lists nine prostitutes altogether, occupying four houses located in the vicinity of Main Street. Two of the houses were occupied by two women apiece, with one of them serving as a "landlady" who ran the house and more than likely serviced clients too. One of them, Paul Gohlke, was found at Irene Lennox's brothel when the census taker came by.

**Prostitutes in Bodie 1910**

| Name | Age | Birthplace | Marital Status | Occupation |
|---|---|---|---|---|
| *House 1:* | | | | |
| Lillian Montague | 40 | Canada (immigrated 1890) | divorced | landlady |
| Pearl Howard | 25 | Canada (immigrated 1900) | divorced | prostitute |
| *House 2:* | | | | |
| Rosie May | 46 | Pennsylvania | single | prostitute |
| *House 3:* | | | | |
| Irene Lennox | 28 | Oregon | single | landlady |
| Grace Morgan | 33 | California | divorced | prostitute |
| *House 4:* | | | | |
| Idelle Russell | 27 | California | divorced | landlady |
| Pearl Bolton | 24 | California | divorced | prostitute |
| Clara Demoss | 26 | Colorado | divorced | prostitute |

Aside from "Rosie" May, virtually nothing is known about the good time girls of Bodie during 1910 except (possibly) one: Grace Morgan. Granted, there is nothing directly linking the Grace of Bodie to a woman of the same name who made the papers of San Francisco during the early part of the century. It is just a guess, however, that the ornery Grace Morgan of the Golden Gate City might have been the same gal who later migrated to Bodie.

The Grace Morgan of San Francisco first appeared in 1906, when an article in the *San Francisco Call* reported that the "comely young woman, nattily costumed in white" was accused by a Chinese cook named Sing Foo of stealing ninety-two dollars from him. Sing Foo explained that he had met Grace when both were working at a hotel at Fort Bragg in Mendocino County. When Sing Foo announced his intention to move to Frisco, Grace "proposed to accompany him." Upon their arrival, the two set up housekeeping in a Japanese lodging house at Clay and Stockton Streets. "She takee monee," Sing Foo told the judge. "He's crazy," said Grace, with a giggle. The judge decided to continue the case.[27]

Four days later, the *Call* wrote a lengthy description of Grace's day in court. As they prepared to see the judge, Grace's cellmates—Mary McDonald and Laura Benzini—noted the woman's stylish outfit. "'With clothes like them o' yours,' said Mrs. McDonald, 'I'd be sure t' git dismissed by th' Judge.'" Laura agreed. "'Well, girls,' responded Miss Morgan, 'as we're all to appear in court together I can't lend ye any of th' things I'm wearin', but I've got a trunkful o' glad rags, an' if the p'lice let me get it I'll fit ye out.'" The jailer complied and allowed Grace access to her trunk. Next, all three ladies appeared before Judge Conlan and his "official aids," who openly "came to gape in wonderment at the three women as a bailiff escorted them into the tribunal."

Grace was described as being "faultlessly garbed in a dark blue silken skirt and white satin waist and snowy picture hat." Mary McDonald, meanwhile, "wore a stunning brown JS automobile coat of insufficient length to conceal the frayed bottom of her black alpaca gown, which in turn was so short as to afford full display of shoes down at heel and striped hosiery in palpable need of laundering. And her black straw headgear, of a shape long obsolete, was decorated with a straggling bunch of feathers, of which a barnyard rooster once was pardonably proud, but which looked quite disreputable as they lolled over the brim of Mrs. McDonald's hat." The reporter further detailed that "Mrs. Benzini's flight at fashion was confined solely to her head, and the wide and towering mass of vari-colored millinery there supported would not have appeared out of place if it were perched atop of a $10,000 prize stage beauty." The hat might have not appeared so awkward if only Laura was wearing something better than a dress that was "housewifely in material, cut and color."

True to her wish, Mary McDonald's charge of disturbing the peace was dismissed, although the judge assured her "that it was the weakness of the prosecution and not her external ensemble that restored her to freedom." Mary turned to leave the courtroom, but not before Grace "sprang forward, grasped a sleeve of the auto coat and exclaimed, 'Gimme that coat, before you go.'" Mary was relieved of her temporary garment as Laura Benzini was bound over for "having neglected to properly provide for her young child." As for Grace, she pleaded innocent to swiping the ninety-two dollars from Sing Foo but her case also was continued. Although it is unknown whether she was found guilty, the *San Francisco Call* "predicted that Mrs. Benzini will wear the auto coat as well as the tremendous hat when she next appears in court."[28]

In 1911, Mono County passed a most curious law. Gambling was outlawed everywhere, except in Bodie's demimonde. The *Bridgeport Chronicle-Union* had something to say about that in an August article, wherein it was noted that the male population of Bodie was no richer than they had been before the new law was passed. Furthermore, said the paper, there wasn't so much as a church or other clean entertainment for them to enjoy. And "yet the boys get rid of their money—and with people who pay neither taxes or license." The article claimed that there were at the time upward of a dozen houses of ill repute in town and that "men who were in the habit of playing a game or two of cards in a saloon now spend their money in less desirable places. . . . If Ordinance No. 113 has improved the moral status of Bodie the betterment is not visible."[29]

The *Chronicle* and its supporters needn't have worried much, for beginning in 1913, the statewide Red Light Abatement Act was passed and officially closed down the prostitution industry. The act coincided with a final downturn in production at Bodie's mines. By 1917, Anna McKenzie remembered, the "red light girls were all gone."[30] After weathering bootlegging busts during the 1920s and a devastating fire in 1932, Bodie's surviving buildings have been preserved as an official state park since 1962. There is still plenty to see—except for the red-light houses of Bonanza Street, which are all gone.

# CHAPTER 3

———— •◆• ————

## *Rosa May: A Mysterious Femme*

No lady of the underworld has been romanced quite like Rosa May of Bodie. The lady has attracted a bevy of admirers over time, people who whimsically imagine she would make a great friend were she alive. They puzzle over her unknown beginnings and ponder her lengthy love affair with Ernest Marks. They mourn her death, and the unfairness at burying her outside of the fence at Bodie's cemetery. Her story has inspired numerous tales and tunes about the legendary lady. But while each tribute to Rosa may contain only an inkling of truth, few care to admit that the lady remains truly enigmatic in her own right.

Although no one source can pin down Rosa's true identity, several historians have tried. Author George Williams, who deserves much credit for his research, believed she was Rosa White who worked for madam Cad Thompson in Carson City, Nevada. Williams based his theory on the fact that Rosa May did work for Cad as late as March of 1880.[1] A website calls her Rosa May Oalaque, but in reality, "Rosa Olaque" was in Bodie during 1879 when Rosa May was in Virginia City.[2] But the lady even called herself Rosa May, and also gave the best reference to her birth, telling census takers in 1900 and 1910 that she was born in Pennsylvania between 1855 and 1864 to Irish immigrants.

Based on the information he found and his interviews with others, Williams believed Rosa first left home in 1871 and may have initially worked as a prostitute in New York, Colorado, California, and Idaho as she made her way west. An 1876 letter to her from Laura Davenport bore a New York address and encouraged Rosa to "come back to New York." A Bodie resident, Father Clarence Birks, also believed Rosa was from upstate New York. Others said she may have lived and worked in the mining camps of Columbia, Lundy, and Masonic near Bodie.[3]

Although Rosa May remains shrouded in mystery, she is unique in that her personal trunk somehow survived after her death. The trunk contained her clothing, at least one photograph, and, most importantly, a series of letters written to and by Rosa between 1876 and 1880. In 1934, after Bodie resident Billy Owens died, the trunk was found in a building he owned and was subsequently auctioned off. The purchaser, B. C. Honea, later sold the trunk to Bodie native Ella Cain. Ella's daughter, Helen Evans, inherited it after Ella died. Through Helen, Williams was able to access and transcribe each letter.[4]

Rosa's letters remain as the earliest verifiable documentation of the lady. The first letter, from Laura Davenport, was addressed to her at 32 South D Street in Virginia City, Nevada—the town's notorious red-light district. The only other letter to her during 1876 came from someone named Jack in San Francisco. Jack was apparently one of Rosa's customers, referring to her as "My Own Darling Rose" and promising to send her "something better than a cane to remember me by." Jack also noted that in a letter Rosa wrote to him, her "natural distrust of me shows up."[5]

In the prostitution realm, soiled doves quickly learned not to trust any man, although it is just a guess that Rosa was inclined by her profession to distrust Jack. Still, her wariness of men extended to the longest known relationship she ever had with a man: Ernest Marks. Born in Prussia in 1853, Marks immigrated to America in 1866. In 1871, he was working as a clerk when he became a United States citizen in Stockton, San Joaquin County, California (but had misplaced his naturalization papers by 1886). With him was his brother, Morris.[6] The brothers parted ways early on but would later reunite in Bodie. By 1878, Ernest was apparently alone when he breezed through Nevada long enough to meet, and fall for, Rosa May.

The letters to Rosa from Marks numbered eighteen and were written between July 7, 1878, and January 1, 1880. All were sent to her at various brothels in Carson City. Notably, the first letter was written from Lake Tahoe, and Marks alternately called the recipient both Jennie and Rosa. The letter was outright immature and raunchy, even by today's standards: Marks apparently had venereal disease, for he wrote of hoping that "pop and gin and medicine" would make him "sound as a roach," and also that "getting up at night to release the Dr. from a crooked [position] is not what it is cracked up to be." In a childish attempt at assuring Rosa of his faith to her, Marks wrote that he had "seen one or two chances to give the Dr. a chance but he and I do not give it a thought. I suppose a great love of Jennie [sic] blinds us to everything else." He also wrote of encountering a woman who queried, "Don't you get lonesome when you have no ladies around," but that "Dr. did not show any symptoms of wanting any and I was very glad to see he had not forgotten his Rosa."[7] One can only imagine how Rosa felt as she read this off-color and rather vulgar first letter from Marks.

Marks eventually moved to Gold Hill some fourteen miles from Carson City, where he remained for at least a year. His next letter, written on July 20, was more polite and thanked Rosa for her "loveing [sic] letter." He claimed he had not seen any other women, but he certainly was familiar with Gold Hill's red-light world, where he spent much of his time with friends. What Rosa thought of romancing a man who had venereal disease, a drinking habit, and friends in the demimonde remains unknown. At the very least, however, this and other letters indicated a budding love affair to which Marks appeared to be dedicated. A letter in December, for example, closed with "my Rosie loves her baby don't you darling," and sent "great love and million kiss [sic]."[8]

There is little doubt that Marks tried to be loyal even as he was uncouth. Subsequent letters to Rosa revealed that he was annoyed that "every man and woman and child knew of you and I. I get it from some quarter every day." Yet such statements were sprinkled with assurances of his fidelity. "I don't propose to break my baby's heart by going around with the dizy [sic] girls and boys," he wrote.[9] Most interesting is that there seemed to be a private agreement between the two: Marks knew exactly what Rosa did for a living, but her business relationships with her clients did not seem to bother him. His expressions of love and faithfulness indicate that in spite of her profession, he was willing to carry on a monogamous relationship with her.

Over time, Marks made more sacrifices on behalf of his affair with Rosa. Later in December he quit drinking, sent Rosa Christmas gifts,

*The Bodie Cemetery, circa 1962, includes the lonely grave of Rosa May on its outskirts.*
Photo by Ronald Partridge, Library of Congress.

and promised to visit her when money allowed. Rosa wrote back that she doubted Marks had remained sober, to which he responded, "I am sorry to think that you do not believe that I had not been drinking." Rosa's doubts were perhaps warranted, for Marks continued to tell her whenever he happened to visit the demimonde in nearby Virginia City and other places. But his letters also averaged two per month during 1879. He continued defending his innocence ("Pet I did not get into some girl's box," he wrote in January), telling of his temperance, and promising to come see her. In one instance, he even wrote her a poem:

> *For today there is no hard task*
> *No burden that I would not bear with grace*
> *No sacrifice I could name or ask*
> *That were granted could I see your sweet face.*[10]

Rosa may have been appreciative of Marks's fidelity, but the man's letters reflect that she often expressed her own self-doubt, jealousy, and worry about herself and their relationship. When Marks at last visited her in February of 1879, it must have been a relief to both of them. "God forgive me Rosa, it's breaking my heart to sit here doing nothing and you in that damn town," he wrote afterward. "I want to take you out of it or help you along." When he was unable to return the favor after he received a valentine from Rosa, however, the lady apparently expressed her discontent. "What is the matter?" Marks queried in his next letter, ending it with "I am always yours. Love and kisses. Erni."[11]

Whatever happened between Rosa and Marks during the spring of 1879 remains a mystery. In his next letter, dated in April, Marks offered no more than casual notes about various friends and their relationships but said very little about his own affair with Rosa. At least one letter was signed "respectfully," while others ended with terms of affection. And, when he didn't return her letters in a timely manner, Rosa was quick to anger. "Your very short and cross letter is at hand today," Marks wrote on July 30, and "I am very, very hurt to see you wrote good-bye."[12]

In August, Rosa left for Virginia City. Her reason for doing so was simple enough: the local harlots were not making enough money to make ends meet and had been forced to "walk the streets in order to hustle up trade." Virginia City was not much better, but Rosa apparently believed she could make more money there. If she took the train, Rosa would have passed through Gold Hill, but there is nothing to indicate that she stopped off for a visit with Ernest Marks. From Virginia City, Rosa wrote a letter to one of her clients, Leo Miller. "Friend Leo," it read, "Having arrived in town again I write to inform you of my address and if you wish to call and see me I would be pleased to have you do so I am living with Mrs. C. Thompson. Hoping to see you soon, I am as ever Yours Respectfully Rosa May No. 18 D St." The letter was returned to Rosa May unclaimed but remains as evidence that she wrote to her clients in an attempt to drum up business at Cad Thompson's brothel. Another note, from clothing dealer Isaac Isaacs, invited Rosa to "come to my room to night if you wish come between 9 and 10. The front door will be open so walk right in to my room and I will be up as soon as I close the store." A p.s. queried, "You know where I live?"[13]

By January of 1880 Rosa was back in Carson City when Ernest Marks wrote to her a final time. "I forgive you darling for thinking that your dear letters disturb me," he assured her. He also talked of bringing her some powder she wanted and announced, "I have not drank a drop today." The letter ended with "May my darling always be happy—Sweet Kisses lots of prosperity for 1880. Yours always, Erni." The only other letter in the collection came from Cad Thompson, who was in San Francisco in March and had apparently left Rosa in charge of her bordello.[14]

Where did Rosa go next? Nobody knows for sure—unless George Williams correctly assessed that she was the same woman, identified as

Rosa E. White, who was living at the brothel of Jennie Moore and Mary Ann Phillips in Carson City as of the June 25, 1880 census. But that woman said she was born in Maine in 1853 and that her parents were born in New Hampshire—quite a different background from the Rosa May of Bodie who said she was born in Pennsylvania. Equally mysterious are the whereabouts of Ernest Marks, who also does not appear in the 1880 census. Did the couple run off together? Or separately? And where were they?

All that is known for sure is that by 1882, Marks had joined his brother Morris in Bodie, where he registered to vote and listed his occupation as "saloonkeeper."[15] In March of 1884, Marks was involved in a shooting scrape with Charles Jardine and sheriff Kirk Steves from nearby Lundy. When Jardine, a local "bad character," exchanged gunfire with Kirk, Marks got off a few shots as well. Only Jardine was wounded, in the leg. A newspaper article on the shooting also said that Marks was working for Morris, who ran Morris Marks and Company—a wholesale liquor business.[16]

Meanwhile, Cad Thompson sold her brothel in Carson City in 1892. If Rosa was still there at the time, that may have been when she decided to move to Bodie as well.[17] Clarence Birks believed she had already been bouncing between the two towns for several years—quite a stretch since Carson City and Bodie are situated roughly one hundred miles apart.[18] In 1956, Ella Cain gave further information about Rosa in her book *The Story of Bodie*. Ella was in her seventies when she wrote about Bodie, and her whimsical account of Rosa May has been largely discounted by other researchers.[19] But although her facts are understandably fuzzy and even romanticized to a great degree, Ella was one of the few people living who actually remembered Rosa May and ended up with her trunk.

Ella wrote that Rosa May, "a dark-eyed, curly headed, petite French girl," first went to work at a brothel called the "Highgrade."[20] In its time, the Highgrade was only one of two "high-class" brothels in town.[21] Rosa quickly became quite popular. One miner commented that "She was a gal who had a smile you'd go to hell for, and never regret it." At the time, Ernest Marks owned the Laurel Palace Saloon. According to Ella, Marks showered Rosa with diamonds and furs and remained dedicated to her. One time, customer Billy Owens made a toast and shouted, "Here's to Rosa May, the darlingest, sweetest little bunch of loveliness that ever came into this camp. She's mine!" Marks threatened to shoot Owens if he drank to his own toast.[22] A Mrs. Bell, whom George Williams interviewed, also verified that Marks "was good to" Rosa and "brought her gifts."[23]

Ella Cain also made an unsubstantiated claim that Rosa "took a trip abroad" to visit "her native Paris" and spent Marks's money gambling at Monte Carlo. With her winnings, she returned to Bodie with "ten or fifteen trunks, which were deposited on her porch in Virgin Alley." It was then that Rosa "replaced the red lantern that hung on her porch with a fine hand wrought iron one with a red panel glass." Other improvements to her house included "silver door knobs, fine furniture and mirrors." Although she was then in her late thirties, Rosa continued doing well. Ella claimed that the famed "Fortuna Ledge" at the Standard Mine had been discovered in Rosa's absence and she was often paid or given the "prettiest and most glistening" chunks of high-grade gold from there. At some point, she hired jeweler Frank Golden to fashion a pair of cuff links and a matchbox from the gold and had Ernest Marks's initials engraved on the latter gift. "It was strange how many cigars he always had to light in the presence of customers," Ella wrote.[24] The best guess is that Ella wrote about Rosa May's adventures when the aging harlot first lived in Bodie during the 1890s. Rosa does not officially appear on record, however, until the census of June 6, 1900. Rosa told the census taker she was born in January of 1855 in Pennsylvania. Her parents were natives of Ireland. She was renting her home on Bonanza Street and working as a "seamstress." Around the corner and up the road on Main Street was Ernest Marks, a saloonkeeper, who also rented his home.

At least one other person who knew Rosa from her days in Nevada was prostitute Emma Goldsmith, who appeared in Bodie after the 1900 census and worked at a brothel known as The Ozark.[25] Guy McInnis recalled that Emma's house was "just north of Jim Cain's bank, near the corner of King and Main Street," and was one of four brothels left in town. Emma was, unfortunately, "a hard drinker" and subject to drug abuse. Her arrests for "using opium and other crimes" appeared frequently in the papers. Back when they were both in Nevada, she had been close enough to Rosa to write her at least one letter. "I have not drawn a sober breath since I have been home," she had written. On August 18, 1900, Emma was found insane and jailed. She was released, but on October 13, the *Bridgeport Chronicle-Union* reported: "Died— Emma Goldsmith—one of Bodie's lowest levels, died about 3 o'clock this morning."[26]

Although they maintained separate addresses on paper, Marks and his old flame apparently continued their relationship in Bodie, just like Ella Cain said they did. George Williams did his level best during the 1970s to find people who had known Rosa and Ernest. One of them was Guy McInnis, who remembered Rosa from when he was in his late teens right around 1900. "It was common knowledge in Bodie that Marks lived down there with her," he said. By then, Marks "didn't mix with society" other than his customers. "He was bummed up with rheumatism. I know he walked with a cane." In spite of their living arrangement, Rosa continued to take customers according to McInnis, who recalled delivering groceries to her. She was "a very quiet woman . . . not very handsome, stout as far as I remember, short and stout. Must have been in her forties. Don't remember what color hair she had."[27]

In 1902, Rosa was able to purchase her house on lot forty-two, block twenty-six on Bonanza Street from former Bodie resident Hugh McCaghren of San Francisco. The price was $175, a little over five thousand dollars by today's standards. Rosa called it the Palace.[28] Some years later between 1908 and 1911, twenty-year-old Herb DeChambeau also remembered seeing Rosa May. She was "about fifty, and too old for prostitution," he said. Instead, Rosa had "three or four girls" working for her. Customers paid a quarter for a beer and two dollars for time with one of Rosa's girls, according to DeChambeau. Sometimes at this point, she also was referred to as Rosie. Like McInnis, DeChambeau said Marks lived with Rosa but never talked about it. Did Rosa capitalize on her business by setting up in other towns? Perhaps. In December of 1909, the *Bridgeport Chronicle-Union* reported that "The tent house in which Rosie and her girls were living caught on fire last Sunday" in a gold camp called Masonic some fifteen miles from Bodie. "One end of the tent was burned out and most of their clothing burnt. It is not known how the fire started."[29]

Other people who remembered Rosa May during the early 1900s included Richie Conway, who delivered milk to Rosa and remembered she was "a dark haired, middle aged woman" with a big heart. Sadie Cain remembered seeing Rosa May sitting in a rocking chair on her porch. Bill Glenn recalled that as a child, he saw Rosa May giving dimes to other local children. Anna McKenzie, who was "twelve or fourteen" when she knew the lady, described her as "a quiet woman who kept to herself."[30] And Lauretta Miller Gray, whose mother owned the Occidental Hotel, said Rosa May and "her girls" came to the hotel each Sunday for dinner. "They were really beautiful people," she recalled, "and they were very nice, too." As for Rosa's manner of dress, Lauretta said, "You'd never take her for a prostitute."[31]

Rosa was still known as "Rosie" during the 1910 census. This time, she told the census taker she was born in 1864, perhaps hoping to make herself appear younger. Around this time, according to Father Clarence Birks, Rosa was married to a man with "a short Anglo-Saxon name with five or six letters."[32] Birks might have been referring to Ernest Marks, who also was in the census, but documented as living on Main

Street—not far from Rosa's house on Bonanza Street. He was now in his late fifties, rooming with two other men, and working as a liquor dealer. But while Marks remained on record in Bodie for several more years, Rosa disappeared into thin air. What happened to her?

The best information comes from Ella Cain, who believed Rosa died in 1912. Ella claimed that Bodie was in the throes of "pneumonia weather" and our heroine traipsed between miners' cabins nursing the sick. "Many a letter she penned home—for the doomed miners—to loved ones," Ella wrote, a claim that was not far-fetched: Rosa's collection of letters included one from Mrs. Carr of New York, who wrote in 1879 to thank the woman for notifying her of the death of her daughter, Mamie Nenninger.[33] Ella declared that Rosa eventually fell sick herself and died that winter. And therein lies the rub: avid research by a number of historians has failed to yield any documentation whatsoever of Rosa May's death in Bodie or anywhere else.[34] Only George Williams came close, noting that by November of 1912, Rosa's property taxes were in arrears. They were never paid, indicating that Rosa likely had either left town or died.[35] Most every admirer, fan, and researcher of the enigmatic Rosa May agrees that she died in Bodie—although one man Williams interviewed, Frank Balfe, said that Father Birks believed the lady actually died in her old hometown of Carson City and was brought to Bodie for burial.[36]

The most popular legend about Rosa May is that, like former prostitute Lottie Johl who died in 1899, the townspeople of Bodie refused to allow the Bonanza Street sweetheart to be buried in Bodie's cemetery. She was buried on the outside of the fence instead, in a place Ella Cain called the "Outcast Cemetery" and "Boot Hill." Ernest Marks, her only real love and oldest friend, "had a picket fence placed around her grave."[37] Later, according to Markham Trailkill whom George Williams also interviewed, the citizens of Bodie felt remorse. They exhumed Rosa's body and buried her a second time inside the graveyard's fence.[38]

True to Williams's research, the June 21, 1913 issue of the *Bridge-port Chronicle-Union* noted that Rosa May's property, now identified as lot forty in block twenty-six, was valued at ten dollars and that the taxes of $210 had not been paid. In 1918, the state of California acquired the property. Rosa May's house was torn down the following year.[39] If Rosa May did die in California, there were no probate records regarding her property. Ella Cain claimed that Ernest received Rosa's personal belongings, including "a fortune in money and diamonds." In time, as Bodie declined, Marks would sell pieces of jewelry to keep his finances afloat.[40] Ella's statement seems logical enough, as Marks's saloon would have been closed by national prohibition in 1920. One of the people Williams interviewed, Bob Bell, claimed, however, that "Marks kept his saloon open until he died."[41]

Ella Cain also claimed that Billy Owens and Marks forgave each other for their riff over the toast to Rosa so many years ago. Theirs was an old friendship. As more and more people abandoned Bodie, the men settled for playing the occasional card game out in front of Marks's empty saloon. "Many times Ernest would take the gold match box from his vest pocket and light a cigar, always holding the side with E. M., and the touching cupid, so that Billy could see them," Ella wrote. "Then Billy would turn his head in the opposite direction, looking in a reminiscent way into space—and would not speak for several minutes."[42] This scenario likely took place during the 1920s, when both men lived just four doors away from each other. Notably, the 1920 census shows that Owens owned his house, while Marks still rented his home.

The matchbox and cuff links appear to have been the only things of value that Marks had left when he died in Mono County, presumably at Bodie, on July 29, 1928. According to Ella Cain, Marks had been ill for some time, had relatives in New York who sent him money, and it was Billy Owens who looked after him toward the end. Marks's last request was to be buried beside Rosa, and Owens, then the town undertaker, dug the grave himself. George Williams, however, found Marks's death certificate which verified that Owens actually buried him in the Odd Fellows section of the cemetery in an unmarked grave.[43]

Billy Owens died in 1933. He, too, was broke according to Ella Cain, and Rosa May's trunk constituted a portion of Owens's belongings that were auctioned to pay his debts. The items included Ernest Marks's beloved matchbox and cuff links, which were found stashed "in a knothole in the wall" with other items. "The bidding was spirited on these," wrote Ella, "and brought in more than a hundred dollars." Given his competition with Marks over Rosa, Billy had at last triumphed. Once upon a time, he had coveted Rosa May; now, the gifts she bestowed on Marks helped with Owens's own funeral expenses.[44]

Over time several markers have been placed at Rosa May's grave, or at least where her grave was believed to be. A wooden fence marked the spot in 1927. A simple wood sign had appeared by 1961. In 1965, Louis Serventi created a cement stone with a simple cross at the top and Rosa May's name. During the 1970s, George Williams rebuilt the 1927 fence. Still, questions remain as to the location of Rosa May's final resting place. Meanwhile, her fancy red lantern and other items remained on display at Bodie's museum as of 2010.[45]

# CHAPTER 4

———•◦•———

## *Coastal Courtesans:*
## *A Seaboard of Sin*

In pioneer California, good time girls quickly found that the largest concentration of men could be found along the budding docks and harbors along the coast. At least some quantity of shady ladies must have accessed the fledgling state aboard ships. Others traveled via rugged and primitive trails. Some of them may have used the trail that Dr. Josiah Gregg forged between Northern California's diggings to the coast during 1849. Gregg's first attempt began at Weaverville and spanned well over one hundred miles to today's Trinidad. Among Gregg's party was L. K. Wood, who remembered the job of constructing the trail as "one of constant and unmitigated toil, hardship, privation and suffering."[1] The group could only progress two miles per day.

At the future site of Trinidad, ship captain Robert Parker laid out the townsite in 1850 as a whaling village. Parker's wife opened the first hotel there, having much experience from running the Parker House in San Francisco—once known as a popular gambling house. Within a year, some three thousand gold seekers were among those who had made it to Trinidad or at least passed through. Saloons, gaming houses, and a few houses of prostitution would open in the coming years, although between 1860 and 1876 another wagon road running south to Arcata remained barely passable. In the latter year, only one harlot has been identified in Trinidad. She was Cockeyed Florence, who is said to have run her brothel from 1876 until she died in 1885. The legend goes that Florence was buried outside of the cemetery in the middle of what was then, or became, the road leading to the burial ground.

Later documentation puts Florence's grave outside the cemetery boundary near the location of some private homes today. At some point, a small wooden heart appeared alongside a shed in the cemetery, reading "Flo + CV." The marker was identified as Florence's grave. As of 2017 a new wooden grave marker stood in the same spot, reading "Florence, b.?, d.1880s?" More solid evidence of Trinidad's red-light district came in a February 1906 notation that "a house which is known as Red Lights has been opened in our town in the old saloon building formerly occupied by W. Pinkham."[2] By then, Trinidad had been enjoying rail service from other cities along the coast for some time. Trinidad remains an enjoyable tourism destination today, sans its former red-light district or much information about the ladies who worked there.

While Cockeyed Florence was shunned by the people of Trinidad, madam Roseanna Keenan, who died at Crescent City just sixty miles to the north in 1865, was not. Roseanna was an unfortunate passenger on the paddle steamer *Brother Jonathan* when it sank in stormy conditions off the coast of Crescent City on July 30. Roseanna and her husband, John, had come to California from Mexico in 1849. The couple first settled in Sacramento, where in 1858 Roseanna was charged with assault and battery on Ann Woods and Melvina White at a place called the "Palace." In court, Roseanna accused Ann with "exhibiting a deadly weapon," but the girl was acquitted.[3] The 1860 census identified "Rosana" as a resident of Sacramento and documented her as being born in Ireland in 1832. John worked as a saloonkeeper, and the couple had four children—one born in New York and the other three, including a set of twins, born in British Columbia.

Just prior to Roseanna's untimely death, John Keenan had himself been a passenger on the *Brother Jonathan*. On June 29, 1865, Keenan had sailed aboard the ship from Portland to San Francisco. Shortly afterward Roseanna boarded the same ship, which was returning to Portland and would sail on to Victoria, British Columbia. With her were "seven ladies."[4] Almost immediately, the steamer encountered a "heavy gale." The sea was so turbulent that most of the passengers became seasick and were confined to their cabins. The ship finally made it to Crescent City on July 30 where it anchored for a few hours before trying to set sail once again. Once again, the *Brother Jonathan* encountered stormy weather, to the extent that the captain ordered the ship to turn around as it approached the Oregon border.

The ship was nearing the harbor at Crescent City when it struck a large rock, ripping a giant hole in the hull. The captain quickly realized the *Brother Jonathan* was sinking fast and ordered everyone to evacuate. There were plenty of lifeboats, but only three were able to be lowered into the water. One of them capsized and another smashed into the side of the sinking ship. Only the third boat was able to carry eleven crewmen, five women, and three children to safety. The *Sacramento Daily Union*, which initially reported that there were four women aboard, noted that "None of the names of these four women is to be found registered at the office of the company in this city, and the explanation given is that they probably belonged to the party of seven women printed on the list as an appendage to the name of Mrs. John C. Keenan. Mrs. Keenan was the keeper of a lager beer saloon at Victoria and the seven women under her charge were on their way thither as waiting-girls."[5]

Newspapers were understandably confused at first about just who was rescued and who wasn't. Later reports identified a Mrs. Stott who made it into the lifeboat with her young son. Five days after its first article about the wreck, the *Sacramento Daily Union* reported that three of the women saved "were women going to Victoria with Mrs. John Keenan.

They returned on the *Del Norte*."[6] The fourth woman, Mrs. Stott, told others that she "saw Mrs. Keenan, who had been sick in her berth all the morning, struggling in the water. She was partially dressed and had two life preservers tied on her. One of the other women in the boat later said that Mrs. Keenan was hit on the head and stunned, either by a plank or one of the boats."[7]

Mrs. Stott also was able to identify at least one of the three harlots who made it ashore in the lifeboat. She was Elizabeth Wild, with whom Mrs. Stott had spent time on the "hurricane deck" before the *Brother Jonathan* sank. Mrs. Stott also verified that "everything was being done by officers, crew and male passengers to save the ladies. She thinks there were no ladies who came on deck who were not got into the boats."[8] As newspapers scrambled for the truth about the wreck, John Keenan also scrambled—to claim his late wife's estate. He was not without reason, for the last mention of Roseanna Keenan stated she "had some seven thousand dollars with her when she was lost."[9] But Keenan himself died in 1869 "from an apparent 'fit' on the steps of his residence at 819 Kearney St." in San Francisco. At the time, he owned a saloon at the corner of Merchant and Montgomery Streets. Roseanna's estate was taken over by George P. Bronner and was still in litigation as late as 1877.[10] A memorial to those lost on the *Brother Jonathan* remains today in Crescent City, with a list of those who either drowned or survived the wreck of the *Brother Jonathan*. Elizabeth Wild appears as "Martha E. Wild." Also on the list is "Mrs. Jno C. Keenan & 7 ladies of the evening" who are not identified. No connection is made between Roseanna and Martha; also, the plaque fails to document whether Roseanna's body was ever recovered.[11]

Further down the coast, San Luis Obispo's soiled doves were defined by their own district along today's Morro Street between Monterey and Palm as of 1886. Five houses of prostitution, ranging in size and services, flourished along the east side of Morro while a dance hall provided entertainment at the northwest corner of Morro and Palm. Two of the brothels were known as the Klondike and the Palace. One of them offered a restaurant. In 2006, nearly a century after the good time girls moved on, an archaeological dig was conducted in San Luis Obispo's former red-light district. The project revealed much about the district's residents. Their diets, for instance, consisted mainly of beef, mutton, pork, chicken, and fish, in order of quantity. Much of it, especially the beef, was of high quality and probably reserved for when customers dined with the ladies. Plenty of liquor bottles, pieces of an opium pipe, and tobacco pipes confirmed the consumption of spirits and drugs. The ladies also purchased their toiletries at Booth's Drug Store, a local pharmacy that supplied them with medicine, Wakelee's Camelline for their complexions, perfume, and grooming items. Brass and porcelain buttons and two button covers, one made of silver, gave insight to the women's wardrobes. Also uncovered were doll fragments, other toys, and game pieces, leading to the assumption that children were perhaps present in the district at one point.

The origin of the brothels of Morro Street begins with Silas Call, who acquired lots five through nine and lot thirteen in block eighteen circa 1870. Call was a longtime citizen, served on the Board of Town Trustees in 1867, and acquired a sizable amount of property in San Luis Obispo. After he died in 1880, his wife, Nancy Emeline Call, took over owner-ship of the properties. Nancy seemed oblivious to an 1884 ordinance which declared that "No person shall keep, or maintain or become an inmate of, or be a visitor to, nor shall any person in any manner contrib-ute to the support of any disorderly house or house of illfame [sic]; and no person shall knowingly let, or under-let, or transfer the possession of any house or lands or other place for use by any person for any of the aforesaid purposes." Those in violation of the ordinance were subject to a maximum fine of three hundred dollars or ninety days in jail.[12] Two years later, brothels had been erected on Nancy's lots. Notably, the lady was a respected citizen with a family, and never made a career out of prostitution. She did, however, rent her buildings to others who operated them as bordellos. The money Nancy received was only a small portion of her income, and she likely gave it little thought—until 1895.

In June of 1895, Nancy was found guilty of renting her houses on both Morro Street and Palm Street exclusively for use as brothels. She was fined seventy-five dollars. In October, she was again charged for renting the "Palace" on Morro Street for the same purpose. This time, Nancy fought back and her attorney, E. Graves, presented several arguments and moved for dismissal of the charge. The judge denied the motion, however, and Nancy had to take the stand. After testifying that she had "not at any time leased the property in question" for prostitution purposes, she was acquitted.[13]

Nancy may have been set free, but the authorities still fretted considerably over their "immoral" houses. Just three months prior to Nancy's acquittal, a Dr. Krill was called to a bordello on Morro Street to tend to a woman named Lena who had shot herself. The .38 caliber revolver had accidentally discharged as Lena carelessly played with it. The bullet was described as "entering her body on the right side in front," and "coming out the back about eight inches from the point of entrance." Luckily for Lena, the wound was "probably not dangerous."[14]

On October 27, the *San Luis Obispo Tribune* reported that Los Angeles detective John Shields had successfully arrested madams May Arlinton [Arlington], Ruby Doe, Trixy Stewart, Martha Dunlap, and Mamie Gear for selling liquor without a license. Each woman paid a bond of two hundred dollars for their release as their court appearances were scheduled.[15] Only a few details are known about the women. Trixy Stewart, for instance, had only been in court one other time back in May for an unknown offense. In November, both she and Mamie Gear's cases of selling liquor without a license were dismissed. Martha Dunlap, however, was convicted of the same offense.

Martha Dunlap actually made the papers quite frequently, largely because she became one of the largest landowners in San Luis Obispo, Santa Barbara, and Santa Maria. Born in 1853, in Connecticut, Martha was in San Francisco when she divorced her husband, newspaper publisher Wilson Dunlap, for "willful neglect" in 1885.[16] Martha next moved to San Luis Obispo, where she began buying all the property she could get her hands on. Between November of 1895 and July of 1896, Martha was noted as being in court several times—once because she lied about her property taxes. But the lady remained steadfast, appearing in the 1900 census as a "proprietress." Her true business was unrecorded, but she did own her residence. The other occupants were Joseph Lind, his wife Carrie, and their two children.

Had Martha retired from the prostitution industry? Hardly. The lady was able to balance her time as a land baron with running various houses of prostitution all along the coast. In 1905 she decided to dispose of some of her Morro Street property and sold it to J. B. Weaver. She had used her money to buy a house at 108 East Mill Street in Santa Maria by 1908. Two years later, Martha and eight other "proprietresses" were arrested during a raid of Santa Maria's red-light houses. There had been a demand for a "moral clean-up" of Santa Maria, which "sprang from the increasing liberties taken by the denizens of the underworld, and their open disregard for any sense of decency." An oil boom was taking place nearby, bringing the ladies plenty of income and, apparently, the said liberties to which they felt entitled.[17]

The raid was well planned, consisting of over thirty-five deputies in order to have "sufficient men to make the arrests simultaneously." Over the course of two hours, the officers raided three Japanese brothels and nine "white" houses—the latter containing some forty women plus their madams. But the *Santa Barbara Morning Press* revealed that sheriff Nat Stewart confined the arrests solely to madams Violet Blake, Jessie Hobart, Lessie Laddie, Margaret Sill, Helen Strong, Hazel Ward,

Virginia Watson, Ethel White, and Martha Dunlap, plus three men who were associated with them. As the madams were hauled off, their employees "were given three days to leave town." Notably, none of the customers found in these houses were arrested. The *Press* made sure to point out that Martha "has been in this business in Santa Maria for many years, and has accumulated a large quantity of property not only in Santa Maria, but also in San Luis Obispo and even in Santa Barbara." Most recently, she had purchased a brothel on Anacapa Street in the latter town.[18]

The plan was to take the madams by train to Santa Barbara for trial. By the time the ladies were transported, more madams had been arrested. Because they arrived on a Sunday, none were able to post bail and were held overnight. In court, only seven madams including Martha and a Japanese madam named Kame Okada were able to pay their fines and were told to leave town or face imprisonment. The exception was the wealthy Martha, who "agreed to live a quiet life hereafter if not molested."[19] Yet in June of 1910, Martha was arrested again for renting out her Anacapa Street property for "purposes of prostitution." This time, the madam was ill and unable to appear in court. The outcome of her eventual trial remains unknown.[20]

Martha never did leave Santa Maria. Newspapers between 1910 and 1917 are rife with her purchases of property, including the St. James Hotel in San Luis Obispo, which she remodeled on at least two occasions. She might have well gone on for several more years had she not suddenly died in Santa Maria on April 23, 1917, after a short illness. The *San Luis Obispo Daily Telegram* finally revealed what everyone really wanted to know: Martha's estate was estimated between seventy-five and one hundred thousand dollars. And her brother, Santa Maria resident Alfred Day, was her only heir.[21]

During her lifetime, Martha Dunlap worked hard for financial success and power at any cost to her reputation. The list of those who attended the funeral from her home on April 26 proves that she had achieved her goal and left this earth as a respected citizen. Her pallbearers—Thomas Boyd, Thomas Tunnell, Geo. A. Harper, A. McNeil, Reuben Hart, and L. C. Bell—were all prominent businessmen. Reverend E. M. Crandall presided over the services before the large funeral procession (including lots of flowers) made its way to Santa Maria's cemetery. Today, Martha's remains are at rest in a vault at the graveyard.

Like Martha Dunlap, Mamie Gear also came from an unhappy marriage. Mamie had apparently come to San Luis Obispo from Los Angeles where, in February of 1888, the *Los Angeles Herald* reported that she had not responded to a telegram addressed to her there. The next time she surfaced, it was in a San Luis Obispo court, where Mamie charged one Jeff Gear with "an assault on her person with intent to kill." A warrant was sworn out against Gear, who had yet to be apprehended.[22] Mamie was forty-five years old when she swore out her complaint against Gear. Like Martha Dunlap, she was far beyond the age of working as a prostitute, but that did not stop her from being a madam. In 1895, both Mamie and Trixy Stewart were in court for selling liquor without a license. Trixy's case came up first and was so lengthy that Mamie's case was postponed. Not until December did she finally go to trial, and the charges against her were dismissed.

The 1900 census found Mamie divorced and running a "lodging house" which was probably her longtime property on Palm Street near the red-light district. The only lodger documented that day was twenty-four-year-old Minnie Taylor, who was employed as a "seamstress." The city directory of 1908 verifies Mamie's address as 956 Palm Street, also that she was the widow of Andrew Gear (not Jeff) and provided "furnished rooms." Mamie was at the same address when she told the 1910 census taker she had given birth to three children who were still living. Residing with her was forty-eight-year-old Annie Dubois who, like Mamie, was making money on her "own account." Two men in the house, Jim Carrol and Gray Huntington, were listed as lodgers. At the time of the census, Mamie was likely suffering from the tuberculosis that would finally kill her in 1912. As with Martha Dunlap, the newspaper reported her death on December 20 as a simple matter of fact: "Mrs. Mamie Gear died today of tuberculosis at her home, corner of Morro and Palm streets. She had been ill several years. Funeral arrangements have not yet been completed. The remains are at the parlors of the P. J. Freeman Co., Monterey street."[23] Mamie's burial place is unknown.

Although Martha Dunlap and Mamie Gear were major players in the prostitution realm of San Luis Obispo, there were certainly other women who kept the newspapers busy. An article in February 1898 reported that a drunken prostitute at the "city bastile" [sic] had made numerous suicide attempts. The woman "managed to swallow the phosphorous upon a bunch of matches. This did not end her existence and she knotted a silk handkerchief around her neck. She was black in the face when discovered. A third attempt was made and defeated by the prompt work of the officers just as strangulation had commenced to set in. The woman had procured a strap and had buckled it tightly about her throat. The strap had to be cut to save the woman's life."[24] No further information was given.

By 1900, the citizens of San Luis Obispo were fed up with their redlight ladies. Attorney A. Nelson duly appeared before the city council on their behalf and asked that the city marshal and his force be instructed to carry out the request to "remove the evil." Councilman Venable accordingly introduced a resolution to carry out Nelson's request. The air must have been thick with tension when nobody seconded the resolution, and the matter was dropped.[25] Eventually, however, San Luis Obispo's citizens won their battle. The 1903 Sanborn map shows that the brothels along Morro Street had been demolished. Longtime brothel owner Emeline Call died in October of 1905. Like Martha Dunlap and Mamie Gear, Emeline was heralded as "quite a social denizen, with membership in clubs such as the San Luis Political Equality Club." Her obituary kindly called her "one of the most estimable and beloved residents" of the city.[26] What the paper did not say was that Emeline's death pretty much signified the official end of prostitution in San Luis Obispo.

*Only one known brothel, on Main Street, survives as a quaint shop in Ferndale today.* Courtesy Jan MacKell Collins.

Sometimes, when city governments could not or would not oversee their prostitution industries, citizens took it upon themselves to handle good time girls in their own way. When Ferndale was founded during the 1850s, the village was a successful leader in the dairy industry. The town incorporated in 1893. But Ferndale was, and is, subject to earthquakes that occasionally knocked buildings from their foundations. When that happened, local citizens would work together to lift and shove the buildings back where they belonged. Records are scant as to the identification of any shady ladies in Ferndale. It is known, however, that attorney Plumer F. Hart paid for the construction of an ornate building at today's 393 Main Street circa 1893, and that over time the structure would serve as a stagecoach stop, saloon, gambling hall, and brothel. It was this same building that some proper Ferndale femmes objected to during the time it was used as a house of ill repute. Local legend goes that the women quietly arranged for a chain to be wrapped around the place in the dead of night, so the building could be pulled off its foundation. If the women hoped the brothel would be deemed unfit, they didn't get their wish. The male friends of the shady ladies managed to pull the building back onto its foundation, and it still stands today.[27]

# CHAPTER 5

————— •◦• —————

## Sin in San Diego:
## The Stingaree District

O ver the centuries, lovely and lively San Diego's history has been divided into four important periods of time. The first of these was the precolonial period when Native Americans exclusively called California's southern tip home. In the 1600s and 1700s, Mission San Diego de Alcala was established under Father Junipero Serra during the Spanish period. The Mexican period began in 1841, after Mexico gained its independence from Spain. The American period, as it is known today, began in 1850 after California became a state.

As early as 1830, San Diego was home to at least one saloon, but more would quickly follow. By 1841, drinking holes were a familiar site up and down the southern coast. When Phineas Banning and D. W. Alexander established the first stage line between Los Angeles and San Diego in 1852, accessing saloons along the route became much easier. The line ran along El Camino Real, an already seasoned road which passed near Mission San Juan Capistrano some sixty miles north of San Diego. Around the same time, or so the legend goes, a poker player in today's Los Rios Historic District won a real live woman of the evening with his winning hand. To keep the shady lady from running off, the man chained her to a rock outside as he finished the game. This incident might have occurred at the 1852 Tomas Ramos adobe, which once served as "a cantina, billiard parlor and dance hall" and was run by Miguel Yorba around 1900. Today the building serves as a cafe.[1]

San Juan Capistrano is also home to a version of La Llorona, the folktale phantom who drowned her children in a creek and whose spirit now walks around crying for her lost babies. In this case, La Llorona was believed to have been a "beautiful young" prostitute—or at least a lady of "loose morals."[2] Unfortunately her real story is lost to history. One tale about her states she threw her newborn infants into nearby Trabuco Creek in order to keep her career on track. At night, her spirit can be heard howling and sobbing, especially when the wind blows. The story was handed down over several generations, with old-timers issuing the dire warning, "Don't go out when La Llorona is out." Mothers especially heeded the caution, lest the woman's spirit steal their own children in the night.[3]

*Stingaree cribs at 303–324 Island Street survived in San Diego when this image was taken circa the 1960s.* Library of Congress

Long after San Juan Capistrano's legendary ladies of the night made their own history, Alonzo Horton founded New San Diego in 1867 and built a wharf at the foot of Fifth Street. The street quickly evolved into the main business thoroughfare, with the Last Chance Saloon serving libations to ship passengers at the corner of Fifth and K Streets. Within a few years, Fifth Street also was home to San Diego's early red-light district, Stingaree. Alternately known as Stingaree Town, the name was no accident: a stingaree is a type of stingray with a most venomous sting, which was likened to the shady ladies of the district. The first mention of Stingaree appeared in the *Los Angeles Herald* in 1879, which reported a ghastly murder. Local residents became alarmed by a series of "cries and noises" near Ninth and X Streets as a man came running and reported a fight between two "Indians." Sheriff Joseph Coyne and several officers rushed to the scene and found the body of a man called Chicano quite literally "cut to pieces" with over twenty stab wounds, including one that "split the chest wide open." Judging from the amount of blood and signs of "a desperate struggle," the fight had carried on for some distance.[4] Another fight was reported in 1881, when a Frenchman was hit in the face with a liquor bottle by a "drunken Indian."[5]

One of the first madams in Stingaree was Belle Ashim, who made the papers after she purchased several items on credit before skipping town aboard a steamer. By now, the locals were complaining about the condition of the buildings on lower Fifth Street which were in severe disrepair. Officials acted quickly to give "an application of paint, soap and water" to the structures, but the effort did little to appease local citizens who were fed up with Stingaree. They called it the "second edition of the Barbary Coast."[6] The complaints extended into 1882, when a letter to the editor of the *Union* pointed out what an eyesore the area was, as well as "a nuisance of flagrant character."[7] For those who had offered up the paint and repairs, however, Stingaree was as good as it was going to get.

Like other red-light districts across the country, Stingaree was not exempt from violence against, or even perpetrated by, its good time girls. In November of 1886, George Bryant was arrested for assaulting Geneva Derby, "an inmate of a house of doubtful character"[8] It is little wonder that violence was a part of everyday life in Stingaree. In April 1887, a reporter for the *San Diego Union* counted thirty-five brothels employing some 121 women, plus other freelancing prostitutes. Notably, however, only those who sold liquor without a license were brought to court. The women included madams Ida Bailey, Mrs. Edna Barstow, Edna and Hazel Russell, and Hattie Ruth, as well as others listed by only their first or last names: Cora, Edna, Georgie, Lizzie, Louise, Ruby, and Stewart. Of these, Ida Bailey was noted as proprietress of the "notorious Sherman House" while Madam Stewart ran an "elegant 7th Street mansion with [her] name in brazen letters over the door." Edna Barstow ran the "Telephone Coffee House" which really was a brothel.[9] Other known women of the night included Kate Clark and Belle Wentworth.

In August, the *Coronado Mercury* reported on a fight that included two "prostitutes from a well known Seventh street bagnio, and though the chastisement each received was deserved, the volley of obscene language used, made the air sulphurous for some time."[10] There was also madam Louise Durant, lately of Paris, who was arrested for keeping a minor, Lulu Gasswell, at her brothel. Lulu, who had just arrived from Paris herself, also was arrested. Certainly, the court must have been torn as to whether Lulu was better off with Louise or her parents, the latter of whom testified that Lulu was "old enough, fat enough and ugly enough to attend to her own affairs."[11]

These incidents and others inspired a reporter from the *San Diego Union* to go undercover and spend several nights on lower Fifth Street in November. The writer took a stroll on his first evening, noting that "the ear is rasped by notes from asthmatic pianos, discordant fiddles and drunken voices boisterously singing ribald songs. Noses are offended by garlic, swill and fried meat coming from some chophouse. The eye is pained to see one, two, or perhaps three men on each corner, so intoxicated that they can barely stand." The reporter concluded that the whole area was "fully bad, if not worse, than the notorious 'Barbary Coast' of San Francisco."[12] Notably, while the man wrote of watching bartenders cheating customers, rolling drunks, and getting nearly every man in sight bombed on liquor, the district's bawdy women were not mentioned at all—nor was San Diego's Chinatown, which had been in place for some time.

By 1888, city attorney Harry Titus had plenty to say about the occupants of Stingaree. "The females who inhabit these dens in Stingaree town are lowest of the low," he stated in disgust. "The women are wrecks of humanity. Blear-eyed, toothless, sallow faced, and hideous under the use of cheap paint and powder as they sit in doorways, dressed in gaudy attire, bedecked with brass jewelry, and coax or invite the passerby to come in."[13] Occasional raids were staged against parlor houses or gambling halls to appease the public but even the famous lawman, "speculator," and "capitalist" Wyatt Earp felt at ease running three different gambling halls in town for a time.[14]

Sometimes newspapers were glib when reporting on instances involving Stingaree. When Henry Preyssing got drunk and wrecked his own home in August 1891, the *San Diego Union* made most light of the situation. After throwing items inside the house and tossing several things out the front door, Preyssing left for a short time before returning home and resuming his melee. "Flat irons, rocking chairs, a press board and other paraphernalia flew around," reported the paper, "occasionally finding an exit through the window or door." At last Preyssing's wife, Bertha, had had enough and began chasing after her husband. Preyssing took off running to Stingaree, where he "entered the apartment of one of the inmates of a house in that quarter, taking refuge under the bed." The man finally fled to Chinatown and was later seen walking on Fifth Street as officers looked for him.[15]

Preyssing wasn't the only one to go on a tear. In September, the "women of the town residing in the Stingaree quarter started out on a 'time'" by getting into a "quarrelsome state of intoxication" before parading up and down the streets and fighting with other prostitutes. The whole group was finally arrested by officer Joe Cota and scheduled for court.[16] Two weeks later, another article revealed that warrants had been issued for four male operators of a notorious dance house in Stingaree. "It is known that a determined fight will be made, as it is intended to make it a test case," reported the *San Diego Union*.[17] Finally, officials were doing something about the Stingaree. By September 29, all dance houses had been commanded to close until they purchased licenses to operate.

Stingaree's good time girls, meanwhile, continued making the papers. In October, Bertha Bernard "raised a hulla-balloa," was hauled into court, and paid a total of thirty dollars in fines and bail money.[18] The next month, Ruby Grant was on trial for hitting May Burton after May said something terrible about Ruby's mother. Ruby, however, was only fined a dollar. By February of 1892, officials were prohibiting the ladies of Stinagree from sitting at their windows, where they were soliciting customers. Even Mary Bowman, a former crib girl of Stingaree, was not beyond the long arm of the law. In September, Mary was living at the Westminster lodging house on G Street when she created such a disturbance that she was arrested. By then, San Diego's city hall had relocated to the corner of Fifth and G Streets in order to be closer to the action.

Stingaree's vice had expanded to an area south of today's Market Street by 1901. By decree, ladies of the night rarely went north of Market, unless it was to advertise their wares from the safety of their madams' fancy carriages. Even the police had to admit that the world's oldest profession was called that for a reason and that so long as the good time girls kept to their "restricted area" and behaved, it was best to just let them alone. But the dawn of the new century was bringing changes in social and economic circles, and the red-light district as designated by the health department spanned an amazing hundred blocks in the downtown area. Within this area, twelve blocks bordered by First and Fifth Streets and Market and K Streets were devoted solely to Stingaree. Outside of Stingaree were more red-light houses, as well as nearly all the city's licensed saloons and the four-block area known as Chinatown. The district also was home to city hall, as well as numerous respectable homes and businesses. In its own way, the red-light district constituted its own annexed village of sorts.

In 1909, Walter Bellon was hired as the plumbing inspector for the city's health department. Because he worked all over the city, Bellon came to know more about Stingaree than most. He remembered notorious saloons like the Old Tub of Blood and the Seven Buckets of Blood at Third and Island Streets. Near the latter tavern was the Green Light, a fancy parlor house. Two rows of cribs, known as the "Stables" or the "Bullpen," were situated in a "courtway" between Third and Fourth Streets. Inside these places was "a bed and chair or two." Nearby were Yankee Doodle Hall and Pacific Squadron Hall, each with upstairs rooms whose entrances featured a red light at the door. Another parlor house, run by Mamie Goldstein, was above the Turf Saloon. Mamie and her black housekeeper, identified as Mrs. Williams, "was responsible for maintaining law and order."[19]

Born in California in 1881, Mamie had been in the San Diego area since at least 1902, when she was arrested for selling liquor without a license. Mamie was a card-carrying Republican who knew her rights. At her trial, Ed Wilson and Ed Kincaide testified that they went to Mamie's and asked for some "booze." Another of Mamie's black servants, Clara Rayford, served the men champagne. Both men were certain that the beverages were "malt brewed." Kincaide, in fact, said that his drink "made him a little frisky." Clara, however, testified she had served the men only nonalcoholic "temperance beer." Also, Mamie verified that Wilson had originally asked for whiskey and that she told him she kept no intoxicating beverages in the house. Mamie's employees Helen Freeman, Margaret Newton, and Azelea Snyder backed up what the madam said. Her case was dismissed.[20]

Between 1904 and 1910, Mamie's parlor house was at 405 Fourth Street. The only known incident Mamie suffered there happened in 1905, when Mike McClure, Al Williams, and Walter Bauer came to the parlor house and demanded something to drink. When they were denied, the men "raised a rough house, tore down curtains, etc." All three were arrested.[21] Five years later, the 1910 census gave little more insight to Mamie's place. The census records the twenty-nine-year-old madam as having five boarders with various "legitimate" occupations. The women—Madeline Wells, Loraine Hill, May Wilson, Cora Johnson, and Myrtle Marshall—ranged in age between twenty-two and thirty-eight.

Later, Mamie lived at 422 Fourth Street. In 1911, she suffered one last indignity in San Diego, and not at the hands of authorities. On a Friday night, three men knocked at the door, which was answered by Mamie's Chinese servant, Charlie. Outside was Tim Collins, who gave Charlie an "unmerciful" beating. Mamie then came to the door and struggled with another man, H. C. Turner. Mamie's girls also heard the fuss and identified a third man, C. G. Underwood, as wearing a white cloth over his face. The men were apparently bent on robbing the house but were unsuccessful at gaining entrance. All three were later arrested.[22] That was it for Mamie, who apparently packed her bags and left town. Madam Kate Clark moved in and took Mamie's place.

Walter Bellon's description of the red-light district in 1905 included another set of cribs located behind Pete Cassidy's saloon on the west side of Fifth Street between Island and J Streets. These were situated in rows and faced a courtyard with no entrance from the street. There were at least fifty cribs, which were rented to girls for fourteen dollars a week, a percentage of the profits, and a fee for a bouncer who kept things in order. The door to each crib had a sign at the top identifying the women by their first name, but Bellon said two women often shared a crib and that while one was engaged the other would be out looking for her next customer. He also remembered that the ladies were in the habit of hanging "a good luck charm, such as a horseshoe tied with a faded ribbon," over their doors. Inside, the walls were decorated with "plaster of Paris angels and cherubs, and often a copy of the Lord's Prayer." Along Fifth Street were some of the "better brick structures" where some women worked legitimate jobs by day and as prostitutes at night. Most of the women used "messenger boys" to deliver their groceries, clothing, toiletries, and liquor. Bellon remembered some of the girls too. One of them, "Dutch Annie," called for a messenger boy each morning to bring her a bottle of alcohol. The young men also brought meals to the women from local restaurants.[23]

In 1910, Dr. Francis Mead of the health department told Bellon that San Diego was being considered to host the upcoming Panama-California Exposition in 1915. At the center of contention was Stingaree, which would need a clean sweep in anticipation of the event. Bellon boldly decided to take on the project. The doctor cautioned him about the dangers of Stingaree, but Bellon reasoned that his combat skills from the army would serve him well. "With that background of basic experience," he later recalled, "I made my first inspection in the Stingaree and Chinatown."

Bellon's experiences were quite interesting. At the cribs in back of Pete Cassidy's, two "shoulder-holster men blocked my entrance and ordered me out, saying, 'No one permitted, these are private grounds.'" Bellon re-introduced himself, explained that he was taking a survey of "how people were living, not what they were doing," and that "health recommendations would follow." He also "quoted the law" before leaving, noticing as "eyes peered from doorways and small windows, and watched as I walked through and out into the street." Later that day, the newspapers announced Bellon's new job to the public. "So it was no surprise when I entered several compounds surrounded by cribs in Chinatown, that no one was around." The residents, he said, would disappear the moment he was spotted.

Bellon also found that when everyone learned that the project entailed cleaning up the area to make it cleaner and safer, "very few of the residents objected." Most everyone "agreed that something had to be done to correct the lack of toilet and other plumbing necessities." Still, the job must have been difficult. By about 1912, it was guessed there were still over one hundred women in the red-light district. And although the district had been repaired and cleaned up to a degree, there was still the question of whether the good time girls of Stingaree were operating within the limits of the law. This time, a Vice Suppression Committee, aka "Purity League," was formed by Reverends L. A. DeJarnett and William Crabtree, as well as several prominent women that included one of San Diego's first female physicians, Dr. Charlotte Baker. The group was backed by over two hundred residents who had signed a petition requesting that the red-light district and Stingaree be closed down for good. With the Panama-California Exposition coming, it was time for the city to do something about May Arlinton [Arlington], Ruby Doe, Trixy Stewart, Martha Dunlap, and Mamie Gear once and for all.[24]

The process began with the opening of a rescue home called the Door of Hope. But that wasn't going to solve the problem of women on the streets, and the public knew it. On October 3, 1912, the *San Diego Union* painted a very clear picture of the future on the front page. "STINGAREE DOOMED, SAY POLICE. VICE CRUSADERS TO WIN FIGHT," blared the headline. Captain of detectives Jack Myers had told the paper that the red-light district was closing soon and that the Door of Hope shelter would open as the "women are driven out" of their cribs and parlor houses.[25] By the fourteenth, numerous letters to the editor had been sent to the *Union's* office both for and against closing Stingaree. "Did it occur to you that half, if not more, of the scarlet women have very poor families and are the sole support of these, either very old or invalid parents?" queried Flora West. Nathaniel Mahoney objected to the Door of Hope operating "where we are raising our children." Another person who signed their letter "Property Owner" reasoned that "these women residents of the Stingaree neither wish, nor will submit to being reformed." Another letter came from a woman in Stingaree: "The Door of Hope is going to be a beautiful place. The name alone would keep me away. I say every woman in this district is just where she wants to be. We don't need anyone to reform us."[26]

The letters against reform fell on deaf ears. Former mayor and current police superintendent John Sehon ordered chief Keno Wilson to close the red-light district as of Sunday, November 10. Early that morning, a few women had already packed their bags and headed to the train station, but many more merely put on their best outfits and waited quietly to see what would happen next. At 8 a.m., Chief Wilson, thirty officers, and "a full detective force" surrounded Stingaree and blocked all the entrances and exits. The remaining prostitutes were told they would be taken to police headquarters in patrol wagons. Notably, the good time girls "were good natured as they piled into the wagons, and laughed and joked as if they were going on a picnic."

Meanwhile, Sergeant Witherbee was at the police station calling members of the Purity League to advise them of the raid and asking them to come to the station. Not one of them could be reached. Only Mrs. F. W. Alexander had appeared by the time 138 women from Stingaree had been brought in. Most of the girls were white, but there was a sprinkling of blacks as well and four Japanese women who "were held for deportation." The one Chinese prostitute "declared her intent to leave." Standing before them all, Mrs. Alexander gently explained to the women that the Purity League "only hoped to be able to bring some happiness into their lives, and to help them reform." The women silently listened to what Mrs. Alexander had to say. When she finished, however, the ladies broke into laughter, joked among themselves, lit their cigarettes, and asked for breakfast.

Upon being fed coffee and sandwiches, each woman was next questioned in Chief Wilson's office in the presence of officers, deputy city attorney D. F. Glidden, and an immigration officer. Understandably, many of the girls refused to answer or lied about their names or former addresses. But at least some of them were willing to talk to the men. One twenty-eight-year-old prostitute told them she "would be glad to quit the sporting life if you could find a job which would enable me to earn enough to meet my expenses. I have a crippled mother and a young sister to support." The woman went on to explain that she had worked legitimate jobs, "but the wages were not enough to keep me alone." She also expressed her reluctance to reform. "I saw one of your Committee this morning and the way she looked at me and the others . . . she walked past us holding her skirts away and looking as if she expected to be contaminated by breathing the same air with us."

One by one, the other ladies told their stories. One said her money went to support her young son who attended school in Sacramento. Another said she was on her own but refused help and stated she preferred to "go her own way in some other place." Yet another, giving her name as "Clara Doe," said she had been hustling since she was fifteen years old and was "well satisfied with her way of life." One more said she had been working as a prostitute for six months and was a "graduate nurse." She was offered a job at the hospital but told the men she was going to look for a job in Los Angeles. Notably, not one of the women blamed the public or "attributed their downfall to the cruel ravages of the world." Most of them had been in San Diego for only a short time. Only two women, one black and one white, accepted any aid; the latter gal had recently spent time in a lunatic asylum.[27]

The remaining soiled doves were instructed by authorities to go pack and be ready to leave town on Monday. When all was said and done, Chief Wilson noted that most of the ladies planned to go to Los Angeles, where prostitution had already been outlawed. For all anyone knew, the soiled doves of the City of Angels were coming to San Diego. "We may drive out the women already here but others will come," he said, "and I see no means of preventing it."[28] What the police might not have told the Stingaree ladies was that before being ordered to leave town on Monday, each would be brought up before the court on charges of prostitution. Justice of the peace George Puterbaugh and assistant city attorney Shelley J. Higgins charged the ladies with vagrancy, a misdemeanor as explained in the penal code section as "Every common prostitute is a vagrant." Puterbaugh fined each woman one hundred dollars, which he would waive if she left town by three o'clock that day. The ladies agreed and went to the train station to purchase their fare, but nearly all of them bought round-trip tickets. Plainclothes policemen were directed to be on hand at each station out of San Diego, where the women were then questioned as to where they were going. But by that evening, Chief Wilson guessed that only half of the women had left town.[29]

The cat and mouse game between the law and San Diego's good time girls continued. It was soon apparent that many prostitutes had simply scattered throughout the city, just like Chief Wilson predicted they would, even as a November 12 editorial claimed that "the redlight district has been summarily closed." Soon too, businesses in Stingaree were complaining they had lost much business because of the Purity League. Several saloons had closed, and San Diego lost its appeal to Navy men coming into port. Prostitution had been the lifeblood of Stingaree, and with the women gone, many of the bars and places of revelry lost the income they needed to survive. As a result, San Diego became unpopular among sailors—for a little while, anyway. An article in the *San Diego Union* noted that while sailors were traveling north to Los Angeles, the Stingaree girls were returning to San Diego where they "invited attention with their eyes and smiles, but [the men] went no further and paid their bills."[30]

Authorities, meanwhile, turned their attention to tearing down Stingaree. None were prepared, however, for the plethora of items that had been left behind. Gold, silver, earthen jars full of money, and jewelry, but also human bones and hair, were found in the intricate mazes of Stingaree's buildings, both above and underground. Mysterious hidden rooms, passageways, and bridges had formed an intimate network that allowed for accessing various resorts and saloons without being seen. More bones were found under a Chinese house. Meanwhile goodhearted citizens grappled with finding homes for the numerous pets left behind by Stingaree residents.

More alarming repercussions included the May 1913 vote of the Navy soldiers who chose San Francisco over San Diego for their "liberty port." Dr. Charlotte Baker promised to provide good, clean, chaperoned entertainment for them, but men looking for love already knew that the good time girls of San Diego were hard to find since they were now living in other parts of town and calling themselves "hostesses" to evade the law. Not until the Red Light Abatement Act of 1913 passed did building owners around town take the law against renting to prostitutes seriously. Authorities, meanwhile, continued swinging the wrecking ball around Stinagree and the waterfront under the health department and Walter Bellon's direction—even as some folks defied the new law. Numerous buildings were demolished, burned, and cleared as a few of their elderly occupants were taken to the county hospital. Residents of Chinatown made a concerted effort to clean up their area, but sixty buildings in the neighborhood were later torn down.

The Panama-California Exposition in Balboa Park opened as planned on January 1, 1915, although Chief Wilson did note that scores of wicked women were once again rampant in the city. This clandestine information was quietly swept under the rug when former president

Theodore Roosevelt visited in July. City fathers gave him a grand tour, including the cleanup efforts along the waterfront. Long after the exposition ended, prostitution as it was known in the Old West continued in San Diego until the 1930s. At last, the remaining good time girls in town grew old and became nothing more than sweet little old ladies. Few cared to reveal their pasts, except to certain friends who enjoyed listening to their stories of the days when San Diego's fun-hearted harlots ruled the Stingaree district.

# CHAPTER 6

*Ida Bailey:*
*A Surrogate Mother and Madam*

Most historians agree that Ida Bailey was among San Diego's most famous madams. She was quite possibly the most generous, as well. Spurned by the public and picked on by the police, Ida remained headstrong and forthright in her business dealings and her personal life. For over sixty years, Ida managed to survive as a parlor house madam, a lodging house landlord, and a mother. But there is one other aspect about the lady that is indeed memorable: Ida had an especially soft spot for children, whose ever they were, and her kind deeds for the orphans she knew are heroic in their own right.

Ida's beginnings are hard to track. In 1900 (as Annie Gould), 1910 (as Annie McLendon), and 1920 (also as Annie McLendon) she told census takers she was born between 1872 and 1877 in Canada and came to America between 1875 and 1879. Her parents are documented as being John and Annie (née O'Connell) Barth. What is known for sure is that Ida was in San Diego by 1885, where she ran a brothel called Sherman House at 502–506 Third Street at the corner of I Street. The Sherman was a large two-story affair, with a wraparound porch that actually extended into the street on each corner. It was probably during this time that, because of her flaming red hair, Ida was alternately known as "Red Headed Ida."[1]

Right off the bat, Ida suffered troubles regarding her liquor license. Newspapers verified that in July of 1886 she applied for one, but was arrested in April, June, and July of 1887 for being without one. The police certainly seemed to have it out for Ida, as well as others: In February of 1888 a special committee, formed by the city attorney to inspect "disreputable houses," paid Ida and several other madams a visit. The women stated they had paid fines or "deposited $100 bonds" in the last month, and also that each had paid for their county licenses and "United States revenue tax." Ida was no snitch, but someone else stated to the committee that one Jim Miggs had told the madams that he was authorized to collect a dollar week from each inmate of San Diego's bawdy houses. The committee recommended "that the matter be referred to the City Attorney, with instructions to examine several witnesses in regard to the manner in which the money has been collected, and if sufficient evidence is found, to prosecute said Jim Miggs."[2]

By 1889, Ida had relocated to 253 Sixth Street, where she employed five other women: Ollie Baker, Rosie Bradley, Lita Garde, Iva Stanley, and Mrs. W. E. Castle. Of these, newspapers in 1892 shed a little bit more on Ollie Baker. By August, the girl had "abandoned a life of shame" and was living at the Salvation Army when "some of the hoodlums, who have been hounding the girls . . . at length succeeded in decoying Ollie Baker away." The guilty party was able to get a note to Ollie during a meeting and she had gone "out to meet them, possibly not knowing who the message was from." Before departing, Ollie's Salvation Army bonnet was "sent into the hall as she was going away."[3] Police unsuccessfully searched for the girl, but nothing was known of her until a month later when Ollie was discovered in Washburn's saloon at Third and I Streets. There, another woman relentlessly "abused" Ollie until the bullied girl brandished a razor. When the weapon was taken from her, Ollie retrieved a "deadly looking revolver" from her room. That too was taken away, and an Officer Northern was summoned to arrest her. There was no other news about what became of Ollie.[4]

Ida, meantime, was continuing to suffer arrests—this time in July of 1891, when she was again found selling liquor without a license. Tired of being harassed, Ida secured an attorney, James S. Callan, who requested a jury trial but was denied. Ida and Attorney Callan next appeared in court on September 17, where the madam testified she had paid twenty-five dollars to ex-city councilman William Lyons. The man had told her the money "gave her immunity from arrest during that month." Although the city ordinance prohibited Ida from getting her license, Lyons also said he was authorized to give the money to Police Chief Crawford. Doing so, Lyons told Ida, would "be considered as a license."

Ida further shocked the court by revealing she had asked for Lyons to be subpoenaed for her case, but the man had not been summoned. Callan asked for a continuance until Lyons could be subpoenaed, but Judge Dudley was not impressed and refused to do so. The defendant,

*One of Ida Bailey's many brothels was once located in the vicinity of the Grand Hotel, shown here circa 1887.* Library of Congress

he said, "was in collusion with another to willfully violate the law," in spite of Ida's testimony that she had paid the money in good faith. Ida furthered her claim of innocence when Callan called his first witness, a notary public whom the madam had "concealed behind a curtain when the money was paid in order to overhear the conversation." That too was thrown out.[5] A few days later, Ida was convicted. She paid a fifty-dollar fine, but her fuming attorney filed a notice of appeal. "It is the intention of J. S. Callen [sic] . . . to carry the case through the courts of last resort if necessary," reported the *San Diego Union*, "in order to test the legality of Judge Dudley's decision in denying a right of trial by jury in violations of the city ordinances."[6] Not surprisingly, nothing happened.

Ida suffered no more court appearances until June of 1899 when she got into a dispute with her landlord, John Kastle. Back in March, Kastle had told Ida she needed to move. Not only did the madam refuse, but she also stopped paying rent. On March 9, Kastle took Ida to court, claiming she owed him seventy dollars in back rent—but he also asked for triple that amount for damages. Shortly afterward, Ida moved and Kastle dropped the case. Given her recent troubles, it is not surprising that in June, Ida finally lost her temper. Around eleven o'clock on the evening of June 17, Ida walked up to Mrs. "Coffee Kate" Grigsby at the corner of Fourth and D Streets and "struck her a stinging blow in the face." Kate already had her own problems, having recently discovered that her husband had two other wives. Whatever the issue was, Ida hopped in a hack and left before police arrived. In reporting the incident, the *Union* said, "Jealousy is said to have prompted the assault."[7]

Ida's new digs at 251 Fifth Street were grander than her old ones. Her parlor house was called the Golden West, and San Diego's 1898 city directory lists four men and eight women, including Ida, living there. Of the men, bar porter Norwood Ellwood likely worked for Ida. The women were properly recorded as Miss Annie Bith and Miss Agnes Bith, Miss Eva Finning, Mrs. W. A. Gould, Freida Meyer, Mrs. Helen

Ordway, and Augustine Lambla. The presence of Augustine Lambla is especially interesting, since the young girl and her brother, George Jules Lambla, would later be taken in as foster children by Ida.

The children's story begins with their parents, Alfred and Winifred Lambla. Alfred was a French immigrant who came to California circa 1871, the same year he became a naturalized United States citizen. In about 1876, he married Winifred in Connecticut. The couple eventually returned to California, where they alternately lived between San Francisco and San Diego. Four children came of the union: an older unnamed son, a daughter who must have been Augustine, and two younger sons, George Jules and Donatus. On the night of May 24, 1898, the Lamblas got drunk and had a horrific argument. "It was the old story of whisky, poverty and jealousy," the *Los Angeles Herald* reported before explaining that Winifred had worked as a housekeeper to keep the family afloat, and that the couple had arrived home in an inebriated state. Eleven-year-old "Donat" and thirteen-year-old George were the only ones there. At seven o'clock that evening, the boys went to their room while their mother retired to hers. Half an hour later, the children "heard a shot in their mother's room, and rushed in and found her dead in bed with the top of her head almost blown off." Another gunshot followed in Alfred's room, and "running in [the boys] found him lying dead on the floor with a shotgun at his side. He had placed the muzzle at his chin and blown the head all to pieces."

The boys went into shock—to the extent that after surveying the scene, they merely "opened the window of their father's room, went to bed and slept all night, got up, prepared and ate breakfast, then lifted the father's body onto the bed, washed the floor clean and hitched up the horse and drove to the Police Station and reported the crime." The officers found a suicide note from Lambla, asking God for forgiveness and explaining that Winifred had been unfaithful and a drunk besides, and that he couldn't stand it anymore. The article closed with mention that "an older son and daughter are living. The former is a printer in Los Angeles."[8] Nothing more was reported about the incident, except for a brief note in the *San Diego Union* in June that the Lambla estate, including a parcel of property in San Diego, was valued at $160.69.

What happened to the children? Notably, they had an aunt and uncle, Augustine and Jules Lambla, who lived in San Francisco during 1898. Neither, however, appears to have been inclined to take in their orphaned niece and nephews. Also, the identity of the eldest son and what became of him remains unknown. Nineteen-year-old Augustine also disappeared from record after she is documented at Ida's in 1899. As of the 1900 census, Donatus had been deposited at the Pajero Valley Roman Catholic Orphan Asylum at Watsonville. Nothing else is known of him. As for George Lambla, he was eventually taken in by Ida.

The madam would later tell census takers that she had previously bore three children and that none were living. The grief over the loss of her own children might explain why Ida exhibited love and sympathy for others. In the 1900 census, George Lambla was living at the Golden West. Also on hand were Ida's girls, Mamie Beck, Dora Henning, and Virna Zelleken. The women were each in their early twenties. Most curiously, Ida told the census taker her name was "Annie Gould." Little else is known about George Lambla's life with Ida although years later, in 1918, one Mattie Macon made mention of him. Mattie was being tried in San Diego for espionage, and Ida, now known as Annie, was called as a witness against her. Mattie's attorney refuted Ida's testimony because Mattie had once reported her "to the authorities for allegedly mistreating her son."[9] It is the only known time that Ida received a black mark on her reputation as a parent. George remained in Ida's care until 1907, when he set out on his own life as a young adult. He died in 1935.

Ida Bailey stayed on the move. By the fall of 1901 she was at a new brothel on lower 4th Avenue when, on October 1, a carriage drove by and someone fired a shot into the open door. The bullet missed Ida by a mere foot. The shooter was never discovered. "It is not thought that shooting was with intent to kill," reported the *San Diego Union*, "but through some crazy freak."[10] But the mysterious gunshot was a sign of things to come. In March of 1902, one of Ida's girls, Madeline Grinder, married Private John Commer. The groom wore his uniform, returning to the barracks afterward as Madeline returned to Ida's house. Rather than a hearty congratulations, however, Commer received a public shaming for wearing his uniform while getting hitched to a prostitute—an unhappy story which surely got back to the brothel. And a month later, Ida was arrested along with madams Ida Gould and Mamie Goldstein for selling liquor without a license. This time, at least, her case was dismissed.

Ever determined, Ida moved again in 1903—this time to the upscale and much celebrated "Canary Cottage." The parlor house was situated at 530 Fourth Street, between Market and Island Streets, and appeared most demure. The pale yellow, one-and-a-half-story building came with a large front yard and a quaint picket fence—as well as two rubber trees near the upper windows to make for a quick escape during police raids. The place appeared so homey that neighborhood children were in the habit of dropping by for candy during daylight hours. Notably, Ida favored small boys over girls, the latter being "shooed along home quite promptly."[11]

At night, the Canary Cottage was a whole different type of cozy. Only the best in food and drink was served. Ida's girls were refined, wearing beautiful dresses and "only light makeup." They were not allowed to smoke. Gentlemen callers were expected to act as such; ill-mannered or rude customers were shown the door by a bouncer. Soon, Ida's elite clientele included prominent society, business, and political men. As a favor to them, the police politely gave advance warning of any raids. Once, however, the notice failed to reach Ida. When the police appeared, "several prominent citizens had to make their getaway down the rubber trees and over the back fence."[12]

The Canary Cottage's glory did not last long. In January of 1904, the *San Diego Union* casually announced that Ida and her well-known competitor Mamie Goldstein "are violating Section 216 of the code in that they are keeping houses of ill fame."[13] To make matters worse, Ida's habit of taking her girls out each Sunday in a rented barouche (a convertible carriage) for a ride around town was drawing the ire of the local wives. Alice Rainford, who ran a florist shop at Fourth and C, recalled that Ida and her girls often stopped to buy flowers for the ride. But the madam's flagrant behavior angered Mrs. J. Cherry and Mrs. Watkins of the Social Purity League, and the women signed complaints.

The arrests of Ida, Mamie Goldstein, and others continued through the summer of 1904. In July Ida was singled out again, for running "a 'parlor' house."[14] It took over a month to find qualified jurors out of 120 selected citizens. Of Mrs. Cherry's testimony the *San Diego Union* wrote, "It was the opinion of many who heard the evidence that it tended rather to the advantage of the defendant, through proving to be largely of heresay [sic] in nature and it was with this idea, apparently, that the defense made use of her testimony." Other witnesses were police officers W. W. Johnson and McCarthy, Sergeant George Couts, Ed Fletcher, and T. R. Gray. Prostitute Beatrice Heald was also placed on the stand and admitted to "being an inmate of the Bailey house and said there had been other girls there, but she did not give their names." Fortunately for Ida, her case ended in an acquittal. A furious district attorney declared he would try the woman again with stronger evidence.[15]

Sure enough, another warrant was sworn out for Ida's arrest just a few days later. The madam posted another bond, and her trial was set for September 1. The court again had a problem finding proper jurors, and the case was postponed even further. But Ida had had enough, finally changed her plea to guilty, paid a twenty-five-dollar fine, and went back to work. The circus that was San Diego's court system was apparently beginning to weigh heavily on her. Perhaps that is why, after years of being single, she decided to marry. Her chosen mate was William Boyd McLendon, a former farmer who had received a dishonorable discharge from the military and spent time in prison around the time Ida was having her issues with the authorities.

Prison record or not, McLendon was just what Ida was looking for. The couple married on October 17, 1905, at St. Joseph's Church. On the marriage certificate, Ida wrote what was possibly her real, legal name: Miss Annie L. M. Barth. George Lambla was there as a witness to the union. Ida remained at the Canary Cottage for about a year before moving, first to 54 Twelfth Street and finally to live with McLendon at 1114 G Street. From all appearances Ida was no longer a madam and likely wanted a family of her own. So when she heard about the case of five-year-old Lucille Harmon in early 1907, she willingly stepped in to help the child.

Lucille was the daughter of a prostitute named Fay Harmon. When the woman's boyfriend, Billy Douglas, "criminally assaulted" Lucille, Fay appealed to the McLendons to take the child and keep her safe. Lucille had no sooner moved in, however, when Fay changed her mind and asked to take her daughter back. The McLendons refused. Fay appealed to the police but was charged with vagrancy instead and Douglas was arrested. Next, Lucille's grandmother, Mrs. Mary C. Curtis of San Pedro, appeared in court asking to be appointed Lucille's guardian. The chief of police agreed that Fay Harmon "is absolutely unfit and improper person to take care of her daughter."[16] They likely felt the same way about Ida. The newspapers never did reveal what became of Lucille, but she was never documented as living with Ida after that.

Ida, now going by Annie McLendon, resigned herself to turning the home she shared with William into a boardinghouse. William worked at a lumber mill, but when he began having heart problems, he fell into a deep depression and began threatening to commit suicide. In early May, Ida stopped him just before he slit his own throat. "I am going to kill myself," he told her, "I am tired of life." A few days later, William came home from work and asked Ida for some bromidia, a sedative containing bromide, cannabis, and alcohol. Ida handed him a small bottle of the stuff and he took a sip. Later, as Ida fixed dinner, he downed the entire bottle. Ida found him unconscious on the floor. The *San Diego Union* told what happened next. "Mrs. McLendon ran aimlessly about the street, crying: 'My husband has taken poison; get me a doctor.' Patrolman Ben Squires, hearing the cries of the woman, hurried down Fifth Street to learn what was the matter. At Fifth and O streets the disheartened wife threw herself into his arms with the plea: 'Get me a doctor, my husband is dying.'" Dr. E. L. Rayber was summoned, but William McLendon died two hours later. Ida told others that she believed her husband must have taken something else in combination with the drug.[17]

Ida's grief for McLendon was genuine. Following his death, she began calling her rooming house "The Marion," perhaps after her husband's birthplace in Marion County, South Carolina. The 1910 census lists Annie McLendon, the once famous madam, as just another boardinghouse keeper. Living with her was yet another child, six-year-old "Ivoal Marze," who was identified as Ida's godson. Ida told the census taker that the child and his father both were born in California, and that his mother was a Spaniard from Mexico. Ten years later, the census recorded the boy as Ivol Marcus. He was still living with Ida and was working a government job. Ivol disappears from record after 1921.

Ida may have been playing the role of mother, but later in 1910, it was revealed that she was back dabbling in the prostitution industry. In October, two "women of the underworld" identified as "Jane Doe" and Virginia Martin were arrested at Ida's "rooming house on G Street."[18] Ida herself seems to have escaped arrest, and it is plausible that she was merely renting rooms to the girls. At any rate, nothing else of note happened to her until 1914, when she moved again to 214 G Street. Ida's kindness was put to the test again in 1916, when she put up a bond for chauffeur

Edward Webb who was charged with manslaughter. When Webb some-how violated the bond, Ida successfully had him arrested. Webb merely "secured another bondsman, V. B. Naylor, and was released."[19]

Even more children would eventually come to live with Ida: The 1920 census identifies seven-year-old Beatrice Edmons [sic] and five-year-old Robert Roy Edmons as her "daughter" and "son." The children's mother, Nellie Edmonds, had lodged with Ida for two years beginning in 1912, but died in 1916. Two other children in the house, Georgia and Patricia Twombly, were children (or possibly grandchildren) of Ida's renter, Arthur Twombly. Ida's support of orphaned children apparently became so well-known that in March of 1921, her name was written in on a ballot for election to the board of education. She did not win.

Later that spring, a *San Diego Union* reporter happened to pen an article about Ida, apparently unaware that she was once the best-known madam in town. Instead, the article focused on two of the family pets, a cat named Malty and a rescued pigeon named Major Hufeland. The pigeon, the writer explained, was Robert Edmons's own pet and had the run of the house. When Malty gave birth to five kittens, the bird protected them fiercely if the mother left them alone. And if someone picked up one of the kittens, Major Hufeland "pecked and scratched" the perpetrator until the kitten was returned to its protective crate.[20] If anyone reading the article recognized Ida from her former career, they did not let on.

Some people did, however, remember Ida from her days as a madam. San Diego resident Jerry MacMullen remembered his father taking him to see the Canary Cottage before it was torn down in about 1911, and also seeing Ida when he was a police reporter for the *San Diego Tribune* in 1921:

> *I was down there on police beat—that's when they had no police station—on Second Street right next door to where the Shore Patrol is now. This dreadful old hag used to come shuffling down the sidewalk in a lousy looking dress and carpet slippers*

*on. Frequently she would stop in front of the police station and*
*chat with some of the older policemen, then go shuffling along*
*on down Second Street. I asked George Pringle one day, one day*
*after he had been talking to her, "George, who is the old lady*
*who comes by and talks to you?" He said, "That's Ida Bailey!"*[21]

Ida may have appeared as an "old hag" to MacMullen, but those who knew her liked her. When a fire broke out at her house in 1922, the fire department was quick to put it out. Ida's biggest loss was some expensive clothing, perhaps left over from her glory days. In 1923, however, she was arrested again—this time for selling moonshine to her former tenant, Roy Staggs. He too was arrested, for disturbing the peace. A search of Ida's house revealed twenty pints of illegal whiskey hidden in a suitcase. Bail was set at two thousand dollars, a far cry from the days Ida bonded out for a mere hundred dollars. She and Stagg were arrested again two months later when a gallon of "white mule" was found during another raid. The lady used her old ruse of pleading guilty, but her fine of $150 was lowered to just fifty dollars when it came to the court's attention that that lady was in the habit of adopting and raising orphans and had made several donations to charities.[22]

By 1926, Ida was living at 141 F Street. But she continued moving around for the several more years, and her last known address was at 41 West 30th Street. As a goodwill gesture toward the elderly woman, the fire department gave her a special basket of treats during their annual Christmas drives. The gesture was most ironic since Ida had spent so many of her years giving to others. Where and when the iconic madam died remains unknown, although one source says that during her last years she lived in an "institution."

# CHAPTER 7

—•◦•—

*Sacramento:*
*The Scarlet Women of "Sactown"*

Sacramento's beginnings date back to the discovery of gold at John A. Sutter's mill at Coloma in 1847. Sutter contracted James Marshall to construct a sawmill, and the following year the builder chanced to find a flake of gold nearby. The great California gold rush was on. Sutter also had planned to establish his own town, Sutterville, around a wharf known as the Embarcadero. Instead, the fledgling community wound up being called Sacramento City, after a nearby river of the same name. By the summer of 1849, gambling houses and saloons had made their inevitable appearance.

The thousands of "forty-niners" who made their way to Sacramento were a motley bunch. They dug for gold as needed, netting tens of thousands of dollars and spending the majority of it on high-priced goods in the saloons and gambling halls—and on the good time girls who fluttered into town seemingly from nowhere. In his book *Forty-Niners*, Archer Butler Hulbert paraphrased the thoughts of a miner at a "palace of refreshment" in Sacramento. There, a "'Sacramento Gal' waved a scarf in Ox Bow's face as she passed, to the mild amusement of Wagonhound; suddenly the latter, just mellow with beer, leaned over to his old pal and said: 'Now, old Ox, if you really want one o' them there gals what yer can't git on your merits, less adopt a strategy. Less half of us go daown [sic] one sider the room, an' t' other half t' other side, and run 'em up the room in relays like them wolves.'"[1]

By 1852 the growing businesses in Sacramento included lingerie shops, indicating the presence of women. But the fledgling city also suffered floods and even burned during a fire that same year. Sacramento naturally survived and was given the honor of state capital in 1854. The massive influx of people over the next six years continued to include prostitutes, many of them of Chinese and Mexican descent. By 1860, Sacramento was fairly overrun with these and other ladies of the evening. One of them was Lucie Octave, who owned property in Sacramento by 1866. Three years later, the city directory listed her at 57 L, the center of Sacramento's red-light district. Her housemate during the 1870 census was identified as "Mary Antoinette," and both women's occupations were documented as "easy virtue." Not until 1873 was Lucie arrested for running a house of ill fame along with the other occupants of the demimonde. She was in San Francisco when she died suddenly of apoplexy on December 7, 1880. The lady left no will, nor heirs, and it was not until 1897 that her estate—initially totaling $950 in cash and household items—was settled. By the time all was said and done, only $454.70 remained. Mary Miller, the wife of the estate's original executor W. B. Miller (who had died in 1896), expressed her willingness to pay the money to the county treasurer. The matter was settled in about 1898, and Lucie, including her burial site, were forgotten.

While Lucie was still alive, Sacramento's proper citizens began taking umbrage to the sin city in their midst. Police officers were pressured into standing guard in front of Sacramento's brothels beginning in 1870, until the madams of the town made a deal with the authorities: The ladies would keep their doors and curtains closed to make their illicit businesses "invisible to people on the street." In exchange, the sentinels in front of the houses of ill repute were to withdraw. The agreement took some time to commence, but by 1872 officers were instructed to cease "entering saloons, theaters, drinking houses, houses of ill fame, balls, circuses or any other place of entertainment."[2]

The new stipulation only encouraged the good time girls and their cohorts to conduct their businesses as they pleased, although violators outside of the red-light realm still answered to the law for breaking ordinances. Over time, the situation spiraled out of control. Finally, in 1878, a group of Sacramento legislators took a trip to the Upper Tenderloin in bawdy San Francisco to observe the anti-prostitution laws in place and whether they might be useful in Sacramento. No such laws, however, came forth as a result of the visit.

Eighteen eighty-five proved to be a banner year for Sacramento's soiled doves. The population had reached about twenty-five thousand and included a bevy of buxom women who came to the attention of authorities. On January 4, the *Sacramento Daily Bee* published a lengthy article about Emma Ossom, a girl of sixteen who was "an overgrown, awkward child with features that indicate weakness of character than evil tendencies." Emma's story began with a visit to her brother in San Francisco. When she returned to Sacramento, instead of going home Emma "fell into the company of Thomas Shields. And his divorced, but attached, wife, and has been with them and Dollie McClintock ever since."

Dollie and the Shields talked Emma into working as a prostitute on the streets. The girl gave Shields half of what she earned, with the promise that he would get her a better job in a house of prostitution he knew of. The two went there on January 3, but the madam "objected to the presence of the girl," perhaps because Emma was so young. The teenager apparently left, but Shields remained at the house where he was arrested in the early morning of January 4. Also arrested was an opium fiend identified as Billy Young, and it was discovered he had offered to take Emma to Oregon. Finally, Emma herself was arrested by an Officer Farrell on J Street.

Emma did not seem to know whether her parents were aware of her return and so was incarcerated for the time being. While she was out in

*Sacramento's J Street, where white slave Emma Ossom was arrested and James Powellson paraded around wearing purple pantaloons.* Library of Congress

the jail yard, Young called to the girl from his cell and warned her "not to tell on him, and saying that he would deny everything." But Emma did tell on him for threatening her. Young was moved to another cell. Emma told more, too. She said that she had "been in company" with one Jerry Burns, and that Gus Freeman had "made overtures to her." But she defended Thomas Shields, even though he had gotten her into trouble in the first place. "The city today is full of these male parasites," the *Sacramento Daily Bee* commented.[3]

What became of Emma Ossom is unknown, but more charges and arrests would be levied against Sacramento's prostitutes. On January 7 Alice Moran, Mollie Clark, and Em Carey were arrested for "exhibiting" and fined five dollars.[4] On March 13, Maggie Wilson also was charged with exhibiting. Then, on March 20, prostitutes Lizzie Bellman and Alice Lapean of L Street appeared in court. Alice was noted as being especially belligerent about officers repeatedly demanding that she keep her doors and window closed over the past year. When an officer decided to close the door of her brothel himself, she defiantly swung it back open. Alice also had been previously arrested for "exhibiting her person and place in such a way as to indicate her business." Police drew the line when Alice installed a bar in her front room as a means to keep her door open. Because she had legally purchased a liquor license, however, they were unable to convict her. Instead, they settled for arresting both her and Lizzie for "violating the ordinance about exhibiting." The jury, however, acquitted the ladies. In reporting the defeat, the *Sacramento Daily Bee* published each juror's name so the public would know who allowed Lizzie and Alice to slide.[5]

In April two more prostitutes, Josephine Macobo and Maty Miller, were accused by Matthew Fox of stealing his money. In court, however, it was noted that Fox was "very vague," perhaps because he did not want to admit that the crime occurred in a brothel. The outcome of the trial remains unknown, but Josephine was arrested again ten days later for exhibiting.[6] Theft from customers also was common. On May 6, prostitutes Louisa Malagee and Irene Sweeney of L Street were accused of "playing the panel game upon G. Cordona, and relieving his pocket of $20." The "panel game" consisted of quietly sliding a hidden panel in a bordello boudoir open and stealing money from the customer's pants while he was engaged with a prostitute. In this case, Cordona's friend was in the next room and witnessed one of the women as she opened the panel adjoining the other room.[7]

Crime among the good time girls of Sacramento apparently came in pairs. In June two more prostitutes, Katie Wilson and Josie Powers, were charged with robbing a Nevada man at their brothel. One of them had kept him engaged while the other reached in through the door and liberated a ten-dollar gold piece from the man's pants. The man witnessed the theft, but when he demanded his money, the girls threatened to charge him with "bestial conduct." He did report the incident to police but was afraid to press charges. Police Chief Jackson and Officer

Kent, however, persuaded him to do so. In court, the ladies followed through on their threat but were duly charged with petit larceny. Had they not been convicted, according to the *Sacramento Daily Bee*, the police had planned to charge them with vagrancy in order to make them leave town. That plan was apparently working, for thirteen other women were indeed charged with vagrancy, "making vacant 13 of the houses about Second and L streets."[8]

Not all bawdy women committed crimes; sometimes they were the victim. Shortly after Katie and Josie were arrested, one George Thomas was charged with making threats against Nettie or Nellie Webster, whom he had brought from San Francisco with another woman to take jobs as "variety actresses" in "Dutch Louise" Strauss's saloon on K Street. The other woman, Lizzie McCarty, went back to San Francisco but Nettie inexplicably remained—until Thomas demanded she give him half of her earnings and pulled a gun on her when she refused. Nettie reported him to police, and surprisingly, Thomas pleaded guilty. He was fined ninety dollars or ninety days in jail, the judge remarking that "we do not want any men or women of this class in our city."[9]

One of the most colorful pimps in Sacramento by far was James Powellson, "an alleged man," who was seen in July of 1885 "promenading J Street, arrayed in lavender colored pantaloons, a cutaway coat, and other fashionable habiliments." The spectacle was quite a shock, with the *Sacramento Daily Bee* commenting, "In the long list of hell's souls there could not be found a lower wretch than this thing." Powellson, it was said, had degraded "three or four girls in Sacramento." Although it was noted that he "is always well dressed, neat and dapper," the man had just recently been released from state prison "for ruining Lillie Nichols, of this city." He was initially sentenced to ten years in jail but appealed and had been discharged on a technicality. The *Bee* expressed its hope that police would eventually find a way to chase the fancy man out of town.[10]

The sale of liquor also was an issue. In July, it came to the attention of authorities that women were selling liquor from their brothels without a license. Four women—Fannie Brown, Kate Thompson, Ella Mills, and C. Dwyer—agreed to buy a license for twenty-five dollars for a year. A fifth woman, Nellie McDowell, refused to do so until she was threatened with arrest. But Nellie was in jail already, charged with "using the machinery of the criminal law" to collect a debt from another prostitute, Hattie Fisk. Hattie owed Nellie thirty-five dollars after she and a man had rented a room but snuck out the next morning without paying. Nellie tracked the couple to Stockton where they were arrested and returned to Sacramento. Hattie told police she had no money but would pay the debt when she acquired the cash.[11]

In August, Nellie made the papers again when her lover, Louis Hansche, was arrested for vagrancy. Hansche lived at 220 L Street with Nellie, in a house that was connected via a hallway to the place next door. One of the arresting officers testified that he told Hansche, "Lou, we don't want to do this, but the newspapers have said so much about this that we have to do it to show the people that we are not accepting money from you fellows to let you go free." On the stand, Hansche testified that he was employed, that he had purchased Nellie's house from her, and that the woman had never given him money. He also claimed that he did not know whether the female boarders of his so-called lodging house were prostitutes. One male boarder, William Gunn, testified that he always paid his rent to Hansche. So did Miss Belle Taylor. As for Nellie, she claimed that she did not support or even live with Hansche and that she only sold him the furniture in the house. Hansche was found guilty anyway to the satisfaction of the *Sacramento Daily Bee*. "Let all these low, contemptible apologies for men be driven out of the city," the paper concluded.[12]

The tirade against pimps continued. On August 18 Louis Robinson, whose companion (and perhaps wife) was prostitute Lillie Robinson, was put on trial for vagrancy. The next day, J. D. Smith was tried for "keeping a disorderly house." In November, William McIntyre was arrested for disturbing the peace at the brothel of Maud Wood on L Street. Both Maud and another girl, May Williams, testified that McIntyre had appeared at the house and offered to bring in a "hooster" who could then be robbed by the three. When Maud noticed a bunch of keys missing, she accused McIntyre, who "raised the disturbance which resulted in his arrest."[13]

The year rounded out with the December 21 arrest of Cora Phelps for disturbing the peace, as well as Sarah Doheny and Kittie McKenna for vagrancy. When the latter two women were deposited in the jail, one of them told others that if she was brought to trial, she planned to "tell all she knew about certain transactions involving several police officers." The girl claimed to know that certain officers were extorting money from various "fallen women" and even named them. As usual, according to the *Sacramento Daily Bee*, the names were supplied neither to officers nor the newspaper.[14]

The incidents and arrests of 1885 are exemplary of Sacramento's battle against its wayward women for well over a decade. It is interesting to note, however, that the numerous arrests of red-light ladies did little to quell the lawbreaking and incidents in the red-light district. As late as 1894, the *San Francisco Call* reported on Lent Burrow, a farmhand who "was shot, and probably fatally, while resisting arrest yesterday afternoon." Burrow and his buddies were at the brothel of Belle Curtis when they "created a disturbance." Belle duly swore out a warrant for Burrows's arrest, but he bolted when two policemen arrived. The officers commanded him to halt, and when he didn't, one of them fired at the man. Burrows kept running but was later found in a barn with a gunshot wound to the abdomen. Doctors, according to the paper, "consider[ed] the chances of recovery as very slim."[15]

By 1895 nearly two entire blocks were devoted to the notorious red-light district on L Street between 2nd and 3rd Streets.[16] Mrs. Florence

Roberts, a self-made missionary, saw plenty of work to be done when she came to California with her miner husband and their son in 1897. It was in Sacramento, while attending the First Baptist Church, that Florence received "my first real knowledge of the unfortunate of my sex." Florence decided that her mission should be to help the women. Years later, she penned a book, *Fifteen Years with the Outcast*, about her experiences.

Florence said that at the sermon she attended, Reverend A. B. Banks asked for volunteers to deliver handbills to the local brothels and invite their occupants to a revival. Florence raised her hand. "How did they accept, you ask?" she later wrote. "Many with tears coursing down their cheeks. Very few but manifested some feeling. Scarcely any, however, promised to come out to the revival services. Nearly all declared that they did not believe they would receive kind treatment if they did come, and none of them wanted to be looked upon or treated as an outcast." Only one woman actually allowed Florence to "come in and pray for her" which, according to the missionary, later resulted in the girl being "saved."[17]

Later that year, a Mrs. Glade and other women from the church acquired a ten-room cottage to open a "rescue home for girls" at the corner of O and 2nd Streets. The place needed repairs and contained only one piece of furniture. Back at her home in Redding, Florence was relegated to seeking donations to furnish the place properly. The lady was indeed devoted to her rescue work. When her husband later told her that she must choose between her mission and him, she chose her work. And when the church summoned her back to the rescue home in Sacramento, she went.[18]

One of Florence's first duties at the home was to accompany thirteen girls to church. Florence feared she might be seen in the company of fallen flowers; sure enough, "we had not traveled half a block when, on turning a corner, I saw a family whom my family held in high estimation. We both received a never-to-be-forgotten shock." Thankfully, Florence's charges "behaved beautifully."[19] Her work paid off; one of her first triumphs was the taming of a girl she called Rita. The child of a Barbary Coast prostitute in San Francisco, Rita was by then twenty-one years old and a "roguish, fun-loving, childish little woman." Somehow, her mother had "guarded her from criminal assault," but Rita had seen the everyday goings-on in the toughest red-light neighborhood in the city and her mother was actually glad to see the girl enter the rescue home.

On Rita's first day at church with Florence and the other girls from the home, the group sat in the second row from the pulpit. Rita was seated next to Florence, but soon "began to embarrass and disconcert me by her actions, causing the rest of the girls to titter (sometimes audibly)." When an usher told Florence to take the girl outside, Rita answered defiantly, "I ain't agoing [sic] out." Her remark was the last straw for Florence, who "let my head sink forward on the back of the pew in front of me," and began to cry. Then she felt a tug on her sleeve. It was Rita, who leaned against her and whispered, "Mother, don't cry; I'll be good. Don't cry." The incident was a turning point for the girl, who eventually learned to read the Bible, moved on to another home in San Francisco, and eventually married.[20]

Not all of Florence's stories had happy endings. Another girl at the home, who she called Leila, was described as a "rather reserved, high-strung aristocratic looking girl." The girl's former homelife with her mother in San Francisco had been far from ideal. The family was poor, and Leila fought with her mother frequently. When she was fifteen, she left school to work as a "waitress" for a family. One day at church, Leila met a seemingly kind man, Claude Forrester, who promised her wealth and gifts. He eventually took her to meet his mother, but the woman turned out to be a madam of Mason Street. A Chinese servant served some refreshments. Leila drank one and the next thing she knew, she had awakened in a room somewhere in the house where she was soon forced into prostitution.

After about a year, Leila was inexplicably turned out of the Mason Street house. A missionary next found her "sitting on a table in a 'Ladies' entrance department of a saloon" and offered to take her to the rescue home in Sacramento. Leila agreed. When her mother discovered where Leila was, she hastened to visit and promised that if Leila could go home with her, "under no circumstances would she ever remind her of the past." Unfortunately, the woman did not keep her promise. During yet another terrible argument, Leila fled. When Florence and her missionaries found her again, the girl was now nineteen and "no language of mine could describe her awful physical condition," said Florence. Worse yet, Leila "was so far gone that she coldly refused all God's and our overtures of mercy." Florence had clearly lost a round with one of her wayward girls. The best she could do was make sure to identify the man who had seduced Leila and sent her on her downward spiral. "Thousands of cases today parallel this one," she warned. Florence eventually relocated to Mrs. Kauffman's rescue home in San Francisco and continued her work.[21]

One of the longest-known madams of Sacramento was Fannie Brown. Born circa 1850 in Ireland, Fannie's first appearance in America was documented by her marriage (as Fannie Watch) to a Russian named Charles Maxmilian Riwotzky. The couple was united in matrimony in 1883 in San Joaquin County.[22] Riwotzky was nearly twenty years older than Fannie, but theirs was a seemingly happy and lengthy marriage. By 1889, the pair was living at 909 2nd Street in Sacramento, where Fannie would remain for over three decades. Around 1893, Fannie began appearing in the city directory as Fannie Brown and running, from all appearances, a house of ill repute. Charles, meanwhile, pursued a career as a "capitalist."[23]

Later directories would show that Fannie's place was quite large. In 1900, however, only one boarder appeared in the census. Her name was Ann Davis, and it was probably she who answered the census taker's questions since Fannie was recorded as being born in 1831 in New York, just like Ann. Most notable is that Fannie was also documented as a prostitute, a label assigned to no other woman in Sacramento at the time. Due to her age, Ann was probably not a prostitute but Fannie's servant.

From all appearances, Fannie ran a good, clean, even respectable house of prostitution. In city directories she was usually listed as keeping furnished rooms, and newspapers are scant on her activities. Not until 1908 did the *Sacramento Union* mention her when Fannie's place, now called the Palace, suffered a fire. It was believed to have been electrical in nature; one of Fannie's girls, Hazel Ashton, told firemen she had left an "electric light" burning when she left her room, where the fire started. Hazel's room was gutted, and she lost most of her clothing. Another woman, Dorothy Doro, "fainted in her room" and was saved by a Patrolman Ryan who "tore through the thick smoke in the upper hallway" and carried the girl downstairs. The paper reported on the madam's reaction to the fire: "'I've been here all these years and never had a thing like this happen before,' moaned Fannie Brown, as she hugged her jewels and nervously watched the firemen work about her." In the end, the Palace mostly suffered water damage. The "paper in the hallway was peeled off and the carpets soaked with the water, so that the total damage is thought to amount to about $3,000, partially covered by insurance."[24]

Fannie prevailed. By 1910 she employed a housekeeper and eight women whose occupations were left blank by the census taker.[25] All was well until 1914, when Fannie's house was condemned in June as part of a "cleanup" crusade in Sacramento's business section.[26] But the building was not torn down, as indicated by Fannie's continued listing in local city directories.[27] She was, however, arrested during a raid in July along with "nearly all of the twenty-eight scarlet women" of the red-light district.[28] After decades of letting the ladies slide, the authorities were at last being pressured into doing something about the naughty women in their midst. The effort was a success, and Fannie and her cohorts were closed down for good.

In 1916, Charles Riwotzky died with Fannie at his side—and newspapers at last revealed that the so-called capitalist's career had actually been that of an "old-time gambler and tenderloin leader." More importantly, Riwotzky left behind a safe deposit box at People's Savings Bank containing $119,000—nearly three million dollars in today's money.[29] Riwotzky's will dictated that Fannie was to receive everything, including his "personal money deposited in several banks." There also was a most interesting caveat in the will: "In the event of any woman, other than my said wife Fannie Riwotzky claiming to be my widow, or in the event of any such woman seeming to established any right to be so recognized, then give and bequeath to such woman the sum of one dollar and no more, herein expressly declaring that I have no other wife than the said Fannie Riwotzky, sometimes known as Fannie Brown." A similar clause verified that Riwotzky had no children.[30] If she hadn't been able to before, Fannie could now enjoy her retirement in style. She died on May 11, 1925, at the age of seventy-six. Today the Riwotzkys share a tombstone in Sacramento's East Lawn Memorial Park.[31]

Fannie Brown may have been shut down in 1914, but in 1917 news came that other good time girls were still plying their trade in Sacramento. On September 15 three reformers against prostitution—Edwin E. Grant, S. C. Barker, and R. Estrada—went into the Art Dance Hall in the two hundred block of L Street. The air inside the place was "hot and smoky"; through it the men observed "thirty to forty women and a large crowd of men." Two of the women came forward and introduced themselves as Ethel and Rose. The ladies offered liquor and sex, the latter which "would only cost a dollar and they could have sex right on the premises" in one of the curtained booths lining the room. Awhile later another woman, May Dixon, asked the men if they wanted to go to her apartment at 417 K Street. There, she said, the men could have sex for a few dollars.[32]

Such antics continued through at least 1921, when police chief Barney McShane announced that due to women violating California's Red Light Abatement Act, "several places in the lower end of the city" would be raided and closed. "We hate to be hard on the owners of the properties," McShane told the *Sacramento Union*, "but they are aware of the use to which their premises are being put and it is up to them to put a stop to it. Unless this is done, we will have to close the houses."[33] Within a few more years, the prostitution industry as Sacramento knew it since the pioneer days would finally draw to a close.

# CHAPTER 8

———◦●◦———

## *San Francisco:*
## *Sin in the City by the Bay*

In 1844, there were only about fifty people living in what would become San Francisco and the surrounding area. This number would change dramatically with the gold rush at Sutter's Mill. The sudden influx of miners, investors, merchants, suppliers, and thousands of others changed the sleepy landscape and its history forever beginning in 1846; ten years later, the blooming city's population was an amazing fifty thousand souls. Some of them were soiled doves, who flew into town so fast that locals called it the "Great Whore Invasion."[1]

The diversity of prostitutes during San Francisco's formative years was quite interesting. Already in place were natives who offered their women for sale or trade. Many of the seven hundred women who arrived during 1849 alone were of Latin American or Mexican descent. The prostitutes among them were initially called "Yankedos," a nickname assigned to those who served soldiers during the Mexican War of 1846–1847.[2] Most arrived each week by ship, their passage paid by others, on the agreement they would give their earnings to their benefactors until the money was paid back. Others were auctioned off, almost always unwillingly, and were forced to share their income with the highest bidder.

The first bawdy houses of San Francisco were primitive bagnios on Telegraph Hill and along the waterfront, where "Chileno" harlots offered sex for sale.[3] Of the women in "Little Chile," it was noted that "their habits were unclean and their manners base. The men seemed deceivers by nature, while the women . . . were immodest and impure to a shocking degree. These were washerwomen by day; by night—and if a dollar could be earned also by day—they were only prostitutes. . . . Their dwellings were dens of infamy, where drunkenness and whoredom, gambling, swindling, cursing and brawling, were constantly going on."[4] Many of these women suffered abuse from the racist general public. In some cases, they were branded with the letters "US." In other cases, their heads were shaved or, even worse, their ears were cut off. A few were murdered. An even worse fate was suffered by Chinese girls, who were now being brought to San Francisco. Those who survived passage on hideous and unhealthy slave ships were auctioned off at the Barracoon, located near a place called Queens Row.

Other prostitutes were Anglo, Australian, French, and German. Most of them could be found at Clark's Point near the bay, operating out of houses scattered among "tough sailor taverns" and gambling dens.[5] Of the foreigners, Frenchwomen would quickly rise to the highest class of prostitutes, largely because of the sex trade skills they had learned in their homeland. Nobody knew that back in Paris and other places, most of these Frenchwomen were common streetwalkers before coming to America. In San Francisco, however, they were considered quite special, establishing their own quarter and putting on airs as though they came from rich and exotic backgrounds. Those men who could afford them had no problem paying higher prices for "French love" or the "French treatment."[6]

As San Francisco grew, a number of fires plagued the budding town, which always managed to rebuild. Eventually the wayward women expanded their quarters to places along Clay, Jackson, Stockton, and Washington Streets, as well as "Cat Alley" on Pike Street and "Lansquenette Row" on Commercial.[7] In time, other streets where the red lantern hung would include California, Kearny, Montgomery, Pacific, and Sacramento Streets. Shorter streets, including Bacon, Belden, and Berry Place were included in the mix. Alleyways called Hinckley, Pinckley, and Virginia also offered pleasures of the flesh. These streets were occupied by all classes of bordellos, from two-room cribs to brothels to fancy parlor houses—but also outrageously huge brothels accommodating a hundred girls or more. Indeed, the first red-light districts grew to be quite large, and quickly. Neither the early harlots of the Bay City, nor their customers, could have realized (or cared) that San Francisco's bawdy districts would eventually make newspapers across America while rivaling those in other big cities.

Although the leading causes of death during this period included cholera, dysentery, scurvy, and various fevers, it was venereal disease that statistically sent the most people to the hospital. Yet women were in such demand at the time that ladies of ill repute were "almost accepted as members of society."[8] In even the city's nicest cafes, "badly drawn paintings of nude women" began appearing on the walls, and business owners began hiring prostitutes to blatantly pose nude as live art displays in their dining halls.[9] Very few people seemed to object to these vulgar and eye-popping public displays. Rather, men seemed to fall all over San Francisco's soiled doves. One young Frenchman talked of the "Countess of Campora" who was "one of the most shameless of women. She was a pseudo Lola Montez, seated like a queen at the counter of her Café restaurant. She was the Flower Queen whose beautiful efflorescence had been the joy and admiration of Chile for many years. But she had imposed on California her too ripe fruits which, although deteriorated, commanded fabulous prizes. At that time, from 1849 to 1852, I never knew of a woman who could procure such a large income by abusing her sex."[10]

The Countess of Campora was perhaps the same woman, lately of New Orleans, who threw a well-publicized soiree during the summer of

1849. The lady had with her "a stable of beautiful and highly cultured girls."[11] Her two-story house on Washington Street, directly across from the city center plaza, featured curtains "of the purest white lace." Inside, "all the fixtures are of a keeping, most expensive, most voluptuous, most gorgeous." The lady had "sent the most polite invitations, got up on the finest and most beautifully embossed note paper, to all the principal men of the city, including the collector of the port, mayor, aldermen, judges of the county, and members of the legislature."[12]

Guests to the party were requested to pay "not less than an ounce" of gold to "the bookkeeper" for the entertainments within—a good bargain since the countess's "six or eight young ladies," as well as other invited harlots, were in attendance. Everything was "very correct, nothing rude, everything refined and elegant, and it was astonishing to see the class of men who gathered there," observed one guest.[13] An orchestra played as guests danced with the girls who "are on their good behavior, and are proud once more to move and act and appear as ladies." Later an elaborate supper was served, complete with champagne at ten dollars per bottle. The countess paid a thousand dollars for the whole affair but would reap much more in profit before the night was through.[14]

Prostitutes who could not afford such a soiree participated in evening "promenades," whereby the women dressed in their best and strolled or rode in carriages down prominent thoroughfares.[15] They could also scare up business at places like the Bella Union, a large entertainment hall on Portsmouth Square, aka The Plaza, at Kearny and Washington Streets. Most of the entertainment at the Bella Union was naughty and bawdy. Although numerous famous performers appeared there, the in-between acts included risqué—and sometimes obscene—shows. Both performers and waiter girls were encouraged to sell sex on the side in curtained booths. The owners of the place liked to call it the "Wickedest Place in the West."[16]

In those early days, high prices were common—largely because San Francisco was growing so fast that there was a shortage of accommodations, food, and other necessary items. One could expect to pay as much as four dollars for a dozen eggs and between $1.50 and five dollars for a meal. An ounce of gold was the weekly price of sleeping on the floor of a gambling house. Most hotel guests were expected to share their rooms with others, paying $1.50 to sleep on the floor with a blanket. Those lucky enough to rent a private room paid between two and three hundred dollars monthly. Fancier places charged between five hundred and a thousand dollars. The prices for sex were equally inflated. Lonely men paid upward of an ounce of gold just to chat or have a drink with a shady lady. Those wishing to spend the night with her paid between two hundred and six hundred dollars.

By now, the respectable ladies of Frisco were uncomfortably aware of the good time girls in their midst. Prostitutes, it seemed, were everywhere—even around the post office and the justice's court on Portsmouth Square. There were incidents: At one of the city's first formal functions, for instance, a number of wives met a prostitute named "Mrs." Irene McCready who dared to attend the party on the arm of James McCabe. The man was one of the wealthiest in town, but his money came from his partial ownership of a brothel called the El Dorado. Everybody at the party knew that the "splendidly dressed" lady was a "disreputable" woman. Pioneer wife Sarah Royce, who was in attendance, recalled that the proper ladies in the room pressured their husbands into making sure McCabe knew that his escort was unacceptable.

Royce and her respectable counterparts were much relieved when Irene and her girls sailed for Oregon in 1850. A bad storm drove the ship back to San Francisco, however, and Irene opened a new parlor house instead. Soon after, she received a bill to pay "her share in the loss suffered by the consignees" of the ship during the storm. Irene demanded an explanation, and the ship's owner sent a young married man to discuss the matter with her. Irene listened politely, and even chatted amicably with the gentleman—before she suddenly accused him of stealing a diamond pin that had been on the table. The madam next scurried to report the theft to Judge Edward P. McGowan, who actually kept quarters with a "lewd" woman himself. McGowan had a chat with the shipowner's attorney, quietly advising him to just pay the cost of the missing pin to avoid a scandal. The matter was settled.[17]

Irene's relationship with McCabe ended in the fall of 1850. The woman was simply too fond of throwing fits about her man's attentions to other women, especially in front of everyone at the El Dorado. One day, McCabe had had enough of her and gave her a sound thrashing. Soon afterward, word came to McCabe that Irene missed him terribly. The gullible man went to see her, and Irene lovingly offered him a glass of wine—which she had laced with drugs. As soon as McCabe passed out Irene set about shaving off every hair on his body. McGowan remembered running into McCabe a short time later and said that the man was "disguised in a slouched hat pulled down over his ears." The judge added that "He did not appear in his usual haunts until his hair had grown out."[18] Irene eventually moved to Sacramento. Meanwhile, McGowan's fondness for hanging out at Madam Du Bon Court's palace of pleasure eventually caught up with him, and the gossip about him inspired him to leave town. They say he too was headed for Sacramento, to the house of a French prostitute known only as Lenny.

McGowan's ousting was a quiet victory for proper folks, but what remained foremost in their thoughts were the women who ended his career. "There are some honest women in San Francisco," wrote Albert Benard de Russailh in his journal in 1851, "but not many."[19] Part of the trouble was that prostitutes were scattered everywhere. Following another catastrophic fire in 1851, the city rebuilt yet again. Within two years some 537 saloons, forty-six gambling houses, and forty-eight brothels were operating. The number of brothels had increased to over one hundred just in the area north of Portsmouth Square by 1855.

Most interesting is the way the general public viewed the fancy French ladies, who were still regarded as women who "gave ease, taste and sprightly elegance to the manners of the town." Jealous wives and women seeking marriage could not miss the well-dressed harlots on the streets, as well as at masquerade balls where everybody wore a mask and nobody, supposedly, was recognizable. No respectable woman dared attend the annual Prostitutes Ball at the Music Hall, the first of which was held in 1855, but certainly prostitutes were a common sight on the streets. Many historians surmise that prostitutes represented the "most elegantly dressed women in San Francisco," and that women of civilized society naturally envied their underworld counterparts.[20] It is not surprising that respectable women worked to keep up with the fashion sense of the shady ladies, ordering and making dresses to match them. And, the Frenchwomen's love of fine clothing "greatly encouraged the splendid character of the shops of jewelers, silk merchants, milliners and others whom women chiefly patronize."[21]

What to do about the painted ladies who seemed to be everywhere? The respectable element turned their attentions to how eastern cities segregated their red-light ladies to their own districts and forbade them from openly soliciting. Their methods especially interested respectable women, for it was they who were forced to pass by prostitutes while shopping along Stockton and Montgomery Streets with their children. Although the women's complaints applied to all tainted women, it was the Anglo prostitutes "who dwell in splendid houses in the principal streets of the city, and endeavor to attract attention by sitting before their open windows and doors" who annoyed them the most. Soon, the *San Francisco Chronicle* was imploring officials to "remove the temptation from those who have not yet fallen into the fatal passion."[22]

With the newspaper backing them up, the proper ladies' voices grew stronger. "Is it not wonderful that young men should nightly spend their evenings, like dogs, smelling out all these vile excrescences, peeking through the cracks and crevices of doors, windows, and blinds in our crowded thoroughfares, in the full face of ladies and gentlemen going to and returning from church?" queried one angry woman. Another noted how men "will pass the early part of the evening in the society of virtuous females, discoursing upon the charms of domestic life, and the solace of home, and virtuous associations! [A]nd directly upon leaving, cross the street and enter a house of ill fame." One woman told of passing a group of harlots who "attracted my attention by giggling, laughing and making impertinent remarks to each other, looking me in the face and passing, and then allowing me to repass them under their licentious stare and meaningless giggle."[23]

Due to pressure from decent society, the good time girls and gamblers along Stockton and Montgomery Streets began gradually relegating their activities to the back rooms, second floors, and other quarters out of sight from the public. Meanwhile, crusaders opened the House of Refuge in 1859, in hopes of reforming fallen women.[24] The city supported the idea, offering funding for the organization. But the "Barbary Coast," as Pacific Street (aka Terrific Street) was called by the mid-1860s, only grew worse. By that time, the area had already been cleaned out twice by do-gooder vigilantes but was growing again. The locale became known for its population of "pirates, cut-throats and dens of thieves," and nearby Kearny Street was so fraught with violence that it was nicknamed "Battle Row." So smelly was one saloon at the corner of Kearny and Pacific that it was christened "The Billy Goat." Worst of all was The Boar's Place, where spectators could watch a woman interacting with a male pig.[25]

Most of the madams of the Barbary Coast rose above the miscreants of Kearny Street and were a diverse bunch. They included Madame

Bertha, who hosted organ recitals each Sunday afternoon for specially invited guests. Bertha played the piano as her girls sang popular songs of the day. Another parlor house was run by Lizzie Oliver, who took over Belle Cora's house after the illustrious madam died in 1862. Almost immediately Lizzie had trouble with one James Dobson, who was refused entry to the house. Declaring that "neither doors nor whores" could keep him out, Dobson forced his way in. Lizzie pressed charges. The pro-prostitution *California Police Gazette* objected to the twenty-five-dollar fine imposed on Dobson, saying it should have been more. "Be these women what they may," the paper editorialized, "they are, nevertheless entitled to protection against a set of loafers who, in their drunken sprees, force themselves into their houses."[26]

Less refined was Johanna Werner of Sacramento Street who employed three French girls, known as the "Three Lively Fleas," to perform "erotic exhibitions."[27] Johanna's employees averaged between fourteen and seventeen years in age, and sometimes even younger. The girls were frequently auctioned off to men, and Johanna had at least one male procurer who willingly went in search of fresh girls on her behalf. Johanna also was the first madam to advertise her house of ill fame outside of San Francisco—by sending images of nude women to those on her carefully crafted mailing list. Naturally, other madams followed suit, although over time the nude pictures were left out so the women could escape prosecution for sending obscene literature through the U.S. mail.

Prostitutes who could not make the grade in parlor houses or even common brothels were relegated to the "cow-yard" cribs. Hell's Kitchen was opened by Ned "Bull Run" Allen in 1868. The building was a three-story combination dance hall and brothel on Pacific Street, with girls operating on the two upper floors. In the theater on the first floor, waitresses were required to wear "short red jackets, black stockings, ruffled silk garters, red slippers and nothing else." The dress code was changed after customers grew too randy, and the girls complained of being cold. But the ladies also were required to drink hard liquor as part of their job. Those who drank enough to pass out "could be had by anyone for twenty-five cents to a dollar, depending on her age and attractiveness." Allen, who was in the habit of drinking to excess at his competitors' places of business, was eventually stabbed to death after picking a fight in the Clover Club.[28]

In 1869, city officials finally passed an ordinance prohibiting women from working in dance halls or saloons. But the red-light ladies were so numerous that it was nearly impossible to enforce the law. Colonel Albert S. Evans explored the Barbary Coast for a night in 1873, noting that the area was "strewn end to end with the wrecks of humanity." In the brothels, he generalized, "A few red-faced, frowzy females will glance inquiringly at you from their seats just inside the doorways of the minor 'dead-falls;' little dens, with the bar stocked with well-drugged liquors—which to taste is to look death in the face and defy him—on one side of the front room, a sofa on the other, and at the rear an arched opening hung with tawdry red and white curtains, communicating with an inner room, into the hidden mysteries of which you and I do not care to penetrate."

Evans's party concluded their visit at the murder scene of a French prostitute in Stout's Alley. The men were escorted inside by an officer to the front room containing "a bed luxuriously furnished, a bureau, wardrobe, table, etc." There lay the "miserable victim" lying "in a pool of blood, the skull fractured by a blow with a chair." The woman's throat had been "cut from ear to ear "with a dull knife." Her bed and a pillow, "thrown against the wall at the other side of the room," were saturated with blood. The men theorized that the woman was hit with the chair as she slept but came to as her murderer retrieved a knife from the kitchen in the back room. "On returning, he found her standing up on the floor, she having staggered to her feet and endeavored to make her way to the door, probably with some dim, undefined, instinctive impulse, to call for assistance," Evans wrote. "He has then got her down upon the floor, stifled her voice with the pillow, and finished his work with the knife." The room had been ransacked, and the killer took time to wash the blood off himself in the kitchen before fleeing. Amazingly, the lady's "male friend" slept through the whole thing in an upstairs bedroom.[29]

The authorities were helpless, it seemed, to do much about the thousands of scarlet women in Frisco. When Johanna Schriffin opened her three-story "House of Blazes" along Chestnut Street, her respectable neighbors discovered the building was actually two or three bordellos in one and rented rooms to streetwalkers. Once, a policeman was sent there to arrest a thief and exited sans his handcuffs, pistol, cap, and blackjack—and no perpetrator. The House of Blazes was closed in November of 1878 while others like it remained open. "God-forsaken women are permitted to stand in their doors and windows dressed, or rather 'undressed' in the most shameful manner, inviting men and boys to enter their vile dens," tattled a local newspaper, the *WASP*, in 1876.[30] And when a wealthy young man dared to complain that his pockets had been picked while he was at a "three-story rookery" in 1884, the girls of the house, and their pimps, beat him to death using pokers and carriage whips.[31] Notably, as much as they reported on such grisly incidents, the newspapers rarely revealed that a good number of brothel properties were owned by groups of businessmen or city officials.

In 1897, Mrs. Elizabeth Kauffman opened the Home of Peace, a rescue mission for wayward girls. Her assistants included Florence Roberts, the rescue home veteran from Sacramento. Florence remembered the first night she and Elizabeth visited the Barbary Coast. The women entered The Klondyke, a combination saloon and dance hall. The place was so awful that Florence declined to describe it in detail in her 1912 book, *Fifteen Years with the Outcast*, lest any young people happen to read it. She did say that "I was looking upon a shameful scene of total depravity participated in by both sexes, some of whom were little more than in their teens." One of them, an intoxicated girl named Hazel, "sidled up to me," she remembered. "Say, what yer got in that case?" Hazel asked. Florence told her that it was an autoharp and began to play a song. "Don't, oh! Don't!" Hazel shrieked. "Oh! For God's sake, don't!" The girl burst into tears and buried her head "with its tawdry covering and matted mop of dirty hair" in Florence's lap. A year ago, she said, her dying mother had made Hazel promise to behave. "Just look how I've kept my word!" she muttered disgustedly. A man whom Florence met while he was in jail in Sacramento happened to be in the dance hall as well. Both he and Hazel agreed to go to the Home of Peace. Hazel, at least, remained there until she procured a domestic job with a Christian family.

Another time, Florence encountered a "beautiful, modest-looking young lady" standing at the bar in a dance hall, trying to repel the advances of a "pompous, sporty-looking middle-aged man." The bartender told her, "Here, none of those monkey-shines, Miss. You tend to business, d'you hear?" When Florence intervened, the man turned on her. "Here you," he sneered, "make yourself scarce. You and your kind are [expletive] hoodoos to our business." Florence refused and was joined by two other women, including Elizabeth Kauffman, who saw the bartender threaten to "brain" Florence with a soda-water bottle. "Go, go! He'll do it," the girl said, and whispered, "He's my father." Florence left and attempted to summon a policeman, who told her, "I can't interfere. The man has a license, his daughter isn't of age, he's her legal guardian." Florence returned the next morning with another officer, but the girl was gone.[32]

As these noble attempts were made to help prostitutes leave their miserable lives, another brothel, the Nymphia, emerged in 1899. Looming three stories tall with hundreds of "cubicles," the new place was the largest brothel on the entire Pacific coast for its time. The owners originally wanted to call the place Hotel Nymphomania, which was rejected by the authorities. Prostitutes were only charged five dollars' rent per night, but with stipulations: Each occupant was to remain completely naked while in her crib and was to service any man regardless of ethnicity. Each crib featured a window covered by a shade, which could be raised at any time by inserting a dime for a peek show—until too many customers were caught using slugs. By opening night three hundred ladies were present in the building and plans were already being made to build an annex for more cubicles. The Nymphia soon raised the ire of Reverend Terence Caraher of the Roman Catholic Church. After witnessing two police officers in front of the place who were instructed to keep order instead of making arrests, Caraher publicly attacked the police force. Within a year the Nymphia was raided. Several women were arrested, and the four male owners ultimately paid a fine of $250 each. The Nymphia finally closed down in 1903.

Unfortunately the Nymphia was only part of the problem. By 1900 the red-light district extended roughly from the bottom of Telegraph Hill and along Pacific Street and Broadway, all the way to the shoreline. Loud music poured from three solid blocks of dance halls as places like Canterbury Hall, the Dew Drop Inn, the Living Flea, Opera Comique, the Sign of the Red Rooster, Ye Olde Whore Shop, and others offered "erotica of a high order." A network of secret tunnels for smuggling girls, drugs, and alcohol ran underneath places called Bull Run, Dead Man's Alley, and Murder Point. All was in close proximity to China-town, whose residents were often blamed for the bawdy antics of the red-light district.

Newspapers did their best to keep up with the antics in the red-light district—although publisher William Randolph Hearst was lambasted for allowing his *San Francisco Examiner* to run "thinly disguised ads for prostitutes in the classified section." Reformers called the newspaper "The Whore's Daily Guide and Handy Compendium." The *San Francisco Call*, meanwhile, frequently published editorials shaming the red-light district. One target in 1902 was the Marsicania, "one of the vilest dens ever operated in San Francisco." The Marsicania housed about one hundred prostitutes who, like at the Nymphia, paid five dollars nightly in rent. According to one source, police "were legally restrained from blockading or entering the premises except under extreme emergencies." It took three years before the Marsicania was finally forced to close. A similar brothel, the Municipal Crib on Jackson Street, opened in 1904. The building spanned four floors: Mexican girls worked in the basement, black women were on the fourth floor, and women of other nationalities worked in between the two. Profits from the Municipal Crib went directly to city officials and prominent politicians—namely Mayor Eugene Schmitz and his attorney sidekick, Abraham Reuf. Police raids were forbidden, at least until Schmitz and Reuf were prosecuted for bribery and extortion. The Municipal Crib was finally closed in 1907.[33]

By 1906, the good people of San Francisco were truly tired of their behemoth demimonde. But their worries were temporarily forgotten on April 18 when, just after five o'clock in the morning, San Francisco began rumbling from beneath as the city's legendary earthquake began. For nearly a minute, the entire city became an upheaval of swaying buildings, roller-coaster roads, and a shaking so severe that hundreds of structures collapsed. An estimated three thousand people were killed, and another four hundred thousand were left homeless. In the aftermath immediately following, hundreds of fires began as survivors regained their bearings, looked for loved ones, assisted the injured, and located the dead. Like much of San Francisco, the entire Barbary Coast was destroyed.

Madam Jessie Hayman bears mention here because today she is heralded as a heroine in the quake's aftermath. Born Annie May Wyant in Louisiana in 1874, the lady arrived in San Francisco as Jessie Mellon in the early 1890s. By 1895 she was employed at the brothel of Mrs. Nina Hayman at 225 Ellis Street. When Nina left and married a wealthy lumber dealer in about 1898, she gave her brothel to Jessie. To honor the madam, Jessie began calling herself "Diamond Jessie Hayman." Even before she took over Nina's, Jessie was known as a "house favorite," and with good reason. The lady was described by San Francisco photographer Arnold Genthe as having "the face and figure of an empress, and the pose and manner of one as well."[34] Genthe was so impressed with Jessie that he included her on the guest list for a lavish dinner at Delmonico's restaurant in honor of a visit from the Grand Duke of Russia. The previously unidentified duke was most likely Boris Vladimirovich, who received his title in 1895 at the age of eighteen.

Even in royal circles Vladimirovich was a known playboy who loved to drink, gamble, and womanize. After a series of scandals, his parents sent him on a world tour in 1902 in an attempt to straighten him up. Little did they know that in San Francisco, the young duke would find more debauchery and wicked pastimes than he ever imagined. Jessie sat next to the duke at Delmonico's. Vladimirovich was smitten. The couple tore up San Francisco together, but when the duke asked her to return to Russia with him, Jessie declined. "No thank you," she is said to have politely responded. "I'm quite talked about enough here."[35] The duke settled for a life-size portrait of Jessie instead, which Genthe obligingly captured with his camera.

Whether Vladimirovich visited Jessie's parlor house is unrecorded, but if he did, he would have been impressed. One source states Jessie's brothel included a saloon, a champagne cellar, three fireplaces, and fifteen luxurious suites. Exactly which brothel it was is unknown, for Jessie owned several parlor houses and was growing quite wealthy. Her Chinese chef served the best in French and other cuisine, and champagne was always a staple. Jessie's boarders were beautiful, and the madam treated them well. Each paid five to fifteen dollars per day in rent, depending on their skills. The ladies kept any money they earned, including tips, and Jessie paid them a commission if she sold more

*The only known image of madam Jessie Hayman appears on her passport record from 1922.* National Archives and Records Administration

champagne than expected. There were, of course, rules: If they were out to dinner with a client, her ladies were to choose one of the many restaurants that offered Jessie a kickback for sending them customers. If an employee's wardrobe failed to meet with Jessie's standards, the madam took her shopping and chose her outfits. The girls were to pay her back out of their income, and the house maid alerted Jessie if anyone looked like they were going to skip with the goods.

Like any other madam in Frisco, Jessie occasionally suffered run-ins with the law. In 1905, for instance, both the madam and another woman, Leona Brooks, were suspected of aiding one Edward Smith who had been pilfering money from the city and had hidden a stash of forty-five thousand dollars somewhere. Even Pinkerton's detective agency suspected that Leona and Jessie, who was "en route to New Orleans," knew where the money was.[36] All of that was forgotten, however, on the day of the earthquake. Jessie and her girls had closed around four o'clock that morning, and the madam was dining at a nearby restaurant when the quake hit. Hastening to her parlor house on Ellis Street, Jessie observed that only the chimney was damaged. She next ordered a car and took her frightened employees with her (as well as much of her wine collection wrapped in their clothes) to her private residence on Post Street. The damage was minimal there, too, and the party stayed the night. In their absence, some soldiers lit a fire inside the empty Delmonico's restaurant to heat up coffee. The flames grew into a conflagration and burned numerous buildings, including Jessie's parlor house.

According to one witness, Jessie was at another of her brothels on Devisadero Street the day after the quake when three businessmen came by. Believing she was open for business, the men knocked on the door which was answered by a distraught Jessie. Two of her girls had already left her, she said, and the others were threatening to flee the city. The men were offered drinks if they agreed to stay "and keep the girls occupied" as Jessie's caretaker managed to round up several boxes of food.[37] Next, three firemen showed up, presumably to help Jessie put wet rags on her roof since fires were still burning throughout the city. Jessie begged them to stay too. She even sent a message to the men's wives, assuring them their husbands were safe, were busy fighting the fires, and were not cavorting with her girls. Then she made dinner for everyone herself.

Another legend states that Jessie and her girls helped other victims of the quake by cooking meals and giving out clothing. If Jessie was indeed a heroine in the aftermath of the quake, her deeds remain unrecorded in any official capacity. She did, however, pick up business faster than her competitors, her only loss being the Ellis Street house. But any good deeds Jessie might have performed in April were quickly overshadowed in August, when district attorney Henry Langdon announced he was going to "close down dens of vice."[38] Jessie was his first victim, arrested at another one of her brothels on Post Street.

Two months later, Henry Goldman took Jessie to court. A month before the earthquake, Goldman said, he had rented the first-floor rooms and the yard at Jessie's place on Devisadero Street to use as a saloon. Now, he claimed, Jessie was "building rooms in the yard" and had "practically blockaded" the entrance to his tavern.[39] As Goldman and the madam battled it out in court, Jessie was arrested again in January of 1907. Another scandal against her erupted in February, when prosecutors linked her to a prominent "club man" named Allen St. John Bowie—the same man Jessie had frantically queried about to the men in her house the day after the earthquake. Jessie later claimed she had married Bowie back in 1899, and it was he who had helped Jessie draw up Goldman's lease and who testified for her defense. The prosecution claimed the two were business partners and even co-owned the Devisadero house.[40] Now, San Francisco scuttlebutts had something they could sink their teeth into. But the only other article about the matter, published in June, merely stated that Goldman was still angry because Jessie was still building onto her own property.

Still, the authorities had it out for Diamond Jessie. In August of 1908, she was arrested again—this time for "harboring an alien," Ethel May Southweed of England. Jessie said she thought the girl was an American, and besides, Ethel was only hired to play piano and sing at her Mason Street brothel. The *San Francisco Call*, however, made it out as if Jessie had hired the girl for immoral purposes as part of her "slave trade" activities—largely because of a new federal law prohibiting "harboring and maintaining in a house of ill fame an alien who has not been in this county three years."[41] The madam was taken to the city prison with a bond of ten thousand dollars. Not surprisingly, Allen St. John Bowie paid the money. After three months of court, Jessie was found guilty, sentenced to a month in jail, and fined two hundred dollars.

Following her release, Jessie maintained two of her other houses on Eddy and Clay Streets for several more years. She, along with the rest of the demimonde, eventually closed for good in 1917 due to new legislation and church crusades. In her retirement, the wealthy madam decided to see the world and traveled to such exotic places as Hong Kong, India, France, Denmark, and Sweden. She was in London in 1923 when she died in her hotel from a heart attack. Her body was shipped back to San Francisco and buried at Cypress Lawn Cemetery in the catacombs. Her funeral cost of $119.25 was paid by one Arthur J. Seed. In its April 2 issue, the *Santa Cruz Evening News* reprinted a London newspaper report that "Jessie May Mellon Bowie" was "said to be the wife of an American millionaire." The *News* followed up by stating that "Allen St. John Bowie, prominent club man, to whom Miss Hayman is said to have been engaged, denied today she was his wife."[42] Had Bowie claimed to be Jessie's husband, he might have received a chunk of her $116,000 estate.

# CHAPTER 9

———— ◆◆ ————

## Sexual Slavery: The Put-Upon Chinagirls

*A green mansion is a place of filth and shame*
*Of lost chastity and lost virtue*
*Most repulsive it is to kiss the customers on the lips*
*And let them fondle every part of my body*
*I hesitate, I resist;*
*All the more shamed, beyond words*
*I must by all means leave this troupe of flowers and rouge;*
*Find a nice man and follow him as his woman.*

—POEM BY A NINETEENTH-CENTURY
CHINESE PROSTITUTE IN CALIFORNIA[1]

Of all the immigrants who came to America in search of a better life, the Chinese stood out more than any other. Unlike those of other nationalities, Asians looked markedly different. They dressed different. They spoke a singsong language that was impossible to comprehend. Their food smelled strange, and they ate with chopsticks instead of the traditional knife and fork. Even their medicine was odd, made with strange herbs and concoctions that were totally foreign to patent pill-taking and syrup-swilling Americans. As their numbers grew, others stereotyped them as weak and weird, and therefore untrustworthy. J. P.

C. Poulton took his opinion of them to the extreme: "The Chinese are an unprincipled, bigoted, and superstitious people. They are self conceited beyond description and are not of any benefit to the country."[2] Anglo laborers soon became angered at the immigrants' willingness to work for less, as well as their refusal to follow American laws. Others saw Chinatowns, like the one which eventually sprang up in San Francisco, as riddled with "filth, disease, opium dens, vice, fire hazard," and other unseemly characteristics.[3]

Much of China was ruled by tongs, businessmen with their own separate factions who were, for lack of a better word, the Chinese version of the mafia. They were among those to migrate to America as early as 1849, when around five thousand Chinamen arrived on the Pacific coast. So many of them settled in a mining camp known as Camp Washington and Washingtonville that the community was eventually renamed Chinese Camp. Within the camp were two tong factions, the Yan-Wo and the Sam Yaps. Their numbers would steadily increase; by 1850, 2,500 more Chinese were at another camp, Weaverville, where they offered highly popular "laundries, joss [a Chinese temple] houses, gambling cribs and opium dens."[4] These places were run by the tongs, whose function was to oversee all businesses, lifestyles, and culture of their people in America. And they did it with a vengeance.

Although the first Chinese immigrants were mostly men, women were eventually brought to America as well. Prior to 1851, only seven known Chinese women were documented in San Francisco. Of these, only one was married. But the vast majority of these and other Chinese women coming to America served one purpose, and one purpose only: They were to sell their bodies for sex with men. The first Chinese prostitutes were allowed to run their own businesses and leave the profession if they married. Their people called them "Baak Haak Chai," which translated to "one hundred men's wife."[5] Later, such freedoms fell to the wayside as tens of thousands of women, girls, and even children were literally enslaved and forced to live in squalid conditions.

One of those first seven women in San Francisco is believed to have been Ah Toy, although at least two sources state that she and a servant constituted the only two Asian girls in San Francisco, and perhaps California, at the time. Whichever is true, her story is remarkable. Born circa 1828 to a poor family in Canton, Ah Toy married and set out for America with her husband sometime after 1848. In one version of her story, the husband died en route and was buried at sea. Ah Toy wisely escaped the putrid living conditions aboard the ship by becoming the mistress of the ship's captain, who gave her several expensive silk outfits. She also managed to squirrel away some gold coins with which to begin her new life. Another source states that Ah Toy's husband was very much alive in China when he sent a letter to San Francisco's tongs and informed them he wanted his wife back. The matter was put to Ah Toy, who denied that she was anyone's wife and declined to go back to China. Other sources disagree whether Ah Toy was a sex slave, whether her husband intended her to work as a prostitute upon their arrival, whether she was forced into the trade to repay the cost of her passage, or whether she was simply forced to work as a prostitute due to her circumstances.

Whatever the case, Ah Toy was able to put on airs as an elite courtesan in San Francisco, with the jewels and wardrobe to prove it. Frenchman Albert Benard described her as "the strangely alluring Achoy [sic], with her slender body and laughing eyes." Writer Frank Soule was not as kind, commenting that "everybody knew that famous or infamous character, who was alternately the laughing-stock and the plague of the place."[6] When she was first taken to court in 1850 on charges of prostitution, Ah Toy employed two of the five women who arrived from China that year. Perhaps that is why she chose to marry one Henry Conrad on May 18 in Sonoma County. An American husband could yield much protection for a Chinese courtesan. Officials noted Conrad's marriage to "a Chinese lady, Assoy [sic]."[7] A newspaper also reported that Conrad married "the well-known China woman, Achoy [sic]."[8] Nobody could spell the lady's name, but they certainly knew who she was.

Henry Conrad did not last long in Ah Toy's life. About a year later, she took a new lover: John Clark, a brothel inspector who was part of the Committee of Vigilance dedicated to sweeping San Francisco clean of its foreign soiled doves. The relationship gave Ah Toy courage, for she was back in court in December of 1851 after catching one of her customers stealing her jewelry. Officers were alerted after hearing of "a series of musical screechings, performed by Miss Atoy [sic], and resembling somewhat a prolonged cry." Ah Toy emitted these alarms as she physically chased down the man herself, "seized him by the collar very much in the style of a police officer, and demanded a diamond pin which he and his party had taken away from her, after politely visiting her house and taking a drink with her." Police arrived at the scene to see Ah Toy making "herself distinctly heard for four squares around, although not very distinctly understood, and the 'volunteer' was marched off to the station house, where the matter was investigated." At the time, Ah Toy was likely running her brothel at 34 and 36 Pike Street, as she was listed there in the 1852–53 city directory. But when she told another man she was John Clark's mistress, Clark gave her a beating. The woman again fled to court in dishevelment with two black eyes. She told Judge Edward McGowan she only wanted an apology. McGowan, himself a red-light ladies' man, knew that Ah Toy regularly gave Clark money and that he would more than likely make up with her in order to keep getting it. With this reasoning in mind, McGowan declined to convict Clark.

Ah Toy was certainly aware that most Chinese women being brought to America were being taken to the joss house in Chinatown where they were "stripped and examined by prospective buyers." She may have even attended an auction, but initially preferred to work alone. Her brothel consisted of a couple of rooms. One of them was outfitted with a stage, from which the woman could perform a striptease before her infatuated, primarily white, customers. In the other room, holes were drilled in the wall for those wanting their own private peep show. A bouncer was employed to collect the money, and within a short time Ah Toy was making a killing in gold for her performances—without having to engage in sex with her customers. They say the line outside of her place sometimes spanned an entire block. To Ah Toy, her business was legitimately beyond that of common prostitution.

Ah Toy quickly gained the power she was seeking, and she was absolutely unwilling to part with it in any way. In 1853, when some men passed some bronze shavings off as gold as payment, Ah Toy boldly took them to court. She was described as being dressed in "an apricot stain jacket and willow-green pantaloons, with a colorful pair of tabis on her small, slightly bound feet. Her hair was arranged in the traditional chignon, her pencil thin black eyebrows contrasting exotically with her white, rice-powdered cheeks." Ah Toy's appearance, her evidence consisting of "a china basin full of brass filings," and her naming of those who had cheated her failed to impress anyone. Not surprisingly, the judge exercised the typical prejudice of the time and dismissed her case. Undaunted, Ah Toy soon sued another man. This time the defendant was Yee Ah Tye, a local tong boss who had been trying to extort a "protection fee" from the madam. This time the court ruled in her favor. It was the first time a Chinese immigrant, and a woman at that, successfully called upon American law to settle her dispute. [9]

By 1854, Ah Toy was actively participating in bringing over Chinese girls from her homeland. She would, over time, import, trick, and enslave thousands of women during her career. Did it bother Ah Toy to forcibly import Chinese girls to America against their will? Not a wit, apparently. She even encouraged the ship's crews to rape the girls on the way to America and to keep them in cages so they would "learn humility." [10] The more broken and submissive the girls were by the time they arrived in America, the less Ah Toy had to do before putting them to work. To assure their compliance, Ah Toy even "taught her girls to fear the police and at all costs to avoid the courts."[11] The practice was common: On his visit to "China Alley" in 1873, Colonel Albert S. Evans noticed that upon seeing him and his party moving down the alley, a Chinese girl, "with hair carefully braided and decked with artificial flowers, and cheeks and lips cunningly painted so as to resemble those of her frail Caucasian sisters," began tapping at the window of her "wicket" to attract their attention. When the girl saw a policeman with the men, however, she "shuts the wicket, and turns away as if she had not seen us at all. The alarm runs down the whole alley in an instant; there is a rattling of wickets, as if a hurricane was sweeping through the place, and in half a minute all is as silent as the grave, and not a head to be seen." The girls not only feared their captors, but also "what is in store for them if they are caught at it by the police."[12]

When she herself was finally arrested for prostitution, Ah Toy called upon her wealthier clients—white businessmen, city officials, judges, miners, and policemen—for defense. Sources differ as to whether Ah Toy won or lost her case, but she did sell her house and leave on a ship bound for China after another arrest in 1857. She was soon back, however, and had resumed business when she was arrested three more times in 1859. One of the arrests was made for beating one of her girls. But the lady was fond of loopholes, and when a new law prohibited bringing single women from China to America during the 1870s, Ah Toy simply claimed that her enslaved girls were married.

Even as Ah Toy abused her girls, she remained active in Chinatown and donated to charities for her people. When a steamer ship full of Chinese somehow exploded mid-voyage, Ah Toy paid half of the expense to transport the bodies back to China. When she eventually retired as a madam, she moved to San Jose where she died in 1928. The *San Francisco Examiner* of February 2, 1928, called her "Mrs. Ah Toy—China

Mary." Her obituary was short, talking briefly of Ah Toy's eighty years as a "familiar character" and noting she was "the wife of a wealthy Chinese gentleman."[13] The *Santa Cruz Evening News* death notice was even shorter, noting that if Ah Toy "had lived three months longer she would have been 100 years old."[14]

The horridly cruel auctions of Chinese women during Ah Toy's time were a sight to see. Upon arriving, the girls were often auctioned off right on the docks, with several observers (including policemen) in attendance. Didn't anyone see the looks of fear and anguish upon the faces of the victims? If they did, they chose not to acknowledge them. Of these events, the *San Francisco Chronicle* merely reported that "each China steamer now brings consignments of women, destined to [be] placed on the market." To the tongs, the auctioning of girls was perfectly acceptable. Back home, female infants were considered a liability by their impoverished families. Both tongs and Anglo merchants could buy these unwanted Celestial daughters for as little as a bag of seeds or sometimes upward of $150. One man who sold his daughter for the latter amount probably did not know that she was later auctioned off on the docks of San Francisco for $2,500. Some families knew exactly what would become of their children when they sold them; others were told their daughters would be married off to wealthy husbands. Either way, Chinese families saw no other way to end their debts or feed the rest of their families.

The auction process was humiliating and brutal. The frightened women were stripped of their clothing and displayed before the public. Those exhibiting too much fear were drugged. Most of them, however, had been taught patience and submission in their native land and simply yielded to their fate. If a girl displeased her client or owner, she was often beaten, branded with hot irons, gang-raped, starved, or even murdered. Some girls committed suicide rather than face a life of imprisonment. In time, other places were similarly auctioning Chinagirls off like cattle.

In the eastern camp of Mokelumne Hill, for instance, a building during the 1850s was expressly used for keeping enslaved Chinagirls who were regularly auctioned to men. Word of the inhumane auctions eventually spread to other parts of the West. "The importation of Chinese women for immoral purposes is a crying disgrace to the United States and to American civilization," wrote a newspaper in Prescott, Arizona. "It is a so-called civilized government acting the part of procuress, but although the better sense of the country has long cried out against it, the infamous traffic still continues."[15]

Occasional raids by San Francisco authorities sometimes netted Chinese girls as young as eight. The children were taken to mission homes or asylums until work could be found for them, but many ended up back in houses of prostitution anyway. Many more girls were taken to the mining camps of the Rocky Mountains, where men could auction or sell them with considerably less interference from authorities. Not until 1859 did newspapers begin publicizing the plights suffered by Chinese immigrants. In reporting the arrest of La You, the *California Police Gazette* commented, "It is a pity officers could not find some better employment than prosecuting these poor Chinese slaves. Do they not know that these poor serfs are obliged to do as they do? The officers do not pitch into WHITE females who pursue the same course. Oh no, they would not do that. Their pleasures and interests would be interfered with." The *Gazette* would pose similar opinions as more Chinese prostitutes were arrested during the 1860s.[16]

By 1860 there were more Chinese prostitutes in Sacramento, California, than any other race. It is believed that nearly 90 percent of Chinese prostitutes were forced into sex work. Yet in his inaugural speech, California governor Leland Stanford called them the "dregs of Asia."[17] At last, citizens got involved. During the late 1860s, police were called when some concerned citizens became aware of a ship bringing Chinagirls into port. The police found forty-five girls, ages eight to thirteen, slated for auction and placement in several predetermined brothels. The public was enraged, and the authorities dutifully sent the children to a halfway house in anticipation of placing them in good homes or orphanages. Their captors, however, simply waited until the public furor subsided, bribed the right people, and successfully sold the girls anyway.

Inhumane treatment of Chinagirls was extreme by 1869. One bill of sale from Loo Wong to Loo Chee, which was published in the *San Francisco Chronicle*, simply listed a "girl" on the document who was sold for $250. The bill of sale did not include the fact that the girl was actually a nine-year-old child. Chinese madams were sometimes appointed to run Chinese brothels. One of them, Dah Pa Tsin of San Francisco, kept over one hundred girls in her brothels along Church Alley. All of them were under fourteen years of age. Dah Pa Tsin and others like her were protected by the tongs. Underground dens of prostitution were another way to keep Chinese slaves under wraps. These places were rife with filth and disease. Their prisoners were frightened, ill, and broken in spirit.

Girls who lost their attractiveness under such conditions were sometimes allowed to "escape" to mission homes, but more often they were taken to an even dingier den and left to die. One such place was described in San Francisco in 1869: "The place is loathsome to the extreme. On one side is a shelf four feet wide and about a yard above the dirty floor, upon which there are two old rice mats. . . . When any of the unfortunate harlots is no longer useful and a Chinese physician passes his opinion that her disease is incurable, she is notified that she must die." Such girls were led to these places, forced through the door, and left with a cup of water, some rice, and a small oil lamp. "Those who have immediate charge of the establishment know how long the oil should last, and when the time is reached they return to the 'hospital,' unbar the door and enter. . . . Generally the woman is dead, either by starvation or from her own hand; but sometimes life is not extinct; the spark yet remains when the 'doctors' enter; yet this makes little difference to them. They come for a corpse, and they never go away without it."[18] If a woman chanced to live through her ordeal and was found too old to work, she could be sold again—to farmers who paid fifty to one hundred dollars—and forced to work for the rest of her life.

In 1869, the Methodist church in San Francisco formed one of a few missions to help enslaved Chinagirls. Other prostitutes did not receive such aid, although at least one writer concluded that they would have been too afraid to accept help anyway. The missions had their work cut out for them; in 1870, the census recorded some 1,500 Chinese prostitutes working out of various brothels and cribs in Chinatown. They were part of the five thousand Chinese women present in all of California, most all of whom were working as prostitutes—sometimes for Chinese men. At the mining town of Cerro Gordo in 1872, the *Inyo Independent* reported on a gunfight between two Chinamen, Lee Tu Pang and See Kee, who were fighting over a Chinagirl. Pang claimed ownership of the young lady, who was seeking protection from Kee. "Pang, in an effort to recover his prize," said the paper, "goes after Kee with a pistol, which he discharged once and received in return a shot in the leg above the knee, sustaining a bad compound fracture." The case was presented to other Chinese men, who apparently decided that Kee was in the wrong and denied amputation of the leg. Kee also appeared in official court, but was "discharged, on evidence as stated."[19]

In 1873, Albert Evans described the Chinagirls he saw in San Francisco by day:

> *You will see coming forth from the various narrow alleys which intersect the main streets, and are known by the expressive designations of 'Murderer's Alley,' 'China Alley,' 'Stout's Alley,' etc., any number of Chinese females, clad in their loose drawers or pants of blue or black cotton goods, straight-cut sacques of broadcloth, satin, or other costly or cheap material, according to their*

*condition and social rank; shoes of blue satin, richly embroidered*
*with bullion, and with thick soles of white felt and white wood,*
*anklets or bangles, and bracelets of silver, gold, or jade-stone,*
*and lustrous blue-black hair, braided in two strands, hanging*
*down the back from beneath coarse-striped gingham handker-*
*chiefs, thrown over the head, and tied beneath the chin as a*
*badge denoting slavery, and a life of hopeless infamy.*

Later that night, Evans also observed the prostitutes of China Alley. "The houses are all small brick affairs, coming flush up to the edge of the alley, and have windows with wickets in them. . . . There is a front and a rear room to each of these little dens. . . . Each of these places appear to be inhabited by from two to half a dozen Chinese girls . . . [who] for the most part are clad in the costume of their own country." The women were all slaves, Evans noted, their situation "more hopeless and terrible than the negro slavery of Louisiana or Cuba could ever be."

Most of the girls were "reared to a life of shame," never went to school, and knew virtually nothing of the outside world. They became "attached to each other in a childish way, frequently being seen walking together on the streets, hand in hand, like little Caucasian sisters going home from school." Although some Chinese prostitutes were allowed to walk the streets as Evans described, none of them dared risking capture if they escaped. Evans did note that some did escape, and even managed to marry in hopes of living "an honest life," but that "their chances of escaping kidnapping, and being dragged away to some distant locality, beaten, and reduced again to prostitution and slavery, are very slim indeed."[20] To the Chinamen who owned them, the girls were lost income. It was an interesting contrast, since Chinese slaves were kept in utterly inhumane conditions by their captors, when they should have been better cared for as valuable assets.

In 1874, after several years of American authorities lambasting the Chinese for leaving their wives in the homeland while importing girls for immoral purposes, one of the tongs, the Six Companies, finally made a formal reply. In their statement, they argued that their families did exist but that "pure and chaste" women had not come to America for fear of defying their old customs. The document openly admitted to bringing prostitutes to the United States, but "at the instigation and for the gratification of white men."[21] The Six Companies had even tried to send some of the women back to China, they said, but were stopped by a white lawyer who maintained the girls' rights to be in America. The Six Companies spoke on behalf of other tongs, who decreed that all Chinese went by Chinese law within their respective Chinatowns. In the outside world, the immigrants were forced to reckon with American laws. Inside, however, matters of interest were settled by Chinatown residents. By this explanation, Chinese prostitution immigration continued, and even expanded to include Portland, Oregon, and Vancouver, Canada, as major ports of entry for girls being imported from China. Part of the reason was because California had enacted an immigration code forbidding "lewd or debauched women" from entering the country.[22]

Finally, the Page Act was passed in 1875, making it illegal to import women for prostitution purposes. The tongs and others, however, found a loophole whereby they simply told officials the girls were already engaged to be married once they were in America. Throughout the 1880s thousands more Chinese girls were induced to leave China as indentured servants and sign contracts to provide sexual services for four to five years upon arriving in the United States. Although those girls who were sold for domestic work brought one hundred to five hundred dollars, the ones who were sold to the sex industry brought between five hundred and two thousand dollars. All were required to sign contracts that were loaded with double standards. Prostitute Xin Jin's contract stipulated that, should she run away, she would pay all costs incurred in finding her and returning her to her brothel. Ah Kam's contract contained a clause that should she attempt to escape or resist, she could be sold. Some contracts even stipulated that runaways, when they were caught, would be required to work as prostitutes for the rest of their lives. A typical contract during the 1880s read as follows:

> *For the consideration of [whatever sum had been agreed upon], paid into my hands this day, I, [name of girl], promise to prostitute my body for the term of _____ years. If, in that time, I am sick one day, two weeks shall be added to my time; and if more than one day, my term of prostitution shall continue an additional month. But if I run away, or escape from the custody of my keeper, then I am to be held as a slave for life.*

Most girls had little knowledge of the legalities of the document or what it actually implied.[23]

Finally, more rescue missions began surfacing. In 1881, the Occidental board of the San Francisco YWCA opened a home for Chinagirls who were rescued from the clutches of prostitution. The home would remain open for several more years as efforts increased. In a more concerted effort to quell prostitution immigration, the Chinese Exclusion Act of 1882 decreed that female Chinese immigrants coming from China must be limited to those who were already United States citizens, women married to Chinese men, or daughters of "domiciled merchants" who were born outside of America. The tongs merely resorted to smuggling girls, bribing customs officials, forging birth certificates and papers, and coaching their charges into lying to officials to procure entry to the United States. In 1888, the act was amended to prohibit reentry of Chinese who had recently departed American shores. Again, many women's papers were simply falsified, but the rising costs of illegal immigration resulted in an increase in the kidnapping of Chinese women within the United States. By 1885, physicians in San Francisco were noting that boys as young as ten and twelve years of age who had been turned away from Anglo houses of prostitution were infected with venereal disease they had contracted from Chinagirls. Members of the board of health, as well as local physicians, testified that they "knew of no city in the world which harbored as many diseased children as San Francisco."[24]

By 1890, respectable women were growing sick of the antics by the authorities, the tongs, and other slave traders. Among them was Mary Edholm of San Francisco, whose mission it became to save those who were still indentured slaves against their will. Mary worried for her own reputation, since her job required her to "mingle among these degraded ones."[25] Crusader Donaldina Cameron, however, knew no such fear. In 1895 Donaldina began working at the Presbyterian Home for women in San Francisco with its director, Margaret Culbertson. The home worked to free indentured Chinese servants, served as a refuge for sex slaves, and gave the girls schooling so they could live normal lives. When Margaret died in 1897, Donaldina became director.

Donaldina's approach to prostitution among the Chinese was by far the boldest, because she and her coworkers actively went looking for Chinese prostitutes to rescue. Together, they learned every back alley, building, tunnel, and hiding place where girls were being held against their will. The determined Donaldina nearly always found and rescued her charges. She was willing to "chop down doors with an ax, and tear away wood with her own hands" to complete her mission. More often than not, police accompanied Donaldina on her raids and would later testify that the captive women left the brothels of their own free will. The women were reunited with their families when possible; others were trained for new jobs or were able to marry. Indeed, Donaldina feared no man, ruthlessly raiding Chinese brothels at will. The tongs called her "Fahn Quai," or "The White Devil," and told their captives that Donaldina "was a she-devil who would drink their blood and show no mercy."[26]

Often, the hardest part of Donaldina's job was convincing her charges that they were safe and rehabilitating them with "faith, strength and love." Her worked eventually paid off, and enslaved women began

*Donaldina Cameron, the woman who saved thousands of Chinese immigrants from the clutches of prostitution.* Library of Congress

finding ways to send word directly to her for help. One of them, Yoke Keen, became the first Chinese woman to graduate from Stanford University in 1928 and returned to her homeland to teach. Other of the girls married, with the prospective bridegroom asking permission from Donaldina first. These grateful women called Donaldina "Lo Mo," which translated to "Beloved Mother." Donaldina retired in 1939. She lived happily in a cottage at Palo Alto with her two sisters, and later, Tien Wu, who had been a slave. She died in 1968 at the ripe age of ninety-nine. All told, Donaldina Cameron rescued more than three thousand Chinese sex slaves during her career.[27]

Donaldina was assisted in her mission by new laws over time. In 1907, a new immigration act forbade the bringing of prostitutes into the United States. Then, in 1910, the Mann Act was passed by Congress which forbade, under heavy penalties, the transportation of women from one state to another for immoral purposes. Although it was often referred to as the "White-Slave Traffic Act," the Mann Act applied to "any woman or girl for the purpose of prostitution or debauchery, or for any other immoral purpose."[28] It would be several more years, however, before the Mann Act, combined with other laws and military efforts, closed down prostitution nationwide during World War I.

# CHAPTER 10

---

## *Belle Cora: She Stood by Her Man*

One of the first named harlots to surface in San Francisco newspapers in 1856 was Belle Cora, whose given name was Arabella Ryan, or possibly Clara Belle Ryan. She was born in Baltimore, Maryland, in about 1827. Tales of her early life vary: In one version, Belle told others that her father was a minister. When she was seventeen, she lost her virginity to "a worldly wise young suitor," who effectively got her pregnant. The young man fled, and Belle's father threw her out. Belle headed south to New Orleans, where her baby was born and subsequently died. As she sat, dead broke and crying at a sidewalk cafe, a fancily dressed woman approached her and heard her story. Belle said she recognized the lady as a procuress for a brothel but accepted her offer of help.

In another version of her story, Belle's father was not a clergyman, and the girl took a job as a seamstress on Baltimore's North Street. Her customers included women from the Lutz, a local brothel. Belle eventually realized that "profits lay not in fashioning fancy dresses, but in wearing them" and went to work at the Lutz.[1] From there she moved to Charleston, South Carolina, and then to New Orleans, where she was by 1849. It was there that Belle encountered two well-dressed men. One of them was gambler Charles Cora, who stepped up to meet the girl.

The Italian Cora was described as having "black hair, a low forehead, large dark eyes, a swarthy complexion, and a mustache so full it hung over his lips." He was over ten years older than Belle, a "brunette, with hazel eyes and a very fair complexion." It was love at first sight. Although Belle went on to work in a New Orleans bawdy house, she told others that "she knew no man but Cora."[2] Another version of pretty much the same story claims Cora and the other man "flipped a coin to see which one was to have" Belle. Cora won. Belle, who "had been reared to the best traditions of the south," had some "negro servants to manage her affairs," and she and Charles "lived quietly together."[3]

However they met, most historians agree that Belle and Charles next boarded a series of ships bound for California. They first landed in Sacramento (or perhaps San Francisco), where Cora tried his luck at the gaming tables. Stories abound of Belle staking his games with twenty thousand dollars, a mighty high amount seeing as she "knew no man but Cora" while working as a prostitute. The devoted soiled dove traipsed after her man as he gambled his way through various mining camps. One story places them at Marysville, where together they ran a place called the New World. The couple might have parted ways for a time, and Belle went to Sonora where she was able to purchase a brothel from madam Cydia Redmon beginning in about 1851. The place was on Stuart Street and Belle ran it under the name Arabelle Ryan.

By November 1852, Belle and Cora had relocated to San Francisco together. One newspaper article, written years after the Coras were dead, verified that Belle owned a fancy hack which she brought with her to San Francisco from New Orleans that year. Edward McIlhany recalled that Cora's "wife or mistress, I do not know which, was a pretty woman and seemed very much devoted to him, as I had often seen her with him in the city."[4] The couple was not yet married, but Belle used Charles's surname when she opened up another brothel in San Francisco. The madam was terribly young, but she appears to have known her business.

Her place was an unpainted two-story affair that appeared drab from outside. Inside, however, was a palatial decor that soon set Belle apart from other madams. She also immediately became a victim of a robbery when a thief stole several items from the room of prostitute Florence Wetmore, as well as from a sleeping customer. Belle overcame the intrusion to become San Francisco's most successful madam for a time. Her girls were fine, and her prices were higher than any other parlor house. Soon, Belle and her man were worth a cool four hundred thousand dollars—over thirteen million dollars in today's currency.

Belle and Charles alternated their time in Frisco with vacation trips to other places. One 1855 record documents Charles Cora as sailing into San Francisco with another person identified only as "lady." That same year, Belle also built a fancy parlor house on Waverly Place near Ah Toy, the famed Chinese courtesan. From outside, the place appeared more as a private residence, complete with a white picket fence and flowers. Belle was given to throwing grand soirees. One of them happened to coincide with a party being hosted by the wife of US Marshal William H. Richardson. Mrs. Richardson's party was far less successful, and not until late in the evening did the proper lady discover why her invited male guests had failed to appear: They had gone to Belle Cora's party instead.

On November 15, Belle was recognized for the harlot she was while openly attending the theater with Charles Cora. The couple's chosen seats were in the coveted first balcony reserved for the wealthiest of theatergoers. As it happened, the Richardsons were there too. When some men turned in their seats to admire and make jovial comments about Belle's presence, Mrs. Richardson—unaware of Belle and Charles's seats directly behind her—thought the men were talking and laughing about her. Richardson went to investigate, discovered the cause of the laughter, raised a ruckus, and attempted to have Belle removed. As there was no law against her presence there, Belle was allowed to stay. The Richardsons flounced out of the theater in a huff.

The following day, Richardson and Cora passed each other on the street and exchanged insults. When they encountered each other again at the Cosmopolitan Saloon later that night, a mutual friend identified as Dr. Mills decided to formally introduce the men to one another as a means of keeping the peace. The twosome acquiesced and even enjoyed a few drinks with each other before leaving the saloon together. Outside, however, Richardson insulted Cora, threatened to slap him, and followed him back into the Cosmopolitan. "I have promised to slap this man's face, and I had better do it now," he declared. Mills and others prevented the man from carrying out his promise.

The next day a sober Richardson set out in search of Cora. Several witnesses attested to Richardson's hunt for Cora, as well as his inexplicable friendliness when the two finally met up and visited two more bars together. The men parted ways afterward, but in the early evening a drunken Richardson was seen talking to Cora once more outside the Blue Wing Saloon. All was well as the pair walked off together, but witnesses differed on just why Cora delivered a fatal shot to his new friend a short time later. "He led his victim to believe the difficulty was at an end, then basely murdered him in an unguarded moment," tattled the *Daily Alta California* newspaper. "We have understood for some time past, that the most abandoned women are taken to the various places of amusement in this city, and seated promiscuously among the audiences; and that it is almost as much as a man's life was worth to object to such a proceeding, particularly when the women are accompanied, as they usually are, by such men as Cora."[5]

Charles Cora was immediately labeled "a dastardly assassin" as newspapers claimed Belle was "mysteriously moving to secure his acquittal by infamous means." But Belle appeared to be on the up and up when she hired three well-known defense attorneys and advanced an amazing fifteen thousand dollars in gold for her husband's defense. Another fifteen thousand was raised by Cora's friends. One of Cora's

*Charles and Belle Cora's palatial home, circa 1853.* Wikimedia Commons

lawyers, Colonel E. D. Baker, tried to back out due to pressure from the newspapers. But Belle refused to let the man off the hook, and a friend of Cora's, Billy Mulligan who was in charge of the county jail, released the prisoner. But the newspapers wanted blood, and the tirade against Cora, as well as chants to hang him, went on for several months.

What was not said outright was that Belle's friends were trying to unduly influence the jury at Charles Cora's trial. Furthermore, a witness named Mrs. Maria Knight testified that she was invited to Belle's parlor house to discuss what she had seen. Maria told the district attorney that she refused any libations at Belle's, fearing they were poisoned. She also said that when she told Belle that Richardson's hands were empty when he was shot, the woman and two men threatened her life before offering her a thousand dollars to change her story. "Woman, if you expect to get out of this house alive, you must say that you saw Richardson with a pistol in his hand," Belle told Maria. "That is the only ground we have to save my husband's life!"[6] Maria agreed, if only as a means to escape the house. Later, however, she would repeat her story for the jury. Belle wisely was not in attendance. When the jury could not decide whether to charge Cora with murder or manslaughter, the *San Francisco Bulletin* was outraged. "Hung be the heavens with black! The money of the gambler and prostitute has succeeded," sneered the paper.[7] In the end the jury was hung, and a second trial was scheduled. Cora was returned to jail.

Cora's final undoing was the fatal shooting of editor James King of William by city supervisor James Casey in May of 1856. As Casey was deposited in jail, Cora made a foretelling comment. "You have put the noose about the necks of both of us,"[8] he said. True to Cora's prediction, both men were hanged on May 22 by the San Francisco Vigilance Committee, a group that had been around since 1851 and was tired of all these renegade murders going on. Belle was devastated and successfully pleaded to stay with her man until his execution. An hour before the hanging, the "nuptials of Cora and Belle Cora, whose real name is Arabella Bryan [sic], was performed by the Rev. Father Maraschi," reported the *Sacramento Daily Union* in its May 24 issue. And it did not go unnoticed that Belle had clung helplessly to her husband before they were "forcibly separated."[9] Cora and Casey swung from a makeshift gallows—a building on Sacramento Street.

Charles's body was taken to the coroner's office and deposited "in a very magnificent mahogany coffin, richly mounted and trimmed," which was likely purchased by Belle.[10] Once the coroner completed his autopsy, the body was removed to Belle's house as a lavish funeral was prepared. The procession to Mission Dolores Cemetery included seven carriages of friends behind a hearse drawn by four black horses. As Belle laid her man to rest, the general public showed no mercy for the widow. When a letter to the editor of the *San Francisco Bulletin* urged officials to make Belle leave the city a few days later, the paper heartlessly published it. The letter was signed, "Many women of San Francisco."[11] At least one citizen, however, pleaded for leniency on Belle. The woman, who signed her name "Adelia," wrote a letter to the editor which read in part, "In my humble opinion, I think that Belle Cora has suffered enough to expiate many faults, in having had torn from her a bosom friend, executed by a powerful association. . . . She has shown herself a true-hearted woman to him, and such a heart covers a multitude of sins."[12]

Belle remained in San Francisco. One legend states she spent a month parading around town in widow's garb before resuming her business. The story may be true, for in August the *Sacramento Daily Union* announced the woman was "having a costly and splendid monument erected to her husband's memory. It is to have, among other inscriptions, the following: 'Murdered by the Vigilance Committee, May 22d, 1855.'"[13] Of her, historian Hubert Howe Bancroft wrote only that she was beautiful "but oh, so foul!"[14] In time, Belle's clients grew to include senators and judges. But she remained true to Charles Cora, even in death. When she discovered that Mission Dolores Cemetery had no room for her own impending grave next to Cora, Belle had him exhumed and reburied at Calvary Cemetery.

Scarred by the death of her husband, the resolute Belle Cora refused to put up with much. In 1857, when an officer entered her brothel looking for a man on a warrant, Belle ordered him out. When he refused to leave, she "went to the door and called the police." Another officer appeared and "put the first officer out by main force." The man struggled free and busted through Belle's front door again. This time, Belle's girls surrounded him as one of them "broke a champagne bottle over his head, inflicting a severe wound."[15] By this time the second officer had come back into the house and made the culprit leave for good.

Eventually, Belle did land on the wrong side of the law. In August of 1859, three girls—Fanny Carrick, Kate Rodgers, and Josephine Jacquot—escaped from San Francisco's House of Refuge. Of the three, only Fanny was arrested when police saw her riding in Belle Cora's carriage. As Fanny was taken to the police station, Belle followed. The madam merely wanted back the clothes she had given Fanny, "which were of the finest quality."[16] Belle did, however, pay for Fanny's lawyers, where a writ of habeas corpus freed the girl. "She is now probably 'safely' lodged in Belle Cora's brothel," reported the *Stockton Independent*.[17] A week or so later, Belle filed a complaint of grand larceny against Fanny. But when the madam failed to appear in court for the proceedings, she was arrested for contempt and paid one hundred dollars in bail money.

Belle could afford the bail money, for she had become quite wealthy. In 1861 it was noted that she was sailing home to San Francisco from New York aboard the *Northern Light*. Nothing more was mentioned about her until February 18, 1862, when she died from an overdose of chloroform—which she had been using for the previous several months after kicking a nasty opium habit (another source says she died from pneumonia). She was buried in Mission Cemetery, but there is some confusion over her final resting place with Charles Cora. Cemetery records show that Charles Cora's body was indeed exhumed from its original spot and reinterred at Calvary Cemetery on February 20, 1862 (not in the 1850s as some say). In 1916, *San Francisco Bulletin* reporter Pauline Jacobson said she visited the mutual grave of Charles and Belle Cora at Calvary Cemetery. Their shared tombstone "stretched the width of both graves, was engraved with two figures standing with heads bowed, under a weeping willow tree."[18] But Calvary Cemetery was quite run-down, and so Jacobson coordinated the moving of both bodies back to Mission Dolores, along with the tombstone.

What little is known about Belle's former life was revealed after her death when her sister, Anastasia Ryan, petitioned "for letters of administration to be issued to Harriet Collins" with regards to Belle's estate. Anastasia claimed she was Belle's only surviving relative.[19] The amount of the estate was deemed "considerable," but her true worth at her death remains unknown.[20] Today, Belle Cora has proven to be one of the most priceless aspects of San Francisco's bawdy history.

# CHAPTER 11

—•◦•—

## Tessie Wall: "How's That for My Big Fat Irish Ass?"

Of all the madams generated during San Francisco's early years, Tessie Wall remains one of the most famous. This "flamboyant, well-upholstered blonde" was best known in the Uptown Tenderloin, where she flourished with a finesse that was envied by other madams.[1] She was born May 26, 1869, as Teresa Susan Donohue to large family. Her parents, John and Sahra Donohoe [sic], were Irish immigrants, and theirs was a typical working-class family of San Francisco. From her home on Mill Street near the financial district and Chinatown, the scrappy Tessie was free to run wild with other children in her neighborhood. Her father worked as a fireman in a local mill, while her mother worked to feed and care for her growing number of children. There would eventually be six of them by 1880.

In 1884, at the age of just fifteen, Tessie married a fireman named Edward M. Wall. Two years later the couple bore a son, Joseph Lawrence, but the baby died four months later. The Walls eventually divorced, and Tessie spent at least some years working as a maid for the family of a banker named Judah Boas. Tessie kept her husband's name and tried to be good. In 1889 she was noted as being in charge of the flower stand during a fair at the Mission Skating Rink that was hosted by St. James Parish. She was living in a fashionable home, or perhaps an apartment, on Dolores Street when she attended a party at the Del Monte Club in 1890, as well as a picnic hosted by the Odd Fellows.

Yes indeed, Miss Tessie Wall loved a party. She also loved to drink. They say that in between attending various soirees, the lady once won a drinking contest against famed boxer John L. Sullivan. The contest might have occurred at a dance hall known as the Cremorne, where Tessie went to work after quitting her maid job. The Cremorne was known for its "pretty waiter girls" and "curtained booths."[2] Although some historians dispute when and where this happened, most agree that Tessie had an amazing ability to hold her liquor, which she drank in great quantities. If she did work at the Cremorne, Tessie could at least make money to support herself while continuing to make the papers as a socialite party girl. And it wasn't long before the young lady figured out that she could do much more for men than just dance with them.

As of 1897, "Mrs." Tessie Wall had installed herself in a fabulous parlor house at 137 O'Farrell Street. Tessie, the spunky Irish lass who grew up poor, had a sense of humor too. A sampler on the wall read, "If every man was as true to his country as he is to his wife—God help the USA."[3] Soon, a bevy of those unfaithful curs were making a beeline for Tessie's, and with good reason: The madam hired only the best of the best courtesans to work for her. Beginning in 1900, Tessie was able to expand to a new place at 147 Powell, which she called the Nelson. This parlor house also was grand, and the furnishings included a gold fireplace. On the day the census was taken, it is interesting that only two of Tessie's girls were on hand: twenty-six-year-old Cassie Harlow and thirty-three-year-old Gertrude Day. In the interest of discretion, the women told the census taker they were employed as a milliner and dressmaker, respectively. Also at the house that day was an apparent customer (or perhaps Gertrude's husband), Albert Day. Tessie also employed a servant, Chai Loy.

The only incident of note at the Nelson took place in 1902, when laborer Clyde Greenacre "sneaked into a house kept by Mrs. Tessie

Wall" and absconded with a fifty-dollar clock.[4] Officer J. B. Collins arrested the man two hours later and he was taken to jail. Following the earthquake and subsequent fires of 1906, Tessie moved again. She managed to salvage her grand golden fireplace and used it in her all-new parlor house at 664 Larkin Street, away from the Tenderloin District. Author Curt Gentry hinted that one of Tessie's investors in the building was Frank Daroux, whom she would later marry.

Built in 1906 by the William Helbing Building Company, the Larkin Street house towered two stories high with a brick exterior featuring Renaissance/Baroque adornments. The building still stands, with thirteen rooms and three bathrooms—likely not much different than the layout Tessie had. It was by far among the finest homes in town. Tessie loved and collected stellar antiques, including a gold Napoleon bed, monogrammed china once owned by William Rockefeller, plus fine furnishings formerly owned by San Francisco's rich and elite citizenry. One of her most notable pieces of furniture was a six-hundred-pound buffet made of iron and gilded gold, and "decorated with love's more athletic scenes."[5] Tessie considered her purchase of fine things as investments. But the madam also was careful with her money: Once, she bought a thousand-dollar painting from Gump's Jade and Oriental Art Emporium. One of Gump's sons delivered the painting, and Tessie invited him to share a bottle of champagne. When the boy returned to his father's store, the money amounted to only $990; the shrewd madam had deducted the ten-dollar cost of the champagne from the price of the painting.

Tessie knew that with money came power. In 1907 for instance, the *San Francisco Call* published an article about Police Captain Mooney of Company E who had staged one too many raids on Tessie's Larkin Street house. Chief of Police Dinan inexplicably suddenly transferred the Larkin beat to the central station under a Captain Martin. Dinan said he had been contemplating the change for several months. When asked about the matter, a grumpy Captain Mooney only said, "All I know is that Larkin Street has been taken off my district. I cannot say whether the raiding of the Wall place had anything to do with it."[6] Did Tessie have a hand in assuring Mooney's transfer? Probably.

Indeed, for the most part Tessie managed to stay out of the newspapers, unless something truly scandalous occurred. In March 1908, the *Santa Cruz Evening News* capitalized on the suicide of a "wealthy manufacturer" named Tuttle. The man appeared to have been emotionally distraught over some unknown problem when he summoned a car and went to the house of his mother-in-law, Mrs. T. L. Seaton. Some sort of "family council" happened there, and when he left the house, according to the paper, Tuttle commanded the chauffeur to "Take me some place, any place where I can forget. Oh, I'm in terrible trouble. I must forget it!" Tuttle ultimately chose Tessie's parlor house, where he "began to imbibe in wine and champagne, spending money with a lavish hand in the company of a female inmate." Tuttle remained in a "high

*Tessie Wall's flamboyant, brash persona made her a good candidate for madam in San Francisco.* Wikimedia Commons

nervous pitch" and continued drinking before scurrying to—and nearly missing—the last boat over to Mill Valley. Upon arriving at his home, the distraught Tuttle shot himself right through the heart. His stepdaughter, Gladys, was the only witness to the act.[7]

The remainder of 1908 was equally interesting for Tessie. In June, her janitor managed to make off with a large roast turkey and some champagne and was duly arrested. Then in November, an extremely intoxicated, well-fed man appeared at Tessie's door around 1 a.m. Claiming he was Chief of Police Biggy, the "short, pudgy man" had begun his spree by kicking in the door at Elfen and Hardin's saloon on Larkin Street before heading to Tessie's. Apparently, he resembled the real Chief Biggy so closely that nobody noticed the difference. Thus the imposter "blustered into the Wall woman's resort, ordered all the inmates into the street, then rescinded his order and set the time for the exodus at 8 o'clock, then had a second attack of kindliness and postponed the fateful hour until December 15." This was accomplished over several minutes as Tessie's frenzied employees hastened to obey the man who kept assuring them, in shouting tones, that he was Chief of Police Biggy. One of the girls, Clarissa Howard, was so upset by the incident that "she suffered from nervous prostration all day."[8]

Clarissa's case of the fantods was not the end of the pudgy man's story. Because he was so easily mistaken for Chief Biggy, word on the street apparently began circulating that it really was the chief of police who made a mess of things at Tessie's. Claiming that "newspapers are hounding me," Biggy committed suicide on December 1. The *Santa Cruz Evening News* expressed dismay at the act, reporting that "anyone who knew him would say that he would never take his life, if only for [his family]. He loved them dearly and his thoughts were always for them."[9] In the wake of the fake's self-appointed raid at Tessie's, the parlor house was closed down for several hours while "two of Chief of Police Biggy's confidential men went to Tessie Wall's resort and had a long conference with the mistress."[10] Exactly what was discussed remains unknown. Chief Biggy received a proper funeral, and San Francisco moved on.

Madam Tessie moved on too, after she understandably became disenchanted with her Larkin Street location. She next hired architect Milton Latham to design a fine parlor house at 337 O'Farrell Street, a few blocks from her old house. Tessie showed Latham through the Larkin Street house to give him an idea of what she wanted. She also seemed especially proud of her Napoleon bed. "How's that for my big fat Irish ass?"[11] she quipped. The bed was a gift from Frank Daroux, the gambler who invested in various brothels and was especially fond of Tessie. During their first date, the lady downed an amazing twenty-two bottles of wine "without once leaving the table." For Frank, it was love at first guzzle. Tessie felt the same way, and eventually purchased over two dozen busts of Napoleon which were scattered throughout her house. "They remind me of Frankie," she explained.[12]

It wasn't long before the madam had matrimony on her mind, but Daroux wasn't an easy catch. It took Tessie nearly nine months to convince the man to marry her, but there were stipulations: Daroux demanded that they marry out of state, and Tessie had to agree to keep the marriage a secret. The couple wed on September 1, 1909, in Philadelphia. Then they returned to San Francisco, where each of them resumed their respective businesses. When Tessie's three-story O'Farrell house was finished, the first floor contained a seldom-used saloon. The second floor featured Tessie's private suite, as well as the kitchen and dining room, parlors for entertaining clients, and a ballroom with floor-to-ceiling mirrors. Twelve bedrooms occupied the third floor.

The 1910 census reveals much about Tessie and her realm in the prostitution industry. Next door to her, madam Pearl Morton employed nine young women. Tessie also had nine ladies working for her. The girls at both houses consistently listed their occupations as clerks, nurses, dressmakers, milliners, and salesladies. Frank Daroux, meanwhile, had become one of the most powerful gambling czars in San Francisco. When police chief John Seymour openly talked of shutting down gambling, Daroux made a bold statement to the press: "My places are running under the law and I defy anybody, police or anybody else, to close them."[13] But the tension mirrored his relationship with Tessie, and neighbors could often hear the couple arguing through the walls of the O'Farrell house. The arguments might have been about Tessie's desire to attend one of the fancy cotillions hosted by Ned Greenway, whom she hated. (Greenway finally told her she could come, but that she and her girls would have to wear a costume disguise; they dressed as champagne bottles.) Or about Tessie's insistence that the couple attend an invitation-only Mardi Gras celebration. (On the way home Tessie lost her diamond brooch, which the newspaper brazenly revealed was a gift from Daroux.) Or they might have even been arguing about Daroux's continued insistence that the couple keep their marital union a secret.

Even as he refused to admit he was married to Tessie Wall, Daroux stubbornly ran his numerous pool halls and other gambling joints very near the O'Farrell house. Tessie, meanwhile, viewed Frank Daroux as a trophy husband if ever there was one, and she wanted to publicly show him off. In 1912, she finally got her wish when Daroux agreed to marry her again, for the public's benefit. The romantic Tessie desired a church wedding and boldly included her male clients on her list of invites. Even those who were married were included, but the uncouth madam likely thought she was following proper etiquette when she invited the wives as well. The guest list wasn't the only problem, however. A dozen ministers were consulted before Tessie found one to perform the ceremony: Reverend William P. Sullivan. But Sullivan no sooner agreed to perform the ceremony at St. Mary's Cathedral when he changed his mind. After much wheedling on Tessie's part, Sullivan finally agreed to marry the couple. He, too, had stipulations, however: The ceremony was to be performed in the rectory, not the gorgeous cathedral, with only the amount of witnesses as required for the marriage. An even bigger problem was that Daroux wanted Tessie to retire from her business. The madam reluctantly agreed and turned over management of her brothel to one of her girls in preparation for the grand ceremony.

Tessie's compromises for the wedding came with her own demands. After the ceremony, she wanted to slip into the cathedral with Daroux and exit the church properly as the couple's friends waited outside. She also wanted a hundred-piece brass band to play "Hail, Hail the Gang's All Here" as the so-called newlyweds descended the steps. Daroux agreed to this last demand, but then threw Tessie's guest list away and did not hire the band. Fortunately for Tessie, most of her guests knew of the upcoming nuptials anyway. The reception was grand and attended by one hundred people who managed to consume eighty cases of champagne. Tessie also got even with Daroux for deceiving her. Apparently, the mayor of San Francisco attended her wedding reception. When she overheard her husband telling him that the couple planned to move to San Mateo, Tessie said loudly, "San Mateo! Why, I'd sooner be under an electric light on Powell Street than to own all of San Mateo!"[14] She must have been pleased, however, that Daroux's wedding gift to her was a ten-thousand-dollar pearl necklace.

Following the reception, the Darouxes retired to a grand house Frank had already purchased at 535 Powell Street (thus Tessie's remark about being under an electric light there). Much to Tessie's dismay, some of her groom's friends had piled a huge amount of manure in front of the only entrance. Tessie was too heavy for Daroux to carry her through it, and the couple was relegated to wading through the muck. To top it off, their two-month honeymoon to Canada was cut short due to their constant fighting. The arguments might have revolved around Tessie's refusal to give up being a parlor house madam, for soon she was back at work. Fourteen girls worked for her, and her biggest rival was madam Jessie Hayman.

Both Jessie and Tessie were in the habit of attending shows at the Orpheum Theater each Sunday night. Management graciously always reserved the first several rows exclusively for women of the demimonde. The madams each took advantage of being seated in the front of the stage, usually waiting until the opening acts began before swishing down the aisles with their girls in their best evening wear. Each madam chose a different aisle for the grand entrance, and each would try to let the other go first so patrons would see, and remember, her girls last. Once, Tessie went so far as to refrain from attending the theater for two consecutive Sundays. This, of course, left audience members and Jessie wondering where the madam and her girls were. On the third Sunday, the clever Tessie waited until mid-show to make her appearance. The performance was stopped and the house lights went up as the madam and her girls triumphantly paraded down the aisle.

Tessie and other madams had other ways to attract business too, such as paying every bellboy, club and hotel steward, maître d', and taxi driver in town to make sure men looking for female entertainment were brought to their parlor houses. Tessie was especially adept at bribery; one time, a cook from the St. Francis Hotel was asked by a guest to give him a tour of the city's nightlife. The cook dutifully delivered him to Tessie's, where he spent his entire evening. The following day, the cook received an envelope containing thirty dollars in gold pieces. The tip was 10 percent of what Tessie made from her customer. When the hotel detective heard about it, he raised a stink, largely because he was already performing the same service for Tessie and others.

Another time, Tessie and her girls decided to attend a charity function at the elite Palace Hotel. The women made their appearance and Tessie probably spent a good deal of money. How could the staff of the Palace refuse her? They really couldn't, since news of an ousting would have given the hotel bad press. Indeed, it was nearly impossible to keep Tessie from attending social functions. She regularly presided over the annual Policeman's Ball, buying lots of tickets and beginning the festivities by slapping a thousand-dollar bill on the bar. "Drink that up, boys!" she would bellow. "Have a drink on Tessie Wall!"[15] Beginning in 1913, Tessie even joined Mayor "Sunny Jim" Rolph as leader of the Grand March at the ball. They say Tessie attended the ball each year until her death.

As Tessie continued storming the town, Frank Daroux sharpened his reputation as a prominent political leader. But his relationship with Tessie remained tempestuous at best, and it was often his own doing. In December of 1915, the couple received an invitation from car mogul Henry Ford to sail with him to Europe. Tessie was naturally enthralled, and even sold her brothel—the price she must pay, said Daroux, if she wanted to go. Tessie acquiesced, only to have Daroux decline the invitation. Tessie somehow managed to get her brothel back, for she remained at "The Wall" on O'Farrell Street for another year according to city directories. Tessie also discovered Daroux was possibly having an affair with a woman named Mary Lind. The incensed madam demanded a meeting with both Mary and Daroux, but both insisted they were innocent. Even so, Tessie told Mary that she would kill her if she ever saw the woman around her husband again.

Things finally came to a head in 1917, starting with the news that Mayor Rolph had been pressured into closing down the Tenderloin in its entirety. Even worse, Daroux filed for divorce. The fight was on again as Tessie contested the divorce while demanding money and jewelry should Daroux get his way. A distraught Tessie would do anything to keep her man. A suicide attempt was thwarted, and newspapers were rife with stories about the Darouxes for months during the proceedings. Each pointed a finger at the other, claiming cruelty, drunkenness, and other charges. Tessie claimed that her husband once called her in the middle of the night and used foul language as he reminded her that "he was political boss of San Francisco, and that he controlled all the

Superior Judges of said city and county, and that he would get a divorce from her whether he had any evidence or not."

Tessie also claimed Daroux slapped her. But Tessie's sister-in-law and even her own sister portrayed Daroux as a good, kind man. In divorce court, however, Tessie testified that Daroux kept her jewelry and that she was now penniless. At one point, as a mutual friend took the stand, Tessie broke down completely. "Oh, God, Charley, don't say that," she pleaded as he testified. "I love him so much. Please don't help to take Frank away from me, Charley. Oh, Charley, if you only knew how much I love him. I have done nothing. I swear I have done nothing. Oh, please, don't help to take him away from me, Charley."[16] And so it went, for years, as Tessie did everything she could to drag the divorce out in court. For Tessie, the only way was her way, and she was not beyond pleading, lying, and applying other histrionics to keep Frank Daroux by her side. When she correctly suspected that he was still seeing Mary Lind, Tessie allegedly sent him a message that "if she couldn't have him, she would fix him so no other woman would ever want him."[17] Daroux just laughed, which probably wasn't the best of ideas. True to her word, Tessie lay in wait for Frank Daroux on December 18. He was living in a suite at the St. Francis Hotel, and when he finally appeared on the street, Tessie fell into step with him. Several witnesses watched the couple make their way down Powell Street as Tessie pleaded for reconciliation and money. Daroux was having none of it. The twosome turned right on Ellis, where Daroux next entered Anna Lane with Tessie on his heels. There, the man "couldn't resist flinging an epithet the newspapers found unprintable" as the pair stood in front of the Vivoli Theater.[18] At that point, Tessie pulled a silver-plated revolver from her handbag and shot Daroux three times.

A crowd slowly gathered as Tessie stood over Daroux, weeping, and the police were summoned. When asked why she had shot her husband, Tessie's anguished reply was, "I shot him because I love him, God damn him!"[19] She also remained concerned about Daroux's condition and was allowed to see him briefly—so that he could identify her as the woman who had fired the gun. "Yes, she shot me. Take her away. I don't want to see her." Daroux said.[20] The *Sacramento Union* would later state that "Daroux was not expected to live for some weeks, so critical was his condition, but on his recovery refused to prosecute his wife."[21] Tessie went free, although the *Oakland Tribune* reported that upon dismissing her case, Judge Fitzpatrick admonished Tessie to "forget the past and not make a similar attempt on Daroux's life." He also told her, "And you must stop making threats against him." Tessie retorted, "He calls me names every time he sees me, and he must stop making threats against me!" The article also said the divorce was soon to be finalized, "immediately after which Daroux has publicly announced he would leave the city for good."[22]

In reporting the shooting incident, the *Santa Cruz Evening News* incorrectly claimed the Daroux divorce had been finalized, and that Tessie had already received one hundred thousand dollars in the settlement. In truth, the "interlocutory decree was granted in July, 1917," explained the *Sacramento Union*, but the divorce did not become final until 1921. Tessie received some "property in San Mateo and in San Francisco and jewelry and furniture, the value of which is estimated at $60,000."[23] Once everything was settled, the unfaithful Daroux indeed married Mary Lind and eventually moved to New York, where he died in 1928. He was buried in Sacramento. Tessie did not attend his funeral.

Following her divorce, Tessie moved into one of the flats in an apartment house she owned, along with as many of her fancy furnishings as she could stuff into the place. She also opened a speakeasy sometime after the onset of Prohibition. One source says she retired in about 1928. She also became preoccupied with death, particularly her own. Fearful of ending up in the potter's field after she died, Tessie made sure to purchase her own plot and moved the remains of her son and some of her family to her designated resting place. She also bought herself a beautiful marble tombstone. The final touch was her obituary, which local newspapers used to keep on file for prominent citizens should they die suddenly. Tessie's reporter friends permitted her to read what they had written, "tears in her eyes, smiling here, sobbing there," and helped her sneak into certain newspaper offices in the dead of night to read more.[24] The lady appeared satisfied with everything written about her.

The 1930 census records Tessie, a widow, living alone at 3569 18th Street in San Francisco. Two years later, just two months after her last public appearance at the Policeman's Ball, the famed madam died at her home on April 28, 1932, from heart troubles stemming from a tooth ailment. Directly above her bed was "a handsome oil painting" of Frank Daroux."[25] Gantner, Felder, and Kenny Funeral Home handled the arrangements for Tessie's funeral on April 30. The madam lay in state in a gold metal casket. Her funeral expenses, including limousines and flowers, cost $879—around fifteen thousand dollars today. Most interestingly, one J. Donohue paid for everything, but whether he was related to her remains unknown.

Those who didn't know about the passing of San Francisco's flamboyant madam soon learned about it from various newspapers which duly published the obituaries they had on file. "Queen of Night Life is Dead," read one of them, the *Madera Tribune*. "Tessie Wall, once famous queen of San Francisco night life, who spent $1,700 on her wedding breakfast, is dead. In seclusion for years, the gray haired woman who once reigned in the Poodle Dog, Silver Dollar, Mason street tenderloin and other rendezvous of world travelers, succumbed to an ulcerated tooth and other ailments last night. . . . Tessie, as she was known from the Shanghai Bund to the Champs Elysee in Paris, reached her pinnacle of fame when she shot her husband, Frank Daroux, famous gamester."[26] Although some of Tessie's property was willed to the ten relatives who survived her, most of it went to the executor of her estate: police captain John J. O'Meara, whom Tessie had known for nearly forty years.

On June 6, the nightlife queen's artwork, wall decor, bedroom sets, furnishings, fancy dinnerware, and jewelry—including her engagement ring, inscribed "Frank to Tessie"—were put up for auction. Most surprisingly, the sale was not as successful as everyone surely believed it would be. On June 7, way back on page 29 of the *Oakland Tribune*, was a list of items that had sold at "low prices." Although plenty of people came to see Tessie's "bizarre furnishings," few cared to bid. Sacramento sheriff Ellis Jones bought Tessie's gold bed for a paltry $105.00. "It was the small things that fetched, relatively, the best prices," commented the *Tribune*. A final report was published on June 12 after the auction had ended. Most of the bidders had "bought for sentiment and for thrift," even though Tessie's house was jam-packed with collectibles. There was William Rockefeller's dinner service. A gold mirror was once owned by silent film actress Edna Wallace Hopper. An oil painting of King Leopold had been a gift from the king of Belgium to opera singer Rosa Shay before Tessie bought it. Rugs, draperies, Turkish chairs, and other wonderful items failed to bring more than a few dollars. "Most interesting, I found," noted the writer of the article, "were the men present who watched the sale and said nothing."[27]

# CHAPTER 12

———— •◦• ————

## Sally Stanford: Madam Mayor of Sausalito

Call her bold, call her brash, but Sally Stanford was a force to be reckoned with. Brought up in a poor family and convicted of forgery at age seventeen, Sally redeemed herself by becoming one of the best-known madams in San Francisco, the mayor of Sausalito, and a restaurant mogul. The lady truly took life on the chin, learning the street smarts she needed to survive. Sally was willing to do anything to achieve success—including shedding six husbands like a pair of worn-out shoes when they got in her way. By the time of her death in 1982, Sally stood out as a brazen woman with a mind for business who had left a trail of success behind her.

Born Janice Busby in Oregon in 1903, Sally spent much of her early life in Baker, a bustling town on the east side of the state. Her father, John, was a laborer with a drinking problem. Her mother, Harriet, was a former schoolteacher who toiled to keep her household together and feed three children. Sally was forced to leave school in the third grade to help her mother peddle goods from the family garden door-to-door. One day in about 1912, Sally's mother took her shopping for shoes at the Golden Rule Department Store. But Sally wasn't interested in shoes, choosing instead to languish in front of a case of colorful ribbons. Suddenly she became aware of someone watching her. Looking up, the girl noticed "the most elegant lady I had ever seen. She had a frilly laced front white silk blouse covered by a small sealskin black jacket. On her head was perched an elaborate black velvet hat with great black ostrich feathers which hung dramatically over one side."

Sally and the beautiful woman were chatting amicably about the pretty ribbons when Sally's mother suddenly appeared, yanked the girl over to the shoe department, and admonished her for talking to strange ladies. The twosome finally selected some shoes, but while her mother paid for them, Sally quickly stole back to the lady at the ribbon counter. It was obvious to the woman that Sally loved the ribbons. "Would you like to have some of those hair ribbons, little girl?" she asked. Sally nodded and watched as her new friend ordered "yards and yards of every type of hair ribbon, in every color." Once they were placed in a bag, the woman placed them on the counter in front of Sally, "winking knowingly and smiling very sweetly as she walked away." Sally stashed the parcel in her jacket and hid it in her bedroom. Later, she prodded her mother about the nice lady. Mrs. Busby told her the woman "was not a nice lady, she was a *painted* lady and I don't want you to ever talk to her again." When Sally's mother eventually saw the hair ribbons, the girl wisely told her they were given to her by a woman whose husband patronized the golf club where Sally worked.[1]

Did the mysterious femme at the Golden Rule inspire Sally to grow up to be one of the most famous madams in California? Perhaps, but Sally later claimed that she "didn't set out to be a madam any more than Arthur Michael Ramsey, when he was a kid, set out to be Archbishop of Canterbury. Things just happened to both of us, I guess." Even, so, Sally soon developed a taste for adventure and a yearning for freedom as the family moved, first to Victorville, California, for a short time and then back to Oregon. In Medford, Sally continued working odd jobs, but there never seemed to be enough money. When Harriet sold the beloved family dog to buy food, something stirred deep inside the girl. One day, after receiving her weekly pay of three dollars as a maid, Sally spied "the most gorgeous, soul-satisfying pair of high-button, high-heeled, black and white shoes, on sale for $1.68." On a whim, she bought the shoes and a pair of stockings before taking herself to dinner at a Chinese restaurant. As she dined on shrimp salad, her father suddenly appeared with his buddy, a local policeman. The men were angry, for Sally's purchases had interfered with their plan to spend the money drinking. Sally considered it a great victory that the store would not refund her shoe purchase. Later, she would remember the encounter with her father and the officer as "my first brush with the law."[2]

*Sally Stanford, the brazen, business-minded madam of San Francisco.*
Courtesy Sausalito Historical Society

Sally's wild streak only grew bigger. In June of 1918, she married a young man she called LeRoy Snyder but whom official records identified as Lee Roy Fansler. According to Sally, she was caring for some cousins in Santa Paula, California, at the time, but another source claims she was working as an "entertainer" in Ventura County. Sally later recalled that after a "respectable period of courting," Lee Roy asked her to marry him. She was only fourteen years old; he was nineteen. Both lied about their ages to secure a marriage license, but Sally was whimsically naive about the whole deal. Later that night, Lee Roy told his new wife, "you're mine now," and next explained to the perplexed girl what to expect for their wedding night. Sally was horrified. "I couldn't believe that anyone, outside of the French whom I'd heard would do anything, could bring themselves to do what LeRoy described," she said. "I was scared out of my wits."[3] So scared, in fact, that the girl bolted out of the house to the nearest bus station for a ticket back to Medford. She didn't have enough money, but most fortunately, a kind army sergeant believed Sally's story that her mother was ill and delivered her back to Medford. Lee Roy later filed for an annulment. A news article on the incident would later claim the marriage lasted only seven hours.

Back in Medford, Sally found a waitress job. She was now blossoming and beginning to notice the men around her. Her observations were reciprocated, and in late 1919 or early 1920 she took up with one of her customers, Dan Goodan, who claimed he was the grandson of a former Colorado governor. The claim was untrue, and Sally's mother didn't like Goodan, but the girl lost her virginity to the man and ran off with him to his hometown of Eaton in Weld County, Colorado. Goodan paid for the trip, as well as some items for Sally and all their furnishings, with a check from the Weiss Lumber Company. In reality, he had absconded with company money. Sally also may have been unaware that Goodan had just recently been released from Folsom Prison.

One day the police showed up in Eaton and arrested Goodan. "Local authorities received word today of the arrest of Dan Goodan, in Eaton, Colorado, for attempting to cash a forged check for $100 on the First National Bank of this city," reported the *Reno Evening Gazette* on May 20, 1920. "Goodan, a former auto truck driver, left Medford a month ago with his wife." Sally also was arrested a couple of days later as the Portland *Oregon Journal* claimed the renegade couple had cashed five hundred dollars' worth of checks in Fresno, California, as well as Pueblo and Colorado Springs, Colorado. Next, according to Colorado's *Greeley Daily Tribune*, "Weld County officers have refused to turn Dan Goodan Jr., late of Medford, Oregon, over to the officers of that place for trial on forgery charge but have consented to allow Mrs. Mabel Goodan, his wife, to go there for trial, as the case against her hero is not so strong as the one in Oregon where she is wanted for forgery."[4]

Sally had passed herself off as Goodan's wife, leading future writers to believe she had married him. The authorities apparently failed to think otherwise as police badgered the girl. "The police sergeant was determined to wring a confession from me," she recalled. "He wanted me to plead guilty, and I said, 'No, I won't do it. . . . I didn't do anything and I'm not going to do it.'" The district attorney promised her probation in exchange for the truth. According to Sally, she was ultimately convicted of merely buying an iron with the stolen money. Even so, she was sentenced to prison in Salem, Oregon, in July of 1920. Seeing as she was the only female prisoner at the time, Sally was allowed to live at the warden's house. But her time there brought her to two realizations. One was "don't take men seriously . . . just 'take' them!"[5] The other was that she never wanted to be poor again.

Sally was eighteen years old when she got out of prison. The state gave her five dollars and a job as a housekeeper in Salem. Upon finishing her parole, the girl's uncle paid her way back to Santa Paula, California, and she began waitressing again. This time, however, Sally decided to supplement her income by bootlegging. By living alone and telling no one of her true occupation, Sally was able to make her own brand of bathtub gin. Her customers, she said, "were just a lot of nice guys from the region with barely enough left over from the necessities of life, like booze, to pay for the luxuries, like bread, potatoes, and shoes." Sally eventually met other bootleggers at a place called The Rincon, where everyone gathered to buy their supplies. The line between Santa Barbara and Ventura Counties ran right through the middle of the house. In a time when police forces operated strictly within their own counties, it was easy enough to dodge them during raids. When she wasn't making liquor, Sally avidly read every book she could get her hands on. "I learned my arithmetic at the cash register," she said. "Chemistry I picked up in my bathtub gin experiments, my customers taught me the rudiments of psychology—and everything else I knew at that time I learned from books."[6]

By 1923, Sally had amassed a small fortune that included a car and her own chauffeur. In 1925, she married again—this time to Ralph Raymond Byham, in Los Angeles. The relationship had ended by 1927, when attorney Ernest Benedetto Diodato Spagnoli waltzed into Sally's life, defended her for a traffic violation in Los Angeles, and paid the five-hundred-dollar fine when she lost. Three days later, Spagnoli proposed. Sally accepted. After the ceremony she drove her new husband to catch a Santa Barbara train headed for his hometown of San Francisco. Sally, who was now using the name Marcia Janus Spagnoli, returned to her bootlegging operation. Her husband had no idea how she was making her money, and Sally intended for it to stay that way. And when Spagnoli demanded that she join him in San Francisco, she closed up shop and went.

At first, Sally was a model housewife and the couple adopted a baby named John. The 1930 census records the little family blissfully living at 75 Chaves Avenue, an address they retained until 1931. But when

Spagnoli inherited a large fortune, Sally said, certain members of his family expressed their distrust of her, and the couple split amicably. In truth, however, Spagnoli had discovered that his betrothed was still married to her last husband. He filed suit in the superior court, and the marriage was annulled. Sally bought a hotel and went back to bootlegging. She wisely kept her car registration under another pseudonym, Marcia Wells, in case of trouble. Eventually, however, police figured out that Sally and Marcia were one and the same and arrested the woman under the thin accusation of leaving her car parked on the street all night. Surely there was more to it than that, as one of the officers, identified as McCausland, broke Sally's arm as she tried to call a bail bondsman. The sympathetic desk sergeant sent her home, and Ernest Spagnoli came to her rescue by threatening to bring McCausland and his partner before the police commission for cruelty.

Unfortunately, Sally's prison record in Oregon came to light in the wake of her trouble with police. Also, one of her renters, Jean Porter, was of particular trouble at the hotel. Not only did she fail to pay rent, but she also was in the habit of bringing various men to her room. One day, Sally and her housekeeper found Jean deathly ill from a self-induced abortion. Sally paid her hospital bills, but Jean went to live with Ella Yates—the woman who had sold the hotel to Sally. Ella happened to be friends with Officer McCausland, who was advised by her to keep an eye on the hotel. Meanwhile, a nice-looking Swedish girl and her husband rented a room at Sally's. One night, in Sally's absence, Ella and Jean set her up by enticing two underage boys to enter the hotel. The police were watching, and when the boys exited the building, they told officers the Swedish woman had propositioned them. The house was raided, and a headline in the paper the next day read, "Wife of Prominent Attorney Arrested for Running Disorderly House."[7]

In court, Jean Porter claimed she had worked for Sally as a prostitute during her time at the hotel. Sally was able to take her adopted son to her mother before police raided her home and took her sixteen-year-old brother, who also had been living with her. In the ensuing mess, Sally's attorneys were able to prove she was framed. But she remained estranged from her brother, who had been convinced to testify against her. In the aftermath, Sally weighed her options. In light of the lies that had been told about her, she boldly decided to become a madam, and a good one at that. Sally began her new career by taking herself to dinner and choosing a name for herself: "Sally," as she heard the song "I Wonder What's Become of Sally?" on the radio, and "Stanford," because the newspaper she was reading announced Stanford University's football victory over the University of California. That very evening, Sally phoned a local theater to reserve tickets for a show and gave her new moniker as the name on the reservation. Sally Stanford was born.

Sally's first brothel was an expansive apartment in an imposing building at 610 Leavenworth Street in San Francisco. By consulting with others in the skin trade, the fledgling madam learned to take only experienced girls and hired six women. A black maid was hired to answer the door, screen callers, and keep out any vulgar men using the f-word. Soon, Sally's place of pleasure was the toast of the town. Even the mayor, future California governor Sunny Jim Rolph, hired Sally and her girls to visit his own secretly kept brothel. "So, you're Sally Stanford," he said at their first meeting. "You're a pretty one." Rolph also gave Sally some sage advice. "Keep them clean and pretty, Sally!" he lectured. "And don't ever lose your class."[8] The two remained friends for life.

Sally fell in love several more times. Her next husband was Lou Rapp, whom she married in 1934 and stayed with for thirteen years. Sally called him handsome, charming, and artistic. And he didn't mind that Sally was a madam. By 1941 she was running several brothels on Geary, Franklin, and Bush Streets, as well as an Oriental parlor in Chinatown. The madam remained stalwart in her business dealings. When the attorney landlord of her Chinese establishment showed up on a business night demanding more rent, he temporarily locked Sally and her associates out of the house. Sally carried out her threat to kick in the glass door and went after the man before he gave up and left.

More fancy pleasure palaces would come. There was the house on Vallejo Street on Russian Hill and 1144 Pine Street on San Francisco's prestigious Nob Hill. To say the houses were palatial is an understatement. At the Pine Street house, each room sported its own decor, ranging from Oriental and Italian provincial to French provincial and Venetian Renaissance. One entire floor was decorated to resemble a fancy hunting lodge. There was a "Pompeian Court" with a fireplace, fountain, and pools. Everything was topped off with gorgeous antique furniture, fine drapes, and expensive carpet. Soft music played on a house-wide system, and only the best of food and wine was served.

Sally's girls, of course, were refined and beautiful. They included former models and showgirls. One of them taught the others ballet when time allowed. All had access to a physician, hairdresser, and dressmaker. But there were rules: Sally's employees were not allowed to associate with one another outside of work, nor were they to visit dive bars. Clients were hands-off outside the confines of the brothel. In return, the ladies received 60 percent of whatever they made. Sally also cautioned her girls against falling in with pimps masquerading as boyfriends, although her advice was rarely followed. Still, guests at the Pine Street house were greeted by a host or hostess and escorted through locked gates to a drawing room. There, the men were treated to an elite party in progress. A Chinese butler served cocktails while the clients were formally introduced to the girls in the room. Their conversations were eloquent, never naughty. Gentleman could visit at their leisure, and only engage in sex if they wanted to. Negotiations were made via the host, after which the client was escorted to the lady's bedroom.

Sally's Vallejo house, the Fortress, was equally palatial. The property was surrounded by a tall stone wall and accessed via a wrought-iron gate, with another gate inside. The interior consisted of a split-level living room running the full width of the house. There also was a large fireplace and a gigantic drawing room, plus a pool. The five-star Fairmont, Mark Hopkins, St. Francis, and Sir Francis Drake Hotels were just a few blocks away, as were several elite men's clubs. As was her habit, Sally furnished the Fortress with beautiful furnishings and staged a masked ball for her grand, invitation-only opening. As the brothel flourished, Sally adopted "two orphaned children" and began using their last name, Owen, in respectable circles. Now, San Francisco had Sally Stanford as reigning madam, but also Marcia Owen, doting mother. One day the children's schoolteacher spotted the madam and her lovely employees at the beach. Believing the girls came from an elite finishing school, the teacher asked if the school was hiring. Sally told her the staff was full. The lady never guessed she was actually admiring some of the best naughty girls San Francisco had to offer.

The clientele at the Fortress did not just include wealthy men. Sally's memoirs were rife with actors, directors, producers, newspapermen, and other famous folks who visited her brothel. Once, she even made an exception for two actresses wishing to spend an evening at the Fortress, but the women did little more than drink too much and caused so much trouble that Sally reinstated her rule that outside ladies were not allowed. Of her male customers, Sally dropped such names as Mark Hellinger, Errol Flynn, and Jean Sablon. Most were fine, generous customers whom the madam appreciated as her guests.

The year 1941 did not start off so great for Sally. In January, she and Louis Rapp had a parting of the ways and divorced. And although neither of Sally's better brothels was ever raided, a military edict in May closed all houses of prostitution throughout San Francisco. Sally remained the exception as the madam secured her Fortress and made sure her staff adhered to strict rules at her houses of pleasure. Double-locked doors, a bevy of security staff inside and outside, connections all over San Francisco, and her own instincts kept her business, her girls, and herself safe. But even California's most prestigious madam was not infallible. One morning in 1947, Sally had retired to her private home on Clay Street when a supposed milkman knocked on the door. Sally was sleeping; when her maid opened the door to take the milk, two men stormed the house to rob it. Fortunately, Sally had had a premonition about the robbery and changed her normal hiding places for her valuables.

The two men—Mark Monroe and Thomas Sitler—were armed and beat the maid "to a bloody pulp" before approaching the room where the madam slept. Sally too was severely beaten but managed to get to a window and screamed for help. She was later able to identify her assailants, and the men were charged with attempted murder. In court, a sometime prostitute identified as Barbara Keilhammer—whom some said was a former employee of Sally's—testified that one of the men was with her during the time Sally was attacked. In truth, Barbara was in Chicago at the time. Likewise, another young woman lied that she was with Sitler. Also, the two men escaped while out on bail but were later caught and sent to prison. Barbara Keilhammer and the other woman were convicted of perjury.

Sally's victory over her assailants coincidentally partnered with a pardon from the state of Oregon for the alleged theft of an iron back when she was a girl. The lady perhaps figured she should quit while she was ahead when she decided to retire in 1949, especially after Sergeant John Dyer relentlessly tried to bust her. Sally would later fondly remember Dyer's attempts, from sending policemen posing as salesmen to her brothel, to sneaking onto the roof in order to catch her girls in the act, to posing as various clients on the phone. According to her, only one successful raid was made—at her private home on Bush Street. In that case, Dyer ordered Sally's girls into the "pie wagon" but ordered Sally to "stand over there. We don't want you."[9] In retrospect, Sally likened herself to the big bass sought out by fisherman, the one who is turned loose upon being caught in order not to end the game. Dyer retired shortly before Sally did and died soon after without ever really catching his favorite fish.

Sally also claimed that her retirement had nothing to do with the efforts of John Dyer. Instead, a teenage tramp whom Sally called Evelyn was responsible. In November of 1949, Evelyn was spotted by officers after she picked up a customer in the Tenderloin. The girl lied to police, claiming that she had worked at several houses of prostitution, including Sally's. Although Evelyn had never worked for Sally (the madam did not even know her), the police bought her story—at least enough to charge several madams with employing her as a prostitute. Sally was of particular interest since she had managed to skillfully evade the law for decades. A month later, Sally's Pine Street bordello was raided. Important items such as her client list were seized, but Sally and her girls had used codes that made the documents look like no more than lengthy shopping lists. But this last accusation was the tipping point for Sally, who decided to finally throw in the towel.

Sally may have retired from the prostitution industry, but she did not retire from business. Following the closure of her houses, she moved to Sausalito and purchased a former German biergarten known as the Walhalla. Built in 1893, the stately building was a former hot spot during Prohibition but by then was in need of some tender loving care. Sally changed the name to Valhalla and got to work. The new restaurant was furnished in Victorian decor. Not until 1952, however, was Sally able to overcome the hurdles of her reputation to get her name on her own liquor license. And it was some time before the general public believed that Sally's Valhalla was serving up fine steaks, not fine women. When the right word got out, however, her clients included such celebrities as Marlon Brando, Bing Crosby, and Lucille Ball.

Sally complemented her success by marrying again, this time to Robert Livingston Gump. The two were united in Reno in April of

1951. Bob Gump was an heir to the famed Gump's retail empire in San Francisco. But he also was the black sheep of the family. Documentary photographer Wayne Miller remembered meeting the newlyweds and recalled that the "understanding was that [Sally] resented the establishment so much she wanted to give them a poke in the nose" by marrying Gump. Miller also remembered Sally was in a "big flamboyant gown and wearing an orchid on her shoulder. She was kind of a short, chunky woman to begin with, so it didn't quite fit." Sally introduced Bob, and Miller took a "wedding photograph" of the couple which later appeared in *Life* magazine. Later, he said, he was having dinner at Valhalla when Gump spotted him. "All of a sudden Gump stands up and points his finger at me," Miller said, "and reaches across the table and says, 'Now I remember you, you're that softcon man who made that picture!' It had evidently been eating on him all those years."[10]

Indeed, Sally's marriage to Bob Gump made the society pages and *Life*—although local columnists persisted in revealing who Mrs. Robert Gump had been in her past life. Predictably, the marriage didn't last. When the couple parted, however, Sally said the divorce was friendly. Divorce proceedings began in January 1952. Not one to let her ring finger grow cold, Sally married a seventh and final time in 1954. This time her chosen mate was her bar manager, Robert "Big Bob" Kenna, and the marriage place was Las Vegas, Nevada. But the relationship soon headed down the same dark road as always, and by their five-month anniversary the couple had separated. The relationship would remain on-again, off-again until a final divorce in 1957.

Whether she knew it or not, Sally was next destined for politics. In 1955, she staged an objection against the impending execution of murderer Barbara Keilhammer, now known as Barbara Graham—the woman who had helped frame her so many years ago. Sally had her reasons: Following Barbara's arrest for lying under oath during the trial of Sally's assailants back in 1947, she had apologized to Sally and "asked me to understand the why of it. I understood."[11] After doing her time, Barbara had hooked up with two men, Jack Santo and Emmet Perkins, who planned to rob a wealthy woman named Mabel Monahan. The threesome entered Mabel's house together. When the men could find no money, they beat Mabel severely, taped a pillow to her head, and left her in a closet to die. Barbara could have plea-bargained her way out of the ensuing trial but chose not to and was convicted of murder. The press called her "Bloody Babs." Several people, including Sally but also newspaper reporters, highly questioned whether Barbara was guilty. Although they tried to have her spared, she was executed in June.

Sally the activist didn't stop with defending Barbara Keilhammer. In 1960 she championed again, this time for convicted robber, kidnapper, and rapist Caryl Chessman. As with Barbara Graham, Sally felt capital punishment of Chessman was not going to solve anything. Claiming the man "was poisoned by the State of California," the former madam converged with others on San Quentin in protest. Afterward, a San Francisco newspaper reported that "Sally Stanford cried when Chessman's death was announced." Ever determined, Sally decided the best way to make a difference was to run for city council in Sausalito, an action which drew insults from everyone from respectable women to the men who knew her. The sly woman drew constituents, however, by campaigning for more money for the local police department and a public restroom for the town. Not surprisingly however, she lost the election.

As one might guess, Sally refused to give up her new endeavor. She ran again in 1964 and lost again. In 1971, the *Daily Review* in Hayward tattled that Sally, birth name Mabel Janice Busby, was "now a restaurateur but once undisputed queen of San Francisco's nightlife," and also that she "used Marsha Owen as her name in her unsuccessful attempts to win election to City Council."[12] Try as they might, nobody could stop Sally from running again and again until 1972 when, on her sixth try, she was finally elected. Perhaps in celebration, and probably to get even,

Sally enlisted newsman Bob Patterson to write her own as-told-to biography, *The Lady of the House: California's Most Notorious Madam*.

As *The Lady of the House* sold like hotcakes, Sally made her next move to successfully win as mayor of Sausalito in 1976. "Ex-madame now her honor," marveled the Long Beach *Independent* on September 20. When her reign was over, she also served as vice mayor. Sally Stanford became a household name, even more so after a television movie about her premiered in 1976. When asked what she thought about actress Dyan Cannon portraying her character, Sally commented, "She just didn't have it in her to play me. I have to admit, it's a hard act to follow."[13]

Sally Stanford—nightlife queen, restaurant VIP, city councilwoman, and mayor—died on February 1, 1982, at Marin General Hospital north of San Francisco. One source stated that Sally had upward of eleven heart attacks in her final years, the last one being strong enough to kill her. She was buried in Mount Tamalpais Cemetery in San Rafael, leaving her two adopted children, John and Hara Owen. John recalled that Sally was "a straight-laced mother" who sent him to military school, lectured him about his dating life as a young adult, and eventually hired him to run the Valhalla. Sally would have liked to have seen Sausalito in the days after her death, when she was given her due respect. All the flags in Sausalito, even the one on the ferryboat, were flown at half-staff in her honor.

# CHAPTER 13

———— •◦• ————

## *Los Angeles:*
## *Lusty Ladies in the City of Angels*

Los Angeles is one of the oldest civilized areas in California. What with the ancient La Brea Tar Pits, settlement by the Chumash, Tataviam, and Tongva peoples, and Portuguese and Spanish explorers, the City of Angels has been drawing people for centuries. When Gaspar de Portola established a trail north to Monterey in 1769 and Father Junipero Serra opened Mission San Gabriel Arcangel in 1771, their efforts paved the way for permanent settlement. The first American trading ship sailed into port in 1805. Some forty-five years later, nearby gold discoveries created a dramatic upswing in the population, leading to the incorporation of Los Angeles when California became the thirty-first state in 1850. At the time, the city was the largest in California.

The 1850s were a boon to the blossoming city. The gold rush caused an upswing in the prices of beef and other goods, bringing much prosperity. Before long, a host of newcomer prostitutes and gamblers moved in from San Francisco and other northern cities. Among the most notorious early resorts was *La Aguila de Oro* ("The Golden Eagle") in *Calle de los Negros*. In this riotous place, armed thugs watched over the gambling tables and they said Los Angeles was "the toughest and most lawless city west of Santa Fe."[1] Things were so rough by 1853 that prominent men of the town formed the Los Angeles Rangers, who oversaw the execution of twenty-two outlaws within the next two years. Not until 1857 did the city settle down some, when the gold rush waned and the price of cattle dropped. As the gamblers and their shady ladies moved on, the landscape of Los Angeles changed as a new generation of the bawdy element, coupled with a growing Chinatown, slowly moved in.

By 1870, the former Plaza—once the crown center of Los Angeles—had deteriorated to a neighborhood "notoriously infested with shameless bawds." A cleanup effort brought upscale hotels and theaters to the area, but also the El Dorado Saloon and Wood's Opera House, which quickly evolved into a variety theater described as "a typical Western song and dance resort, the gallery being cut up into boxes where the actresses between acts mingled with the crowd; patrons indulged in drinking and smoking, and the bar in front did a thriving business."[2] Other theaters followed suit. Beginning in 1876, railroads and other modern modes of transportation brought more and more people to Los Angeles. They included a number of naughty ladies. Within ten years, another new generation of bars and bawdy houses were scattered throughout the city, to the effect that authorities established a sizable official red-light district, as well as the necessary laws to regulate it.

The designated red-light district of the 1880s began

> at the center of High Street and New High Street, and thence southerly along New High Street to the center of Temple Street; thence westerly along the center of Temple Street to the center of Fort Street, thence southerly along the center of Fort Street to the center of Third Street; thence easterly along the center of Third Street to the center of Main Street; thence southerly along the center of Main Street to the center of Mayo Street; thence easterly along the center of Mayo Street to the center of Los Angeles Street; thence northerly along the center of Los Angeles Street to the center of First Street; thence along the center of First Street easterly to a point 200 feet east of the east line of Alameda

*Alameda Street and 1st Street in Little Tokyo as it appeared in 1918.* Metro Transportation Library and Archive

*Street; thence northerly parallel with Alameda Street to its intersection with a prolongation of center line of High Street.*[3]

Within these confusing boundaries, brothel business was relegated to the upper floors of two-story houses only. Fines of up to two hundred dollars and/or six months in jail would be imposed on any houses posing a nuisance.

Los Angeles's demimonde, now known as Hell's Half Acre, was soon well-known to tourists on the Southern Pacific Railroad, who "would eagerly ask their porters to let them know when the train passed by an infamous stretch of Alameda Street, southeast of the old Plaza."[4] From the train, passengers could catch a long glimpse of the saloons, restaurants, and cribs of Alameda Street. The ladies of the line knew that if they stood out front, they could show off for anyone who might be inclined to visit them upon disembarking from the train. The finer folk of Los Angeles objected to such antics and voiced their opinions to the *Los Angeles Times* concerning the girls being highly visible on "one of the principal thoroughfares, where they constantly hail passersby."[5]

What many respectable people did not know was that many of these soiled doves were controlled by pimps and landlords who constantly demanded that they work at one dollar per customer and pay high rents. Fancier parlor houses were located along Commercial and New High Streets, but the crib girls near the tracks tended to draw seedier, less refined customers. Their business transactions were conducted in "their squalid cribs, which often consisted of nothing more than a makeshift bed and wash basin."[6] Most crib girls merely rented the cribs for as much as eighteen dollars each week while paying additional rent to a boardinghouse elsewhere.

A real estate boom in 1885 contributed heavily to the growth of Los Angeles. Hundreds of people came to buy land as cement sidewalks were installed, railroad lines were built, and newcomers were plied with music and free "cold lunches" in saloons offering whiskey and wine. Colleges were built. Orange groves were planted, and irrigation ditches were constructed to water them. A new harbor at today's Redondo Beach promised plenty of trade. Los Angeles soon bloomed as a first-class city.

The red-light district also grew. Some brothels had infiltrated formerly respectable homes. A 1999 excavation of a brothel privy on Costello Street revealed the place was once a parlor house. Discarded items included "gaudy decorations, formal dining settings, and oil lamps."[7] More common properties included that of Gussie Bland who owned a combination bordello and saloon at 128 North Alameda Street. One of her favorite consorts was William Hogg Wolseley Markham whom she met on a trip to Shanghai. But Markham also was a thief, stealing thirteen thousand dollars as assistant paymaster for the HMS *Espoir*. In 1886 Markham was in disguise and on his way to visit his beloved Gussie but changed his course to Kansas City when he realized Pinkerton agents were after him. The agents caught up with him after getting Gussie drunk, wherein she told them Markham was masquerading under the name Luke Charles Rich in Kansas.

Los Angeles authorities spent much of their time trying to control their red-light district during the late 1880s. Reformers emerged as it was revealed that, like many other cities, Los Angeles's political and city officials were corrupt to a great degree with hush money and clandestine investments from the Tenderloin passing through their hands. Groups like the Board of Freeholders, the League for Better City Government, and the Municipal Reform Association began forming, primarily to point out publicly that such corruption had direct links to the red-light district. But their platform was imbalanced: How could these groups really focus on reform for the red-light ladies when they were already busy trying to improve the city's political structure? In the meantime, even common washerwomen like Sylvia Daniels found themselves forced to pursue prostitution as a means to make real money in order to survive but went largely unnoticed by reform groups.

Then there was Bartolo Ballerino, known as the "father of the cribs" of Los Angeles. Ballerino's biggest holding was the Ballerino block in old "Negro Alley," where the man and his wife, Maria, exacted two dollars in rent each day from prostitutes. The couple tended to turn a blind— and cold—eye to those renters who suffered illness or violence. One of these women was identified only as Adele, a prostitute who was beaten so severely by one of her customers that she was bedridden for over two weeks. Ballerino demanded the full month's rent. Adele refused at first, but "finally compromised on $25, deducting $5 for the time she did not occupy the place." Unwilling to accept the deal, Ballerino had his son and another man "dig a hole in the sidewalk in front of the door. The slabs of paving stone were set up against the woman's door, blocking ingress, and when she remonstrated she was assaulted."[8] Ballerino and others like him continued running cribs in Los Angeles for many more years.

Ballerino's cribs were not the only ones in use during the late 1880s and '90s. Near Aliso Street and Alameda Street was a place known as Easy Jeanette Street, which was guessed to have been constructed as late as 1894. The women of Easy Jeanette Street lived elsewhere but rented cribs consisting of small rooms furnished with little more than a bed and a wash sink and shared a common privy. They advertised their wares by sitting on the edge of the windowsill and beckoning customers in. Although the cost for time with a crib girl was only around a dollar, most women paid seventy-five dollars in monthly rent. There were inherent dangers of working in such a place, including arrests, but also depression and the likelihood of alcohol or opium use to fight that depression. Suicides occurred on occasion, and the ladies also lived in fear of being beaten by their customers.

One of the biggest differences between crib girls and parlor house ladies was that the latter nearly always lived on the premises. Also, their money came from wealthier clients. In a parlor house, men could expect to be served fine food, fine liquor (which was seldom offered in a crib), and sex. In 1897, a group of madams dared to publish *La Fiesta de Los Angeles Souvenir Sporting Guide*, a whimsical directory to the finest palaces of pleasure the city had to offer. Among those to appear in the guide was Hattie Wilson, whose advertisement for her Oakwood Inn read, "Mrs. Hattie Wilson who keeps the Oakwood Inn on the old Adobe Road, about six blocks from the terminus of the Downey Avenue car line, has one of the most secluded little nooks in the country. Here you can go and take your lady friend day or night and be free from observation, and by the way she has fine furnished apartments, where she serves as fine a meal as can be found in the city. A choice selection of wines and liquors are kept constantly on hand."

Other advertisers included Miss Ella Rorich and her four girls, who occupied "the mansion" at 419 Commercial Street, and Florence Laddy at 148 San Pedro Street. "If you are looking for a good time and a place where you will be well entertained you should certainly call at Florence Laddy's," read the advertisement. "Miss Florence has a wide reputation as an entertainer and for hospitality. She has three young ladies who are chuck full of fun and give you a good time."[9] Nobody would realize from the frivolous ad that just the previous December, Florence had been in court—not to answer charges of prostitution, but rather, charges that she had served liquor in her place. It took a while to actually find Florence when she was charged, but she eventually popped up in time for her trial. With her was a "ravishing blonde," Addie Wilson, who testified that it was she, not Florence, who served beer to some customers. Florence wasn't even there, Addie said, a claim backed up by the very customers the girl had served. Although the *Los Angeles Herald* labored over the details of the trial for several days, Florence's case was finally dismissed.[10]

Hattie Wilson, Ella Rorich, and Florence Laddy seem to have avoided many run-ins with city officers, as well as the women's aid groups which began focusing on the cribs after the turn of 1900. Reformers also concentrated their efforts on Bortolo Ballerino and another known crib pimp, Chris Buckley, and the politicians they supported. "Between them they control property that is said to produce an income of nearly $100,000 a year," wrote one reporter, "an income that is a direct rake-off from the wages of sin." The *Los Angeles Times* also jumped into the mix. Reporters held back little, lambasting city officials and the police force as a well-known evangelist and reformer, Mrs. Charlton Edholm, gave a fiery speech at the East Los Angeles Christian Church in 1903. "Buckley and Ballerino are renting those cribs every night near the heart of this city in direct violation of the laws of the state of California," she told the crowd. "When Mayor [Meredith] Snyder and Chief of Police [Charles] Elton took office they swore to uphold, without favor, the laws of the commonwealth, which they know do not countenance the existence of houses of prostitution."[11]

Those listening to Mrs. Edholm, including about every newspaper in town, were fueled to action. Female progressive groups began making regular visits to Hell's Half Acre and other Tenderloin areas, offering to help those prostitutes who wanted to leave and giving them literature for various rescue homes, including the Door of Hope that had been in place since the 1880s. These actions finally caught the attention of Mayor Snyder. Ballerino was at last arrested for renting a crib for prostitution, but the pimp fought the charges and threatened his renters. Because of Ballerino's intimidations, crib girls who were called to court seldom showed, or pretended to forget who Ballerino was if they did appear at the trial. Ballerino, meanwhile, was caught trying to bribe a city clerk. Fences soon appeared around his cribs as well, to keep reformers from knocking on the doors.

In December 1903, police at last raided Hell's Half Acre and kicked out a number of soiled doves and their pimps. The *Los Angeles Times* described the exodus with a rather whimsical and romantic pen:

*Darkness like a great mantle of charity settled down and softly stretched its folds of somber shadow over the erstwhile red-light district last night. . . . The 300 members of the demimonde, who have been inmates of the cribs and stalls, had flown to escape the dragnet of the police and the stern justice of the city's courts. For the first time in the history of modern Los Angeles, the ribald jest, the vulgar song, the cheap and flashy show of finery on the be-painted and bespangled damsels . . . were not on exhibition for the gaze and gratification of the youths and men who seek such things. Instead of the myriad of twinkling red lights and the glow of incandescent bulbs that were always a striking feature of these houses of the Scarlett [sic] women, last night the American section was in complete darkness . . . the atmosphere was as peaceful and as serene as was that which surrounded the cross-surmounted old adobe pile just over the other side of the Plaza, where the . . . Church of Our Lady of Angels, stands in its solitude.*[12]

Naturally, Ballerino threw a fit, blaming everyone but himself for what had happened. But the man also had a plan: shortly after Hell's Half Acre was silenced, Ballerino set about erecting a whole new set of cribs on the second floor of the International Hotel in January 1904. "The preachers say one story no good," he told a couple of police commissioners who came by. "The Salvation Army say it make people bad. I am willing to do the right thing, so I make [the cribs] all two stories. It will be the great International Hotel and will have more rooms than any other hotel in the state. . . . Then I invite all the good people of the city to come down here and have champagne." Ballerino further assured the officers that there would be music, and also that the cribs would be finished within another week. When the men asked him the purpose of the second story, Ballerino shrugged. "That is not for the public," he said frankly. "It is for my—what you call it? Oh, yes; for my harem. I keep my women up there."[13]

Chris Buckley took a different route, preferring to change the fronts of his cribs into legitimate-looking businesses. *Los Angeles Times* reporters, alerted by the crowds who watched the transformation taking place, were no dummies. It was observed in one article that "In each of the places was placed a small counter and tier of shelves . . . these 'improvements' were placed near the front of the cribs and behind them board partitions have been erected, thus making two small rooms out of one. These counters and shelves will be used for the sale of cigars, tobacco, chewing [gum] and the like. In a word, every crib woman will go into the cigar business today." Ballerino followed suit, and several prostitutes intimated to the *Times* that they too would soon "go into the 'cigar business'" on the first floor of the International.[14]

Ballerino especially was amazingly brazen; a visit by a *Los Angeles Herald* reporter in February revealed that the pimp had followed in Buckley's footsteps by having signage installed in front of his cribs off Alameda Street. The reporter noted that "Each 'crib' displays a brand new sign such as an enterprising tradesman would fling out to catch the passing trade. 'Annette' sits behind a window which bears the caption 'Dry Goods Store.' 'Marcelle' waits for customers behind a 'Stationery' sign. In each window is displayed a meager stock. Paper collars [descend] from strings stretched behind the little panes. Cheap neckties are displayed on hastily constructed counters. Poor tobacco is arranged in gaudy pouches on [the] shelf and window ledge." The women, meanwhile, "stand boldly forth in open doors, nor do they seek to hide their calling in the guise of shop keeping." The writer then sauntered over to the "Great International" to see a "jostling crowd" as the ladies beckoned customers. "They sang, they laughed, they joked and now and then hailed some familiar habitué with shouts of welcome. They made merry in their own debauched way." The reporter also saw only one policeman in the entire area. "He was in semi-uniform and explained his presence by saying that 'he was on his way home and just dropped in to see what was going on.' He found a good deal going on."[15]

The very next day, Ballerino and his agent, Joe Wiot, were summoned to court where they were found guilty of renting an apartment to prostitute Rose West for immoral purposes. The men were convicted in just twenty minutes. Seventeen women at the Great International were arrested as Ballerino was sentenced to thirty days in jail and charged a five hundred dollar fine. The sentence seemed light enough, but apparently took the wind out of his sails. For the rest of his days, Ballerino lived in one of his own dingy cribs at the International, telling a reporter, "This town is going to the dogs. It's getting too darned good."[16]

In the midst of the 1903–4 cleanup campaign came crib girl Ella Powers, who made the mistake of telling her pimp, Michael "George" Walsh, that she wanted to leave the profession. Ella, who had formerly lived in Oxnard with her widowed mother, had already been arrested twice: once in 1901 after she was involved in a drunken scuffle on Leroy Street, and again in 1902 when she was tagged a vagrant and told to leave the city. On December 8, 1903, Ella told Walsh that she wanted to quit her life as a prostitute. The next day, the *Los Angeles Herald* provided details on what happened next. Ella, said the paper, was often the victim of Walsh's abuse when she didn't make enough money to suit him. Disheartened and disgusted with her life, Ella found a good job as a chambermaid at the St. Lawrence house. Just over a week later, Walsh visited Ella at her new place of work and demanded she leave with him. When she refused, the heartless pimp "grabbed a case knife from a table and stabbed her in the side. He then cut her in the side of the face, knocking her down. While she was prostrate he kicked her." That time, Walsh was arrested and given ninety days' probation.

After being treated, Ella returned to the "receiving hospital" to have her stitches removed. While there, she begged Police Surgeon Smith to have someone lock Walsh up but refused to swear out a warrant. Upon returning to work, Ella next discovered that Walsh had taken a room at St. Lawrence and constantly badgered her to go back to work for him. One day he was drunk when he approached Ella as she scrubbed the floor. "I said I'd get you and now I'll finish you," he said. The man fired five shots at Ella. The first of these hit her in the arm. Screaming with pain and fear, Ella ran into another room as Walsh followed, firing. He missed twice, but the fourth bullet hit her in the nose and split, with one portion of it lodging above Ella's eye. The last bullet stuck the poor girl above the ear "and glancing around the skull, lodged beneath the scalp at the base of the brain." A crowd began gathering as the ruthless cur Walsh jumped into a waiting buggy and quickly left the scene.

Ella was taken to the hospital. Her wounds were not serious, although they did further scar her once-pretty face. Police, meanwhile, apprehended Walsh at Black's poolroom. Ella told them that all she had done was profess her desire to leave her life as Walsh's prostitute. Most interestingly, the outcome of Walsh's trial appeared not in the front pages of the *Herald*, but way in the back on page 12. Walsh, it was reported in

March of 1904, was sentenced to five years at Folsom Prison for intent to murder. The callous *Herald* seemingly took into account that Walsh had, after all, taken Ella in off the streets and gave her money and clothing. And besides, Walsh was a "hard-working man with a previously good reputation, but the woman did not even seem to be grateful to him for having given her a home." In sentencing him, Judge Smith told Walsh that he was indeed "a very fortunate young man."[17] The *Herald* turned its attentions to other matters as Ella was left to recover and attempt to resume her life.

The battle to close down Hell's Half Acre was waged for several more years. An all-new cleanup campaign was staged again in 1909, wherein police physically padlocked several places of vice. The cribs and saloons were finally closed altogether. But what happened to their occupants? Many prostitutes had no place else to go, settling instead for operating on the streets, in various apartment houses, and in more clandestine brothels in the hills around town. But now, the new and morally improved city of Los Angeles exhibited a kinder, gentler attitude toward wayward women. When Prescott, Arizona, prostitute Gabriell "Dollie" Wiley shot her abusive lover in a Los Angeles liquor store, newspapers ran to cover her story like moths to a light bulb.

Gabe was an Italian immigrant orphan who had lost her father soon after her family came to America. Her mother had died in the aftermath of the San Francisco earthquake of 1906. Alone with no family, Gabe worked her way east, finding employment as a waitress by day and a prostitute by night in the Nevada goldfields before moving to Prescott. A series of bad relationships included her marriage to boxer Ernest Presti, who was believed to have beaten her and was eventually shot to death by another man. In 1912, she fell for Leonard Topp, a striking middle-aged man of Canadian and Chippewa descent who had recently received an honorable discharge from nearby Fort Whipple. Topp was no better than Presti, sharing Gabe's room above the Palace Saloon but beating her and stealing her money. Still, Gabe, suffering from some sort of Stockholm syndrome, hoped to marry Topp. When the man suddenly left her in 1915 and departed for Los Angeles, the woman came completely unstrung.

Gabe soon learned that Topp had left her for another woman, Bonnie Elliott. "When I got [to Los Angeles], I saw him with another woman," she later explained. "I tried for some time to get him to talk to me, but he always refused."[18] When Gabe discovered that Topp intended to marry Bonnie, she hatched a plan. On January 1, 1916, the girl was dressed to the nines as she secretly followed Topp into a liquor store on West Seventh Street. "Hello, Leonard," Gabe said. When Topp turned around, she pulled a small gun from her hand muff and shot him square in the chest.

Liquor store owner John Donohue was kneeling behind the counter when Topp came in and heard the shot. When he stood up, Donohue said, he saw "a woman lying on her back on the floor and Topp on his knees beside her. He had his hands around either her throat or the lower part of her head and was beating her head up and down on the floor." Not realizing exactly what had happened, Donohue said, "Shame on you, what are you doing?"[19] Topp stood up and took a step or two toward the man before falling dead to the floor; the bullet had nicked his heart. Police found Gabe unconscious on the floor. She was taken to the hospital, then to the jail, where she remained in a daze and called out for her dead lover.

Newspapers throughout California and Arizona simply went wild for the story of the unfortunate, abused woman who went crazy and killed her man. Enter Los Angeles attorney Earl Rogers, who agreed to defend Gabe. The woman couldn't pay him, but an unidentified prostitute visited Rogers's office the day before the trial and presented him with a cigar box containing three thousand dollars' worth of gems to pay for Gabe's defense. The papers ate this up as the trial commenced. An eager, all-male jury lent a sympathetic ear as Gabe told her tale. "I killed him because I loved him," Gabe concluded, adding that "for a while we were happy. He was my master. I was content to do anything he ordered me to do, just so he would reward me by saying he loved me." The hapless victim also said she remembered nothing of the shooting, saying only, "Oh I loved him too much. I would never have been here today, if I had not loved him so."

Gabe's testimony drew the sympathy of a number of prominent society women, as well as Salvation Army workers and preachers' wives, all of whom attended the proceedings. The jurors were especially moved when Gabe's friend from Prescott, a striking blonde named Pearl Valley, testified that Topp's favorite pastime was to "scuff the toes of his boots against" Gabe. By now Gabe's story was being closely followed by her attorney's daughter, Adela Rogers-St. Johns, who covered the trial extensively for the *Los Angeles Herald*. In the end, it took the jury just ten minutes to acquit Gabe of murder. Within minutes, famed soprano Ellen Beach Yaw spirited Gabe away to her own expansive estate for some rest and recuperation. While there Gabe promised reporters, "From this moment on, I shall live so that good women will not draw aside their skirts when they pass by me."[20]

Gabe's sympathizers might have changed their minds if they knew that Gabe married again, had her husband jailed for robbing her at gunpoint, divorced him, and married someone else—all while working as a prominent madam back in Prescott. But that news failed to come to light in Los Angeles, even after Gabe sued Hollywood producer Dorothy Davenport Reid. At issue was the movie *The Red Kimona*, which Reid collaborated on with Adela Rogers-St. Johns about the murder of Leonard Topp—without Gabe's knowledge or permission. The film focused on "Gabrielle Darcy" who, just like Gabe, tracks down her abusive lover and kills him. Gabe said she had no idea the movie was about herself when she happened to see it at a Prescott theater. In 1928 she filed suit against Reid and All-Star Features Distributors Inc., claiming the film portrayed her "as a woman of lewd characteristic, a prostitute and a murderess." She also requested damages in the amount of fifty thousand dollars. Such a lawsuit was quite novel, even for Hollywood, at the time. The *New York Times* ran a story about it, and writers who had covered Topp's killing were happy to pick up where they left off. The suit was settled in 1931, causing Reid to file bankruptcy in 1933. Gabe, meanwhile, remained a successful madam in Prescott before moving to Salome, Arizona, and eventually retiring. She died in 1962.[21]

# CHAPTER 14

———— •◦• ————

## *Cora Phillips: The 24-Carat Queen*

B y the mid-1870s, it seemed that everybody in Los Angeles knew who Cora Phillips was. Where she came from and why she was there remains a mystery, even though she was at one time a reigning madam in the City of Angels. But Cora had her secrets, and she kept them well. Not until she died did the papers reveal that Cora was actually married to a prominent politician named Joe Manning, to whom she left her small fortune.

Aside from her birth in Ohio in 1853, the earliest documentation of Cora is found in a *Los Angeles Herald* article dated February 24, 1876. Cora, along with two other soiled doves identified as Mary Holmes and Annie Sattelie, were arrested for prostitution. "Their trial comes off at 10 o'clock this morning in Judge Gray's Court," reported the *Herald*, "and it remains to be seen whether the righteous indignation of the Council against bawdy houses will amount to anything." Apparently, it didn't, for all three women were released on their own recognizance. Annie left town, but Cora and Mary duly appeared in court the next day. The trial was well attended, and the *Herald* reporter covering it commented that "We thought that we noticed several men dodge out of their sight as they came into the room, but we might have been mistaken."[1] Much to the crowd's disappointment, all that happened was that the ladies bonded out at one hundred dollars apiece.

Both the crowd and the *Herald* were further disappointed in the inevitable trial of Cora Phillips. Witnesses were reluctant to testify against her, the exception being prominent citizens who simply talked about how bad Cora was, and one Officer McFadden who "produced some ugly facts that will hardly bear publication." As for the defense, Cora's attorney merely based his rebuttals "on technicalities of law and definitions of terms." The jury retired for only a few minutes before finding Cora not guilty. The *Herald* apparently hoped that finding her guilty might lead to a clean sweep of the city's bawdy houses, but that didn't happen. "Here was a woman, one of the most notorious in Los Angeles, whom even the little children would point their fingers at on the street," thundered the *Herald*, "and it is impossible to make an intelligent and unbiased Jury believe that she is an immoral character."[2]

Was Cora really corrupting Los Angeles as willfully as the newspaper said she was? It's hard to tell, since the only other news of note on the woman was published in November of 1877, well over a year after her trial. In this instance it was reported that a woman named Carrie Rice, who was somehow associated with Cora, tried to overdose on laudanum. In this case, however, the only paper to report the incident seems to be *Crónica*, a Mexican newspaper which published the article in Spanish. Also, the 1880 census merely notes that Cora resided with two other women on Wilmington Avenue. Several single women were living in the same neighborhood. None of them, however, appear to have been associated with Los Angeles's red-light district some blocks away. But secrets were a specialty of women like Cora, who likewise probably never revealed just why she visited San Francisco a month later, returning by ship with three friends, or what she was doing when she took the Southern Pacific train back to San Francisco via Mojave the month after that or who was with her when she returned, again via Mojave, in September.

It is easy enough to speculate that Cora's mysterious trips were actually recruiting missions for girls. When she was arrested a second time in 1882, she was officially charged with "keeping a house of prostitution." Three women—Minnie Chandler, Ruby Tilden, and Eva Walker—were identified as "inmates of the same" and a trial date was set. Cora, however, already knew that certain citizens of Los Angeles had it out for her. The clever madam and her girls filed an affidavit with the court, explaining that they believed "the prejudice of the citizens of Los Angeles was such that they would not be accorded a fair trial."[3] The women asked for a change of venue, and the case was transferred to the justice's court in Pasadena. But for some reason, the case was never tried.

Just over a week after getting her trial moved, Cora took out an advertisement in the *Herald*. "$100 Reward!" the ad read. "LOST, on Tuesday, June 13th, a CRESCENT BREAST-PIN, with diamond star. The above reward will be paid for its return to MISS CORA PHILLIPS, No. 84 Los Angeles St."[4] Cora's reward of one hundred dollars would be equivalent to around $2,400 by today's standards, illustrating how valuable her breastpin was. The advertisement ran for several weeks, but it is not known whether someone returned the pin or Cora just gave up on the lost item. Besides, she soon had bigger fish to fry, whether she liked it or not.

In July, a special meeting of the Los Angeles City Council focused on an investigation of police chief Henry King. At issue were the bawdy houses along Arcadia Street, as well as illegal activities in Chinatown, which King had previously refused to address. Assistant City Attorney Gage testified that King was uncooperative when shown a diagram of the problem area "and deliberately walked off." Another time, after the arrest of some prostitutes, Gage arrived at their trial only to find King "in consultation with Mr. Wilson, counsel for the defense." Gage's list of wrongdoings by the chief was quite extensive, and his testimony showed that King had refused to prosecute certain lawbreakers. When it came to Cora Phillips, Gage attacked police officials for failing to make sure she was tried in Pasadena. To the jury at hand, it appeared (and probably rightfully so) that Cora and her cohorts in the red-light realm had King in their pocket, paying him off as needed to look the other way when the ladies were arrested.[5]

Perhaps the outing of Chief King to the public is why Cora began shopping for a man in her life, one who was just important enough to shield her from the law but would never be suspected of doing so. She seemed to have found one in Joe Manning, a sometime fireman and housepainter with fair hair and dreamy blue eyes who was well-known in social circles. Manning had been in Los Angeles for a while and was well liked. At a Christmas gala in 1878 hosted by the "hall of the Confidence boys," the *Herald* noted lightheartedly that he "was made happy with a box of toy paints" as his Christmas gift.[6] Manning resided at 59 Main Street, not too far from the red-light district. By the following year, he had moved a few doors up to 76 Main Street when he was elected marshal of the Central Republican Club and ran for county assessor. And during the Fourth of July parade just before Chief King's trial, people just adored Joe Manning as he sailed by in a "triumphal car" for the Confidence Exempt Association. Also in the car was the "Goddess of Liberty, represented by little Daisy Moore."[7]

Cora Phillips might have very well been one of the pretty ladies in the crowd, waving her scented handkerchief as Manning drove by. No documents or witnesses can attest to when the two officially got together. Whenever it was, Manning was just Cora's cup of tea. Within a year, he was residing at the "Phillips Block" on Court Street, nestled between Spring and Main Streets (it is unknown if the block was so named because of Cora). He would remain there during 1883 and 1884 as he continued his occupation as a painter. Cora, meanwhile, had moved into her stately parlor house at 203 Alameda Street. It was hard to miss Cora's place, The Golden Lion. Two life-size stone lions sat at the entrance. Inside, the house was decorated with "lush fabrics, decadent furniture, plush carpets, plus two Steinway pianos."[8] Henry Carr, who knew Cora, described her as the "24-carat Queen of Bohemia" who eventually "retired with a fortune." Likewise, the *Los Angeles Tribune* acknowledged that the Golden Lion was "an upper-class establishment." Once, when the house was raided, police found two wealthy men "who put up their little ten dollars and vanished after telling the officers, 'don't give us away.'"[9] On another occasion, police raided the house and arrested ten women who were employed by the madam.

The raid on Cora's might have taken place in 1887, when fifty-seven men and women in the red-light district were arrested, including the madam herself. If Manning was involved with Cora at that date, he likely heard of the proceedings but was apparently not present. Notably, city

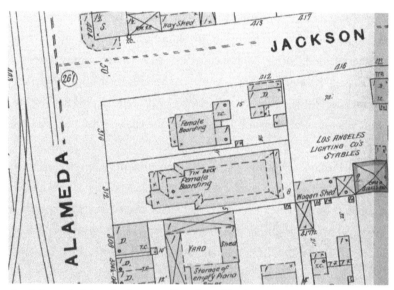

*Cora's last palatial parlor house at Alameda and Jackson Streets, circa 1890.* Library of Congress, Geography and Map Division

directories dated 1887 through 1890 showed him living at 54 North Los Angeles Street, and in 1889 he was simultaneously identified as residing back at 59 Main Street. Cora made the newspapers again in 1888 when Mr. M. Dodd accused the lady of trying to close down some cribs he had built at the corner of Alameda and Turner Streets. Cora wasn't the only one to object to the cribs; a councilman named Collins felt the small houses were a disgrace to the city. In reporting on Dodd's stormy conversation with Collins, the *Los Angeles Herald* declined to comment on the irony of a known madam and a councilman agreeing on the same issue for different reasons. Dodd wasn't through with Cora. About a week later, at a meeting of police commissioners, the crib owner approached the board and told them he "still wants his property, at the corner of Turner and Alameda streets, to be occupied by the gay maidens who abound there. He thinks no discrimination should be used against his tenants when others of the same kind in the vicinity are let alone." He also specifically "charged that Cora Phillips influences the officers of the law to raid his tenants." Police Chief Cuddy told Dodd to "keep on the side of truth and not mislead the Board."[10]

Dodd's rantings left Cora unimpressed—or did they? Within six months of the man's accusations, the madam began looking to branch out or perhaps even move altogether. In March of 1889, the *Herald* reported that Cora had purchased "a cottage adjoining the Jackson Hotel" in Santa Monica, much to the embarrassment of the city officials there. The purchase price was a cool four thousand dollars. As officials tried to find a way from stopping Cora "and her friends" from moving into the cottage, the madam made preparations "to beautify the ground in front of the cottage." The city fathers weren't buying the ploy. "It is understood that the Clerk of the Santa Monica City Council notified Miss Phillips that the water would be turned off on her lot," said the *Herald*, "and that this has been done. . . . It is said that Miss Cora is determined to stand by her asserted rights as a property holder of the

City by the Sea, and that the authorities are equally determined that she shall not be permitted to occupy the cottage."[11] No follow-up article was forthcoming. Apparently, Cora lost a round.

In 1890, Joseph Manning did something seemingly out of character: He applied for a liquor license for a saloon at Washington Gardens, a lavish amusement park that included a picnic area, live ostriches, a merry-go-round, Ferris wheel, roller coaster, and even hot-air balloon rides. There also was a bowling alley, dance pavilion, a theater with seating for four thousand people, and a baseball field with seating for up to ten thousand spectators. Manning's application was referred to the city police chief for further investigation. But Manning apparently lost interest in the endeavor, and Washington Gardens was up for sale by August. Next, Manning focused instead on a saloon license at 114 Court Street in September as his application at Washington Gardens was revoked. The new place was the address of the Tivoli Theatre, which was actually advertised as a "strictly family theatre" in October and was closed by December.[12] In the end, Manning settled for returning to politics, announcing he would "pose as a representative Republican at the next county convention" on September 28.[13]

It would have been fun to see what Manning did by mixing liquor licenses and politics, especially with Cora by his side—but the lady died unexpectedly "of apoplexy" on January 1, 1891. She was only thirty-eight years old. Newspapers all over the state carried snippets of her obituary, revealing at last that her real name was Ada Manning, wife of Joe Manning. Naturally the writers at the *Los Angeles Herald* also could not resist revealing that the woman "was known in certain circles as 'Cora Phillips,' and for many years was the leader of the members of the half world in this city."[14] All of Cora's secrets were told, and not all of them were bad. The *Daily Alta California* remembered that she "was noted for many quiet deeds of charity, and especially to flood sufferers several years ago." Also, the woman left "an estate valued at $100,000 to $150,000" to Joe Manning, her "well-known local politician" husband.[15] Cora's funeral, at her home on West Sixth Street, was "largely attended" with an elaborate floral display. The madam was laid to rest in Evergreen Cemetery.

A few days after Cora's funeral, Manning hustled to apply for the necessary paperwork to claim his wife's estate. The newspapers had overshot their guestimate, but he still received around $22,500. Included was Cora's Sixth Street house, which Manning officially moved into later that year, and her last fancy parlor house at 312 Alameda Street. By 1892, however, voter records show Manning had moved again, to 115-1/2 Main Street. He was employed by the Vienna Buffet which had opened in the former Tivoli Theatre. The Vienna Buffet was now known as a "den of vice," but Manning, described as a "man-about-town," apparently didn't mind.[16]

If Cora taught Manning anything, it was to keep her house of pleasure afloat. So the widower immediately rented it to a madam, known in 1893 as Grace Pomeroy. But Grace's demeanor was a far cry from that of Cora Phillips. In January, a "notorious woman beater" named Frank Powelson was arrested at the brothel after he raised "a general disturbance" and pummeled one of Grace's girls, Helen Lewis.[17] Powelson was a habitual offender, but was somehow acquitted a week later. He was, however, charged with a misdemeanor for chucking a rock through the window of the house. Grace eventually disappeared, but Helen Lewis was still around in 1895 when another prostitute, Ethel Wilson, pleaded guilty to battery and paid a twenty-dollar fine. "She is the female who blackened the hazel eyes of one Helen Lewis," the *Los Angeles Herald* explained.[18]

Something in Helen must have stirred Joseph Manning, for one source says the two married. The union didn't last, however, and Helen moved to Stockton. When Cora's former resort next surfaced in the newspapers, it had been empty for a time when five young men broke into the place in May of 1897. The *Los Angeles Herald* verified that the house had only recently been vacated, but that "the upper part of the house was left furnished, and the lower floor, or basement, has been used as a dance hall." Shortly after the would-be thieves broke in, one Officer Davis was summoned. Manning was notified, and together the men started for the brothel. "When they arrived one of the gang, who had been placed on guard, gave the alarm and the whole lot rushed out at once and made a break to get away," explained the *Herald*. "The officer gave chase and succeeded in overhauling three of them, who gave their names as Will Roach, Earl Young and B. Reddrick. The names of the two boys who escaped could not be learned."[19] The young men were boys, really, their ages ranging from sixteen to twenty years. Fortunately, the thugs had only taken a garden hose, which was found hidden under a hedge.

Manning remained employed at the Vienna Buffet and was probably still there when he too died suddenly on January 14, 1901—nearly ten years to the day after Cora. His obituary revealed that he had been a founding member of Confidence Engine Company No. 2, "the second permanent, paid group of volunteer firemen in Los Angeles, formed in May of 1875."[20] Cora was mentioned, of course, as well as several relatives who survived Manning. His funeral took place at Orr & Hines funeral parlor. Between what Cora left him and the money he had made over the last decade, Manning left an estate worth ten thousand dollars— a bit over three hundred thousand dollars today. He also paid one last respect to his beloved Cora: Joe Manning's will decreed that she be reinterred next to him at Los Angeles's Evergreen Cemetery.

# CHAPTER 15

———— •◦• ————

## Sex with the Stars: Hollywood Madams

W hen the farming town of Nopalera was established way back in 1853, little did anyone realize that a single adobe house would eventually grow into America's Tinseltown. By 1870, the sleepy suburb of Los Angeles was regarded as a "thriving agricultural community."[1] That all changed in 1887, however, when Daeida and Harvey Henderson Wilcox moved to Los Angeles from Kansas, bought 160 acres of land that included Nopalera, and platted a new subdivision. They named it Hollywood.

Wilcox was a prohibitionist, and he intended Hollywood to be a religious, wealthy, and upper-class community. For over a decade, with the help of real estate investor H. J. Whitley, Hollywood was developed to include electricity, gas, and telephone lines. The main thoroughfare, Hollywood Boulevard, offered spacious lots landscaped with pepper trees. By 1900, five hundred people called Hollywood home. Two years later, the Hollywood Hotel began construction as filmmakers—many of them tired of being under the thumb of New Jersey motion picture magnate Thomas Edison—found Hollywood more conducive to making movies. By 1915, motion picture studios were rampant in town as movie stars and their accompanying entourages came west to bask in the limelight of Tinseltown. What better place for a madam and her girls to rub elbows (among other things) with the rich and famous?

One of Hollywood's first and most famous good time girls of note was Lee Francis, aka Beverly "Bee" Davis. Lee told her biographer, Serge Wolsey, that she was born to French immigrants named Dubois in San Francisco around the turn of 1900. Her mother was the victim of an arranged marriage: After her parents spurned her relationship with a man named Beverly, she was married off to a man twenty-one years older. Five children came from the union, the youngest child being Lee. Her father named her Isabel, but her mother called her Beverly in memory of the man she really wanted to marry. Lee's father, who resented her nickname, sent her away to a Los Angeles reform school at the age of six, which devastated her mother. Furthermore, she discovered that her father had instructed the mother superior to circumvent any communication from her mother. Lee only found out about it when she was asked to distribute the mail among students one day and found a note from her mother asking where her child was.

Soon after, Lee schemed to escape the convent. It was poorly planned; Lee still wore her school uniform as she boarded a train for the Sacramento address on her mother's letter. Also on the train was a woman Lee called Hilda Fernald, who paid for the girl's ticket and took her to the address on the envelope. It turned out the address was that of her brother and her mother was not there. The brother agreed to let her stay with him while they contacted their mother, an idea that did not go over well with the brother's wife. After two months of being mistreated by her sister-in-law, Lee was at her wits end when Hilda called out of the blue. Lee agreed to go to the theater with her, little knowing that she was leaving her brother's house for good.

Instead of helping Lee find her mother, Hilda introduced the child to a sixty-year-old man, a Colonel Dashfield. The nice man purchased candy for Lee before he and Hilda took the girl to a matinee and dinner.

They even let her have a cocktail, the last thing Lee remembered before she woke up the next morning. She was in Dashfield's bed and had lost her virginity. Dashfield had stepped out while she slept, buying fancy lingerie and clothing for her. Young Lee was impressed, and when Dashfield and Hilda instructed her to stay at the hotel and keep the door locked, she obeyed. For three months, the couple wined and dined the girl, taking her out for dinner and to the theater as Dashfield continued having his way with her. When she became pregnant, Hilda took her to get an abortion and Dashfield's attorneys gave Lee a check for ten thousand dollars to shut her up about what had been going on.

So began the flesh-trade career of Beverly Davis as she called herself, who eventually left San Francisco for Reno before arriving in Los Angeles around 1920. But as happens in making a legend as a madam, Lee's trail becomes scattered by would-be historians seeking the truth about her. Writer Jon Ponder seems to have come closest to identifying Lee's whereabouts in her formative years as a Hollywood madam, starting with "a small house" she purchased in the early 1920s "a half mile south of the [Sunset] Strip on Norton Avenue." Going by Lee's own memoirs, Ponder guessed that the madam was running "brothels in a series of mansions—she mentions one on Bedford Drive in Beverly Hills, for example, where she operated in 1936, and another on Kings Road—and at least one apartment building on the Westside."

Wherever she operated, Lee was forced to keep on the move. It is true that her customers included celebrities and some of the biggest names in the movie industry, but being high-class likely meant more exposure than the average bordello keeper. Lee's houses were fine and included swimming pools, tennis courts, a well-stocked bar, fine dining, and, of course, ladies of the evening, but as Ponder wrote, "she didn't own these places . . . she was at constant risk of having to move [her] house overnight when neighbors realized she was operating a brothel in their ritzy enclaves."[2] Lucky for Lee, the police were in her pocket and would notify her of upcoming raids.

Much of what has been written about Lee centers on her residency at 8439 West Sunset Boulevard. Built in 1927 as the Hacienda Park

*Even actress Jean Harlow used Lee Francis's services, sometimes renting prostitutes for her own entertainment.* Wikimedia Commons

Apartments, the expansive Italian Renaissance Revival structure was one of many like it that was intended as a luxury apartment building. But if Lee had really managed to utilize the entire place spanning over fifty thousand square feet as one gigantic brothel dubbed "The House of Francis," it would have been quite a feat. Rather, the Hacienda was initially home to several famous actors when Lee rented an apartment there beginning in 1937. The best guess is that the apartment functioned as a headquarters for Lee, who hired out young actresses who were doubling as prostitutes—and making upward of a thousand dollars per week before the madam's cut. Lee was highly successful and most popular; stories are rampant about her famous clients. One of them, Jean Harlow, allegedly hired prostitutes from Lee for her own personal entertainment. Other notable customers included actors Errol Flynn, Clark Gable, and Spencer Tracy. But these men and others, according to Ponder, were most likely entertained by Lee's employees at various hotels. And although some of them may have resided at the Hacienda as well as other apartment complexes such as Chateau Marmont and Sunset Tower, they dared not risk being seen cavorting by other more respectable residents.

It is probably true that Lee paid upward of 40 percent of her profits to police and politicians and plied them with champagne and caviar—and perhaps even sex—to avoid being arrested. But around the same time she moved into the Hacienda, according to Ponder, Lee said she also decided to "go legit" and commissioned a nightclub to be built at 8588 West Sunset. Contractors and interior designers were hired to spruce up the new "Club Versailles" and invitations were sent for a grand opening. Unfortunately, her permits were denied just before the opening. Lee later insinuated that mob leader Bugsy Siegel offered to buy the place from her. But he never paid the four thousand dollars he promised.[3]

There is surely more to the story, but even Lee's own autobiography, *Hollywood Madam*, and Serge G. Wolsey's book, *Call House Madam*, fail to clarify why she elected to stop paying off the authorities after the failure of Club Versailles. In January of 1940, police raided Lee's house on Norton Avenue, arresting the madam and two other women. It was the only time Lee ever suffered an arrest. In March, she was fined $250 and sentenced to thirty days in jail. Upon her release, Lee laid low but quietly continued her call-girl business. Her last known public appearance was in 1959, when she and her girls attended a farewell party at the famed Garden of Allah Hotel before its demolition. What became of her after that nobody seems to know.

Lee Francis's reign happened during a most important time in Hollywood. By 1923 stars were indeed flocking into town, and the most prominent landmark was the famed "Hollywoodland" sign which appeared just below the ridge of Mount Bee. Hollywood had hit the "golden age" by 1927, with five major film studios making movies starring such notables as Clark Gable, Judy Garland, Cary Grant, Ronald Reagan, Will Rogers, John Wayne, Mae West, and many others. The first Academy Awards took place in 1929. Lee Francis was not the only madam to take cool advantage of the budding stars and their money. Indeed, one of her competitors, Ann Forrester, was so scandalous she made Lee Davis look like a June bride.

Born in Texas in 1907, Ann was legally known as Almerdell Forester. She married at some point, and divorced, but who her husband was remains unknown. By the 1930s Ann (sometimes known as Ann Forst) had managed to form her own little clandestine company which managed various bordellos up and down the coast, from El Centro to as far north as Seattle. Ann's companion, Bristol Barrett, acted as a procurer of girls for the houses. From her office in a hotel on Spring Street in Los Angeles, Ann was in charge of paying bills and arranging sex-trade transactions with businessmen, politicians, and even higher-ups in the Los Angeles police department. What few people realized, however, was that Ann and Barrett conducted a white-slave prostitution ring, wherein many of the women hired were kept as virtual prisoners. The madam also was selective, firing those girls who failed to meet her standards. At one time, they said, she had as many as two hundred girls working for her.

One of the reasons Ann and her cohort operated with little trouble was because of Los Angeles mayor Frank Shaw, who was elected in 1933. For five glorious years, Shaw offered Ann the protection she needed to conduct business without interference from the law. But the wily madam wisely kept a little black book as well, containing names of important clients and other prominent men, as a means to keep her business afloat. Ann kept the book on her at all times and likely used it on more than one occasion to keep her "friends" in check lest she feel threatened. The calculated move earned her the nickname of the "Black Widow" by police and the press. But when Shaw was recalled in 1938, Ann's little tangled web began to unweave.

It was guessed that Ann was making upward of five thousand dollars a week by the late 1930s. Her house on Devonshire Street in an upscale neighborhood cost thirty-five thousand dollars to build and was large enough to include lodging for her parents, identified by the 1940 census as Mack and Minnie Clingan. (Ann's occupation was listed as "gameing [sic], sports.") Also in the house was thirty-nine-year-old George Lenhart. Things fell apart when, in April of 1940, one of Ann's employees, Maxine Rayle, phoned sheriff Walter Hunter of the Los Angeles Police Department. Maxine told Hunter she and another woman, Helen Smith, were being held against their will in one of Ann's brothels. Officers arrived at the address Maxine gave and rescued the women.

The *San Bernardino Sun* told the story, naming a woman called Helen Reed and two men, Charles Montgomery and Bristol Barrett, as the guilty parties. Ann was identified as the "payoff woman" and was arrested too, along with another woman named Donna Stewart.[4] The *Sun* said little else about the case until August, when Ann, along with

Edith Johnson and Charles W. Montgomery, was arrested for their participation in a prostitution ring. Ann was convicted on pandering charges but was able to post bail in the amount of five thousand dollars. If Ann felt like she still had an upper hand because of her little black book, she was wrong. In the ensuing trial in late 1941, a number of "disgruntled employees" willingly testified about their working conditions, "including being forced to service several men a day, not being allowed to rest when ill, and only getting half their promised pay."[5]

Notably Los Angeles's new mayor Fletcher Bowron testified on Ann's behalf. He was lambasted by the newspapers for his trouble. In December of 1941, Ann was found guilty and sentenced to ten years in the State Institution for Women, a minimum-security facility at Tehachapi. Ann's buddies, Montgomery and Barrett, were sentenced to an unknown amount of time in prison for their part in the prostitution ring. As for Ann, she was duly incarcerated at Tehachapi, and was likely pleased to find that prisoners actually lived in cottages instead of cells. She was released in 1946 and remarried to a hotel mogul with properties in Arizona and Nevada. She died in 1998.

One of the women who testified in the trial against Helen Reed and Ann Forrester was a twenty-one-year-old prostitute named Brenda Allen. Notably, at the trial Brenda said it was Bristol Barrett, not Ann, who talked her into working as a prostitute. The other witnesses were said to have appreciated Brenda's straightforward testimony and how she avoided accusing any of the defendants of anything. But Brenda certainly learned something from her predecessor, for she had soon replaced Ann Forrester as Hollywood's newest elite madam to the stars. Her protection? A little black book similar to Ann's, but also her lover and cohort: Hollywood vice cop Elmer V. Jackson.

For eight glorious years, Brenda ran amok among Hollywood's elite, at one time making upward of one hundred thousand dollars a year. Over one hundred women were in her employ, their customers paying between twenty and one hundred dollars for services. The take was around nine thousand dollars daily, which Brenda split with her girls. Some of the money was used to pay off policemen, doctors, lawyers, and bail bondsmen as needed. And although she was arrested nineteen times, the clever Brenda would simply pack up and move to a new brothel from which to operate. Her reign ended in 1948 after the Los Angeles Police Department managed to tap an incriminating telephone conversation between the madam and Jackson. The ensuing sting named not just Jackson but also several other vice cops who were "paid to protect prostitutes."[6] Police chief Clemence B. Horrall was forced into early retirement. Even Jackson went down after Brenda testified that she paid him fifty dollars per week for each of her employees and had also paid off others. One article recalled that Brenda was "a Hollywood disorderly house operator" who was charged with paying protection money in the amount of $1,200 to "certain members of the vice squad."[7]

In court, Brenda's alleged "three-inch index [sic] which reportedly lists the names of prominent film celebrities" was introduced, but the defense denied it belonged to the woman.[8] Even so, the so-called "black book" was confiscated by Judge Joseph Call, who was told it contained "names of dignitaries in the radio and motion picture field and of prominent executives" and ordered it sealed. "And keep it sealed," he said.[9] Brenda, meanwhile, was fined five hundred dollars, presumably for bribing a public official. A year into her sentence for "pandering," however, a Los Angeles policewoman admitted to perjury in Brenda's trial. The madam was able to bail out for two thousand dollars. After that, Brenda laid low. She was working as a beautician under the name Marie Brooks when she married Robert Henry Cash on May 1, 1960. Unfortunately, Cash had no idea his wife was once the harlot queen of Hollywood. Upon discovering her true identity, Cash immediately filed for an annulment. That was the last anyone heard of the once infamous Brenda Allen.

# NOTES

---•●•---

## INTRODUCTION

1. Curt Gentry, *The Madams of San Francisco: An Irreverent History of the City by the Golden Gate* (New York: Ballantine Books, 1964), 17–18.

2. Ibid., 19.

3. Ibid., 19. Gentry refers to the *alcalde* as a Spanish official, unusual since Mexico presided over California during Dana's time there.

4. Ibid., 19–20.

5. Elizabeth C. MacPhail, "Shady Ladies in the 'Stingaree District,' When the Red Lights Went Out in San Diego: The Little Known Story of San Diego's 'Restricted' District," The Journal of San Diego History, Spring 1974, Volume 20, Number 2, San Diego History Center, https://sandiegohistory.org/journal/1974/april/stingaree/, accessed June 1, 2019.

6. Chauncey L. Canfield, ed., *Diary of a Forty-Niner*, reprint from 1881 (Stanford: James Ladd Delkin, 1947), n.p.

7. Joel E. Ferris, "Hiram Gano Ferris of Illinois and California," *California Historical Society Quarterly*, XXVI, 1947, 296.

8. Dee Brown, *The Gentle Tamers: Women of the Old Wild West* (Lincoln, NE and London: University of Nebraska Press, 1958), 86–88.

9. Ibid.

10. Frank Soule, John H. Gihon, and Jim Nisbet, *The Annals of San Francisco: Containing a Summary of the History of California, and a Complete History of Its Great City: to which are Added, Biographical Memoirs of Some Prominent Citizen* (Cambridge, MA: Harvard University, 1855), 83.

11. J. Ross Browne, "Down in the Cinnabar Mines," *Harper's New Monthly Magazine*, October 1865, 553.

12. Robin Flinchum, *Red Light Women of Death Valley* (Charleston, SC: The History Press, 2015), 52–54.

13. Ibid., 52–57.

14. *San Francisco Call*, Vol. 67, No. 136, April 5, 1890, 8.

15. University of California, Hastings College of the Law UC Hastings Scholarship Repository, "1914 Voter Information Guide for 1914, General Election," https://

repository.uchastings.edu/cgi/viewcontent.cgi?referer=&httpsredir=1&article=1081&
context=ca_ballot_props, accessed September 18, 2019.

16.  "California Nuisance Abatement, Proposition 4 (1914)," Ballotpedia, https://
ballotpedia.org/California_Nuisance_Abatement,_Proposition_4_(1914), accessed
September 18, 2019.

17.  Ibid.

18.  Sally Stanford, *The Lady of the House: California's Most Notorious Madam* (New
York: Ballantine Books, 1972), 30–31.

## CHAPTER 1: GILDED GIRLS:
## THE COURTESANS OF CALIFORNIA'S MINING CAMPS

1.  Mickey Broman, *California Ghost Town Trails* (Baldwin Park, CA: Gem Guides
Book Co., 1981, rev. 1985 Russ Leadabrand, ed.), 8–9.

2.  B. A. Botkin, ed., *A Treasury of Western Folklore* (New York: Crown Publishers
Inc., 1951), 37.

3.  Archer Butler Hulbert, *Forty-Niners* (Boston: Little, Brown and Company, 1931),
205.

4.  Ibid., 240.

5.  Suzanne Ashe, "Old fashioned hanging re-enacted in Columbia," (Senora) *Union
Democrat*, August 23, 2015, https://www.uniondemocrat.com/csp/mediapool/sites
/UnionDemocrat/LocalNews/story.csp?cid=3716620&sid=753&fid=151, accessed
May 20, 2019; Lambert Florin, *Ghost Towns of the Pacific Frontier* (New York: Prom-
ontory Press, 1987), 198.

6.  Florin, *Ghost Towns of the Pacific Frontier*, 279.

7.  Ibid., 228.

8.  Florin, *Ghost Towns of the West* (New York: Superior Publishing/Promontory
Press, 1971), 263.

9.  An alternate version of this tale states that Cannon actually went to Juanita's on a
pleasure call. Florin, *Ghost Towns of the Pacific Frontier*, 208.

10.  "Downieville, California," Back Country Explorers, https://www.backcountry
explorers.com/downieville-california.html, accessed May 20, 2019.

11.  Herbert Asbury, *The Barbary Coast: An Informal History of the San Francisco
Underworld* (New York: Pocket Books Inc., 1957), 35.

12.  Dame Shirley, *The Shirley Letters from California Mines in 1851–52: Being a
Series of Twenty-three Letters from Dame Shirley (Mtrs. Louise Amelia Knapp Smith
Clappe) to Her Sister in Massachusetts and Now Reprinted from the Pioneer Magazine of
1854–55, with Synopses of the Letters, a Foreword, and Many Typographical and Other
Corrections and Emendations by Thomas C. Russell; Together with "An Appreciation" by
Mrs. M. V. T. Lawrence* (San Francisco: T. C. Russell, 1922), 35–39.

13. Curt Gentry, *The Madams of San Francisco: An Irreverent History of the City by the Golden Gate* (New York: Ballantine Books, 1964), 55.
14. "Cerro Gordo," Digital Desert: Mojave Desert, http://mojavedesert.net/cerro-gordo/.
15. Robin Flinchum, *Red Light Women of Death Valley* (Charleston, SC: The History Press, 2015), 15–19, 22.
16. Ibid., 16–19, 20–21.
17. Ibid., 22–23.
18. Ibid., 24–28.
19. Florin, *Ghost Towns of the Pacific Frontier*, 188.
20. "Panamint City, California," wikipedia.org.
21. Flinchum, *Red Light Women of Death Valley*, 22, 44–45, 47.
22. Ibid., 47–48.
23. Lucius Beebe, "Panamint: Suburb of Hell," *American Heritage* magazine, December 1954, https://www.americanheritage.com/panamint-suburb-hell, accessed September 21, 2019.
24. Flinchum, *Red Light Women of Death Valley*, 48–49; Florin, *Ghost Towns of the West*, 195.
25. Cecile Page Vargo, "Enterprising Women of the Western Mojave Mining Camps: First Came the 'Ladies,'" Explore California History, magazine for enthusiasts, February 2004, http://explorehistoricalif.com/ehc_legacy/feb2004.html, accessed September 21, 2019.
26. Ibid.
27. "Marguerite Roberts," findagrave.com.
28. Vargo, "Enterprising Women of the Western Mojave Mining Camps."
29. Ibid.
30. Ibid.
31. "Marguerite Roberts," findagrave.com.
32. Natasha Petrosova, "Randsburg Mining District: Part II: Red Mountain-The Sin City," August 25, 2016, Forgotten Destinations, http://forgotten-destinations.blogspot.com/2016/08/randsburg-mining-district-part-ii-red.html, accessed October 4, 2019.
33. Vargo, "Enterprising Women of the Western Mojave Mining Camps."
34. Ibid.
35. Petrosova, "Randsburg Mining District."

# CHAPTER 2: BODIE:
## WHERE BAD GIRLS CAME TO STAY AND PLAY

1. Lambert Florin, *Ghost Towns of the Pacific Frontier* (New York: Promontory Press, 1987), 179.
2. Douglas McDonald, *Bodie, Boom Town—Gold Town! The Last of California's Old Time Mining Camps* (Las Vegas, NV: Nevada Publications, 1988), 9.

3. Jeremy Agnew, *Brides of the Multitude: Prostitution in the Old West* (Lake City, CO: Western Reflections Publishing Co., 2008), 94.

4. *Weekly Bodie Standard*, December 25, 1878, n.p.

5. Robin Flinchum, *Red Light Women of Death Valley* (Charleston, SC: The History Press, 2015), 49; Charles E. DeLong, *Life and Confession of John Millian: (properly, Jean Marie A. Villain) Convicted as the Murderer of Julia Bulett, as Given by Him to His Attorney* (Virginia City, NV: Lammon, Gregory & Palmer, 1868), 4.

6. *Butte Daily Miner*, September 8, 1869, 4:3; *Butte Weekly Miner*, September 23, 1879, 7:2.

7. Herbert Asbury, *The Barbary Coast : An Informal History of the San Francisco Underworld* (New York: Pocket Books, Inc., Cardinal Edition, 1957), 22; Jay R. Nash, *Encyclopedia of Western Lawmen and Outlaws* (New York: Paragon House, 1992), 108–109.

8. Robert A. Hereford, *Old Man River: The Memories of Captain Louis Rosche, Pioneer Steamboatman* (Caldwell, ID: Caxton Printers, Ltd., 1942), 105, 200, 204–233.

9. "Simone 'Eleanore Dumont, Madam Mustache' Jules," findagrave.com; New York *National Police Gazette*, October 4, 1879, 10.

10. *Tonopah* (Nevada) *Daily Bonanza*, April 14, 1907, 7:4.

11. *Gold Hill* (Nevada) *Daily News*, September 1, 1877; J. G. Weaver, "Madam Mustache, 'The Queen of the Green Cloth,' Noted Female Gamblers of the West," *Truth, the Western Weekly* (Salt Lake City, UT), March 28, 1908, 4–5, 9.

12. *Bodie Weekly Standard*, May 29, 1878, n.p.; *Daily Bodie Standard*, September 8, 1879, n.p.

13. *Bodie Morning News*, September 9, 1879, n.p.

14. *National Police Gazette*, October 4, 1879, 10.

15. *Bodie Morning News*, September 9, 1879, n.p.

16. *Bridgeport Chronicle-Union*, January 11, 1922, n.p.

17. *Butte Weekly Miner*, September 23, 1879, 7:2.

18. *Sacramento Union*, September 18, 1879, n.p.

19. *National Police Gazette*, October 4, 1879, 10.

20. McDonald, *Bodie, Boom Town—Gold Town!*, 11, 28.

21. Florin, *Ghost Towns of the Pacific Frontier*, 180.

22. *Sacramento Daily Record*, April 1, 1880, 1:6.

23. McDonald, *Bodie, Boom Town—Gold Town!*, 28.

24. Anne Seagraves, *Soiled Doves: Prostitution in the Old West* (Hayden, ID: Wesanne Publications, 1994), 75–80.

25. George Williams III, *Rosa May: The Search for a Mining Camp Legend* (Riverside, CA: Tree by the River Publishing, 1982), 67, 181.

26. Ibid., 67, 176, 179.

27. *San Francisco Call*, March 31, 1906.

28. *San Francisco Call*, April 4, 1906.

29. Williams, *Rosa May*, 176–177.

30. Ibid., 68.

## CHAPTER 3: ROSA MAY: A MYSTERIOUS FEMME

1. George Williams III, *Rosa May: The Search for a Mining Camp Legend* (Riverside, CA: Tree by the River Publishing, 1982), 130, 187.

2. Frank S. Wedertz, *Bodie 1859–1900* (Bishop, CA: Chalfant Press, 1969), 30.

3. "Rosa May Oalaque," Bodie, California, https://www.bodie.com/history/cemetery /78-rosa-may-oalaque/, accessed October 10, 2019; Williams, *Rosa May*, 49–51, 86–87, 188.

4. Williams, *Rosa May*, 37, 84.

5. Ibid., 89.

6. *California Voter Registers, 1866–1898*, Ancestry.com.

7. Williams, *Rosa May*, 84–85, 91–93.

8. Ibid., 94–96.

9. Ibid., 94–95, 113.

10. Ibid., 99–102, 105–108.

11. Ibid., 110–112, 114.

12. Ibid., 117–124.

13. Ibid., 128, 157–158.

14. Ibid., 129.

15. *California Voter Registers, 1866–1898*. For Morris Marks, see *Tenth Census of the United States, 1880*. (NARA microfilm publication T9, 1,454 rolls.)

16. Williams, *Rosa May*, 174.

17. Michael Rutter, *Upstairs Girls: Prostitution in the American West* (Helena, MT: 2005), 195.

18. Williams, *Rosa May*, 50.

19. *Fifteenth Census of the United States, 1930* (Washington, DC: National Archives and Records Administration, 1930).

20. Ella M. Cain, *The Story of Bodie* (USA: Pickle Partners Publishing, 2018), n.p.

21. "The Love Story of Lottie Johl," Colorful Ladies of the Old West—Stories, fold3, https://www.fold3.com/page/2711-colorful-ladies-of-the-old-west/stories, accessed October 12, 2019.

22. Cain, *The Story of Bodie*, n.p.

23. Williams, *Rosa May*, 62.

24. Cain, *The Story of Bodie*, n.p.

25. Ibid.

26. Williams, *Rosa May*, 125–127, 175, 181.

27. Ibid., 50, 181.

28. Williams, *Rosa May*, illustrations insert; Alton Pryor, *Classic Tales in California History* (Roseville, CA: Stagecoach Publishing, 1999), 102–103.

29. Williams, *Rosa May*, 183.

30. Ibid., 42, 66–67, 157.

31. Marguerite Sprague, *Bodie's Gold: Tall Tales and True History from a California Mining Town* (Reno, NV: University of Nevada Press, 2005), n.p.; *Fourteenth Census of the United States, 1920.* (NARA microfilm publication T625, 2076 rolls.)
32. Williams, *Rosa May*, 50.
33. Cain, *The Story of Bodie*, n.p.; Williams, *Rosa May*, 103–108.
34. Cain, *The Story of Bodie*, n.p.
35. Williams, *Rosa May*, 179.
36. Ibid., 50.
37. Cain, *The Story of Bodie*, n.p.
38. Williams, *Rosa May*, 61.
39. Ibid., 179.
40. Cain, *The Story of Bodie*, n.p.
41. Williams, *Rosa May*, 52.
42. Cain, *The Story of Bodie*, n.p.
43. *California Death Index, 1905–1939*, Ancestry.com; Cain, *The Story of Bodie*, n.p.; Williams, *Rosa May*, 37.
44. Cain, *The Story of Bodie*, n.p.
45. "Bodie's Dead: Rosa May," The Great Silence, December 14, 2010, http://the-great-silence.blogspot.com/2010/12/bodies-dead-rosa-may.html, accessed October 12, 2019; Williams, *Rosa May*, illustrations insert.

## CHAPTER 4: COASTAL COURTESANS: A SEABOARD OF SIN

1. John Meyers, *Trinidad: Looking Back From My Front Porch* (Trinidad, CA: self-published, 2016), 15.
2. Miscellaneous bound documents, Trinidad Museum, Trinidad, California.
3. *Sacramento Daily Union*, December 15, 1858, 3:1.
4. "Brother Jonathan (steamer)", Wikipedia.org; *Daily Alta California*, August 2, 1865, 1:3.
5. *Sacramento Daily Union*, August 5, 1865, 3:2.
6. Ibid., August 10, 1865, 3:2.
7. *Daily Alta California*, August 10, 1865, 1:2.
8. *Marysville* (California) *Daily Appeal*, August 12, 1865, 1:6.
9. *Sacramento Daily Union*, August 8, 1865, 2:3; *Grass Valley Daily Union*, August 30, 1865, 1:2.
10. "Roseanna Keenan," findagrave.com; *Sacramento Daily Union*, May 2, 1877, 3:4.
11. "Brother Jonathan Memorial," findagrave.com.
12. Wendy M. Nettles, "Neophytes, Shopkeepers and the Soiled Doves of San Louis Obispo," "The Copelands Project," prepared by Applied Earthworks, Inc., Fresno, CA, October 2006, 148.

13. Ibid.
14. *San Luis Obispo Morning Tribune*, March 10, 1895, 1:3.
15. *San Luis Obispo Tribune*, October 27, 1895, 3:4.
16. *Daily Alta California*, January 23, 1885, 8:2.
17. *Santa Barbara Morning Press*, January 30, 1910. 1:6,7.
18. Ibid.
19. *Lompoc Journal*, February 5, 1910, 5:3.
20. *Santa Barbara Morning Press*, June 23, 1910, 5:1.
21. *San Luis Obispo Daily Telegram*, April 24, 1917, 5:2.
22. *San Luis Obispo Morning Telegram*, February 24, 1889, 3:6.
23. *San Luis Obispo Daily Telegram*, December 20, 1912, 1:3.
24. *San Luis Obispo Morning Tribune*, February 3, 1898 2:3.
25. Nettles, "Neophytes, Shopkeepers and the Soiled Doves of San Louis Obispo," 209.
26. *San Luis Obispo Semi-Weekly Breeze*, 1905, 1; Nettles, "Neophytes, Shopkeepers and the Soiled Doves of San Louis Obispo," 149.
27. Ferndale Museum docents, Ferndale, California, interview by author, February 5, 2017.

# CHAPTER 5: SIN IN SAN DIEGO:
# THE STINGAREE DISTRICT

1. Pamela Hallan, *Dos Cientos Anos en San Juan Capistrano* (Irvine, CA: Walker Color Graphics: Lehmann Publishing Co., 1975), 98.
2. Ibid., 53.
3. Nada Chatwell, "Are You of This World?," Dana Point Historical Society, October 31, 2012, http://www.danapointhistorical.org/are-you-of-this-world/, accessed October 23, 2019.
4. *Los Angeles Herald*, December 16, 1879, 4:1.
5. *San Diego Union*, October 19, 1881, 3:1.
6. Sherry Monahan, *California Madams* (Helena, MT: Farcountry Press, 2019), 107.
7. Elizabeth C. MacPhail, "Shady Ladies in the 'Stingaree District,' When the Red Lights Went Out in San Diego: The Little Known Story of San Diego's 'Restricted' District," *The Journal of San Diego History*, Spring 1974, Volume 20, Number 2, San Diego History Center, https://sandiegohistory.org/journal/1974/april/stingaree/, accessed September 10, 2019.
8. *San Diego Union*, November 12, 1886, 3:2.
9. Ibid., April 3, 1887, 5:3.
10. *Coronado Mercury*, August 17, 1887, 4:1.
11. Monahan, *California Madams*, 108.
12. *San Diego Union*, November 3, 1887, 5:1.

13. Monahan, *California Madams*, 108–109.
14. MacPhail, "Shady Ladies in the 'Stingaree District.'"
15. *San Diego Union*, August 13, 1891, 1:6.
16. Ibid., September 3, 1891, 5:3.
17. Ibid., September 26, 1891, 5:3.
18. Ibid., October 17, 1891, 5:3.
19. MacPhail, "Shady Ladies in the 'Stingaree District.'"
20. *San Diego Union*, April 16, 1902, 5:3.
21. Ibid., September 7, 1905, 8:2.
22. Ibid., May 1, 1911, 6:6.
23. MacPhail, "Shady Ladies in the 'Stingaree District.'"
24. Ibid.
25. *San Diego Union*, October 3, 1912, 1:1.
26. Ibid., October 14, 1912, 10:2.
27. MacPhail, "Shady Ladies in the 'Stingaree District.'"
28. *San Diego Union*, November 11, 1912, 9:1.
29. Ibid., November 12, 1912, 13:2.
30. Ibid., November 23, 1912, 5:4.

## CHAPTER 6: IDA BAILEY:
## A SURROGATE MOTHER AND MADAM

1. Sherry Monahan, *California Madams* (Helena, MT: Farcountry Press, 2019), 116.
2. *San Diego Union*, February 22, 1888, 5:1.
3. Ibid., August 18, 1892, 5:2.
4. Ibid., September 18, 1892, 5:2.
5. Ibid., September 18, 1891, 5:3.
6. Ibid., September 22, 1891, 5:1.
7. Ibid., June 18, 1899, 3:1.
8. *Los Angeles Herald*, May 26, 1898, 9:5.
9. Theodore Kornweibel Jr., *"Investigate Everything": Federal Efforts to Ensure Black Loyalty During World War I* (Bloomington, IN: Indiana University Press, 2002), 185.
10. *San Diego Union*, October 2, 1901, 4:3.
11. Elizabeth C. MacPhail, "Shady Ladies in the 'Stingaree District,' When the Red Lights Went Out in San Diego: The Little Known Story of San Diego's 'Restricted' District," The Journal of San Diego History, Spring 1974, Volume 20, Number 2, San Diego History Center, https://sandiegohistory.org/journal/1974/april/stingaree/.
12. Jerry MacMullen, "Sad Passing of Canary Cottage," *San Diego Union*, Jan. 9, 1966, p. G3.
13. *San Diego Union*, January 10, 1904, 8:1.
14. Ibid., July 17, 1904, 9:2.

15. Ibid., August 2, 1904, 2:3 and August 4, 1904, 3:1.
16. Ibid., January 17, 1907, 5:2.
17. Ibid., May 4, 1907, 6:1.
18. Ibid., October 30, 1910, 17:3.
19. Ibid., March 29, 1916, 14:5.
20. Monahan, *California Madams*, 121–122.
21. "An interview with Gerald F. "Jerry" MacMullen, 1897–1981 September 5, 1971," San Diego History Center, Oral History Program, https://library.ucsd.edu/dc/object/bb74756107/_1_1.pdf, accessed October 30, 2019.
22. Monahan, *California Madams*, 122–123.

# CHAPTER 7: SACRAMENTO: THE SCARLET WOMEN OF "SACTOWN"

1. Archer Butler Hulbert, *Forty-Niners* (Boston: Little, Brown and Company, 1931), 319–320.
2. Sherry Monahan, *California Madams* (Helena, MT: Farcountry Press, 2019), 54.
3. *Sacramento Daily Bee*, January 4, 1885, from Jay Moynahan, *Red Light Revelations: A Glance into Sacramento's Bawdy Past of 1885* (Spokane, WA: Chickadee Publishing, 2001).
4. Ibid., January 7, 1885, from Moynahan, *Red Light Revelations*.
5. Ibid., March 13 and March 20, 1885, from Moynahan, *Red Light Revelations*.
6. Ibid., April 20, 1885 and April 30, 1885, from Moynahan, *Red Light Revelations*.
7. Ibid., May 6, 1885, from Moynahan, *Red Light Revelations*.
8. Ibid., June 11, 1885, from Moynahan, *Red Light Revelations*.
9. Ibid., June 16, 1885, from Moynahan, *Red Light Revelations*.
10. Ibid., July 10, 1885, from Moynahan, *Red Light Revelations*.
11. Ibid., July 25, 1885, from Moynahan, *Red Light Revelations*.
12. Ibid., August 12, 1885, from Moynahan, *Red Light Revelations*.
13. Ibid., August 18, August 19, and November 21, 1885, from Moynahan, *Red Light Revelations*.
14. Ibid., December 21 and December 22, 1885, from Moynahan, *Red Light Revelations*.
15. *San Francisco Call*, September 18, 1894, 10:3.
16. Sanborn Fire Insurance Map from Sacramento, Sacramento County, California. Sanborn Map Company, 1895.
17. Florence Roberts, *Fifteen Years with the Outcast* (Anderson, IN: Gospel Trumpet Company, 1912), 22, 38–39.
18. Ibid., 39–47.
19. Ibid., 52–53.
20. Ibid., 55–60.

21. Ibid., 67–73, 91.
22. *California, Select Marriages, 1850–1945*, Ancestry.com.
23. *US City Directories, 1822–1995*, and *California, Voter Registers, 1866–1898*, Ancestry.com.
24. *Sacramento Union*, July 2, 1908, 10:2.
25. *Thirteenth Census of the United States, 1910* (NARA microfilm publication T624, 1,178 rolls.)
26. *Sacramento Union*, June 12, 1914, 14:1.
27. *US City Directories, 1822–1995.*
28. *Sacramento Union*, October 8, 1914, 3:4.
29. Ibid., December 16, 1916, 7:2.
30. *California, Wills and Probate Records, 1850–1953.*
31. *US City Directories, 1822–1995*; "Fannie Riwotzky," findagrave.com.
32. Peter C. Hennigan, "Property War: Prostitution, Red-Light Districts, and the Transformation of Public Nuisance Law in the Progressive Era," *Yale Journal of Law & the Humanities*, Volume 16, Issue 1, Article 5, January 2004, 125.
33. *Sacramento Union*, August 3, 1921, 10:3.

## CHAPTER 8: SAN FRANCISCO:
## SIN IN THE CITY BY THE BAY

1. Jeremy Agnew, *Brides of the Multitude: Prostitution in the Old West* (Lake City, CO: Western Reflections Publishing Co., 2008), 201.
2. Ibid., 200.
3. Herbert Asbury, *The Barbary Coast: An Informal History of the San Francisco Underworld* (New York: Pocket Books Inc., 1957), 220.
4. Frank Soule, John H. Gihon, and Jim Nisbet, *The Annals of San Francisco: Containing a Summary of the History of California, and a Complete History of Its Great City: to which are Added, Biographical Memoirs of Some Prominent Citizens* (Cambridge, MA: Harvard University, 1855), 412, 555.
5. Roger W. Lotchin, *San Francisco 1846–1856: From Hamlet to City* (Lincoln, NE and London: University of Nebraska Press, 1974), 206.
6. Agnew, *Brides of the Multitude*, 200–201.
7. Lotchin, *San Francisco 1846–1856*, 206.
8. Ibid., 18, 248.
9. Daniel Steven Crafts, "Barbary Coast," Found San Francisco, www.foundsf.org/index.php?title=BARBARY_COAST, accessed September 21, 2019.
10. Ernest de Massey, "Some Phases of French Society in San Francisco in the 'Fifties,'" *California Historical Society Quarterly*, XXVIII (1953), 118.
11. Curt Gentry, *The Madams of San Francisco: An Irreverent History of the City by the Golden Gate* (New York: Ballantine Books, 1964), 39.

12. Soule, Gihon, and Nisbet, *The Annals of San Francisco*, 668–669.

13. Jacqueline Baker Barnhart, *The Fair But Frail: Prostitution in San Francisco, 1849–1900* (Reno, NV: University of Nevada Press, 1986), 28.

14. Soule, Gihon, and Nisbet, *The Annals of San Francisco*, 668–669.

15. Jacqueline Baker Barnhart, *The Fair But Frail: Prostitution in San Francisco, 1849–1900* (Reno, NV: Univeristy of Nevada Press, 1986), 28.

16. Agnew, *Brides of the Multitude*, 205.

17. Gentry, *The Madams of San Francisco*, 41–47; Barnhart, *The Fair But Frail*, 76.

18. Gentry, *The Madams of San Francisco*, 47.

19. Lotchin, *San Francisco 1846–1856*, 303.

20. Barnhart, *The Fair But Frail*, 23, 29–30, 52.

21. Soule, Gihon, and Nisbet, *Annals of San Francisco*, 364, 463.

22. Lotchin, *San Francisco 1846–1856*, 206–207.

23. Ibid., 257–258.

24. *California Police Gazette*, October 8, 1859, n.p.

25. Agnew, *Brides of the Multitude*, 206–207.

26. Barnhart, *The Fair But Frail*, 76.

27. Asbury, *The Barbary Coast*, 236–237.

28. Agnew, *Brides of the Multitude*, 204–205.

29. Albert S. Evans, *A La California: Sketch of Life in the Golden State* (San Francisco: A. L. Bancroft & Co. 1873), Chapter 12, n.p., http://www.sfmuseum.org/hist6/evans.html, accessed June 6, 2019.

30. Barnhart, *The Fair But Frail*, 31.

31. Hillyer Best, *Julia Bulette and other Red Light Ladies: An Altogether Stimulating Treatise on the Madams of the Far West* (Sparks, NV: Western Printing & Publishing Co., 1959), 30.

32. Florence Roberts, *Fifteen Years with the Outcast* (Anderson, IN: Gospel Trumpet Company, 1912), 91, 105–108.

33. Crafts, "Barbary Coast."

34. Ernest Beyl, "A short history of bordellos in San Francisco, part 3," *Marina Times*, October 2012, https://www.marinatimes.com/2012/10/a-short-history-of-bordellos-in-san-francisco-part-3/, accessed November 15, 2019.

35. Gentry, *The Madams of San Francisco*, 180.

36. *Santa Cruz Sentinel*, May 14, 1905, 11:3.

37. Gentry, *The Madams of San Francisco*, 191–192.

38. *San Francisco Call*, August 29, 1906, 14:5.

39. Ibid., November 8, 1906, 9:4.

40. Ibid., February 14, 1907, 7:3.

41. Ibid., August 26, 1908, 16:3.

42. *Santa Cruz Evening News*, April 2, 1923, 1:6.

# CHAPTER 9: SEXUAL SLAVERY:
# THE PUT-UPON CHINAGIRLS

1. Jean Pfaelzer. *Driven Out: The Forgotten War Against Chinese Americans* (Manhattan, NY: Random House Publishing Group, 2007), 92–93.

2. Michael Rutter, *Upstairs Girls: Prostitution in the American West* (Helena, MT: 2005), 127–128.

3. Roger W. Lotchin, *San Francisco 1846–1856: From Hamlet to City* (Lincoln, NE and London: University of Nebraska Press, 1974), 125.

4. Lambert Florin, *Ghost Towns of the West* (New York: Superior Publishing/ Promontory Press, 1971), 274.

5. Jay Moynahan, *Photographs of the Red Light Ladies 1865–1920* (Spokane, WA: Chickadee Publishing, 2005), 101.

6. Curt Gentry, *The Madams of San Francisco: An Irreverent History of the City by the Golden Gate* (New York: Ballantine Books, 1964), 58, 60–61.

7. *California, County Birth, Marriage, and Death Records, 1849–1980*, Ancestry .com.

8. Gentry, *The Madams of San Francisco*, 60.

9. Ibid., 58–61, 63–64.

10. Rutter, *Upstairs Girls*, 131–132.

11. Gentry, *The Madams of San Francisco*, 58.

12. Albert S. Evans, *A La California: Sketch of Life in the Golden State* (San Francisco: A. L. Bancroft & Co. 1873), Chapter 12, n.p., http://www.sfmuseum.org/hist6 /evans.html, accessed June 6, 2019

13. Gentry, *The Madams of San Francisco*, 65.

14. *Santa Cruz Evening News*, February 1, 1928, 1:5.

15. Jan MacKell Collins, *Wild Women of Prescott, Arizona* (Charleston, SC: The History Press, 2015), 34.

16. *California Police Gazette*, August 20, 1859, n.p.

17. Rutter, *Upstairs Girls*, 43.

18. Herbert Asbury, *The Barbary Coast: An Informal History of the San Francisco Underworld* (New York: Pocket Books Inc., 1957), 171.

19. Robin Flinchum, *Red Light Women of Death Valley* (Charleston, SC: The History Press, 2015), 65.

20. Evans, *A La California*.

21. Asbury, *The Barbary Coast*, 137.

22. Alexy Simmons, "Red Light Ladies: Settlement Patterns and Material Culture on the Mining Frontier." *Anthropology Northwest* (Corvallis, OR: Department of Anthropology, Oregon State University, Number 4, 1989), 17.

23. Asbury, *The Barbary Coast*, 168.

24. Ibid., 166, 259.

25. Jacqueline Baker Barnhart, *The Fair But Frail: Prostitution in San Francisco, 1849–1900* (Reno, NV: University of Nevada Press, 1986), 80–81.
26. Anne Seagraves, *Soiled Doves: Prostitution in the Old West* (Hayden, ID: Wesanne Publications, 1994), 140–141.
27. Ibid., 140–142.
28. "What is the Mann Act?" FindLaw, https://criminal.findlaw.com/criminal-charges/what-is-the-mann-act.html, accessed November 25, 2019.

## CHAPTER 10: BELLE CORA: SHE STOOD BY HER MAN

1. JoAnn Levy, *They Saw the Elephant: Women in the California Gold Rush* (Norman, OK: University of Oklahoma Press, 2013), 149.
2. Curt Gentry, *The Madams of San Francisco: An Irreverent History of the City by the Golden Gate* (New York: Ballantine Books, 1964), 81–82.
3. Edna Bryan Buckbee, *The Saga of Old Tuolumne* (New York: The Press of the Pioneers, 1935), 191.
4. Gentry, *The Madams of San Francisco*, 85–86.
5. *Daily Alta California*, November 21, November 1855, 2:2.
6. Levy, *They Saw the Elephant*, 171.
7. Roger W. Lotchin, *San Francisco 1846–1856: From Hamlet to City* (Lincoln, NE and London: University of Nebraska Press, 2013), 197.
8. Gentry, *The Madams of San Francisco*, 100–101.
9. Ibid., 108.
10. Hubert Howe Bancroft, "Trial and Execution of Casey and Cora," *The Works of Hubert Howe Bancroft*, Vol. XXXVII (San Francisco, A. L. Bancroft & company, 1882–90), 240–241.
11. Ibid., 109.
12. Ibid., 240–241.
13. *Sacramento Daily Union*, August 25, 1856, 2:2.
14. Bancroft, "Trial and Execution of Casey and Cora."
15. *Daily Alta California*, September 16, 1857, 2:3.
16. *Sacramento Daily Union*, August 12, 1859, 2:5.
17. *Stockton Independent*, August 20, 1859, 3:4.
18. Levy, *They Saw the Elephant*, 222.
19. *Sacramento Daily Union*, February 22, 1862, 2:1.
20. *Shasta Courier*, March 1, 1862, 2:2.

## CHAPTER 11: TESSIE WALL:
## "HOW'S THAT FOR MY BIG FAT IRISH ASS?"

1. Herbert Asbury, *The Barbary Coast: An Informal History of the San Francisco Underworld* (New York: Pocket Books Inc., 1957), 227.

2. Curt Gentry, *The Madams of San Francisco: An Irreverent History of the City by the Golden Gate* (New York: Ballantine Books, 1964), 205.

3. Ibid., 202.

4. *San Francisco Call*, February 24, 1902, 2:6.

5. Gentry, *The Madams of San Francisco*, 207.

6. *San Francisco Call*, March 6, 1907, 6:5.

7. *Santa Cruz Evening News*, March 31, 1908, 1:1.

8. *San Francisco Call*, November 30, 1908, 1:1.

9. *Santa Cruz Evening News*, December 1, 1908, 5:1.

10. *Los Angeles Herald*, December 2, 1908, 1:4.

11. Gentry, *The Madams of San Francisco*, 209–210.

12. Asbury, *The Barbary Coast*, 227.

13. Gentry, *The Madams of San Francisco*, 211.

14. Ibid., 215.

15. Ibid., 207, 216.

16. Ibid., 217–222.

17. Asbury, *The Barbary Coast*, 228.

18. Gentry, *The Madams of San Francisco*, 203.

19. Ibid.

20. *Oakland Tribune*, April 29, 1932, 1:7.

21. *Sacramento Union*, August 20, 1921, 10:3.

22. *Oakland Tribune*, March 11, 1918, 1:1.

23. *Sacramento Union*, August 20, 1921, 10:3.

24. Gentry, *The Madams of San Francisco*, 225–226.

25. *Oakland Tribune*, April 29, 1932, 1:7.

26. *Madera Tribune*, April 29, 1932, 4:5.

27. *Oakland Tribune*, June 7, 1932, 12:2 and June 12, 1932, 33:2.

## CHAPTER 12: SALLY STANFORD: MADAM MAYOR OF SAUSALITO

1. Jan MacKell Collins, *Good Time Girls of the Pacific Northwest: A Red-Light History of Washington, Oregon, and Alaska* (Guilford, CT: Rowman & Littlefield Publishing Group, Inc., 2020), 96–97.

2. Sally Stanford, *The Lady of the House: California's Most Notorious Madam* (New York: Ballantine Books, 1972), vii, 14–15, 17.

3. Ibid., 18–21.

4. *Greeley* (Colorado) *Daily Tribune*, May 27, 1920, 2:5.

5. Stanford, *The Lady of the House*, 23–24.

6. Ibid., 25–26.

7. Ibid., 38.

8. Ibid., 60.

9. Ibid., 119.

10. Wayne F. Miller, "An Eye on the World: Reviewing a Lifetime in Photography," an oral history conducted in 2001, by Suzanne B. Riess, Regional Oral History Office, The Bancroft Library, University of California, Berkeley, 2003, https://digitalassets.lib .berkeley.edu/roho/ucb/text/MillerBook.pdf, accessed February 6, 2020.

11. Stanford, *The Lady of the House*, 109.

12. *Hayward Daily Review*, January 25, 1971, 3:1.

13. Marc Bonagura, "The Tiger is Dead: Sally Stanford's Obituary," http://www.the tigerisdead.com/sallystanford.html, accessed December 12, 2019.

# CHAPTER 13: LOS ANGELES:
# LUSTY LADIES IN THE CITY OF ANGELS

1. W. W. Robinson, *Los Angeles From the Days of the Pueblo: A Brief History and a Guide to the Plaza Area* (San Francisco: California Historical Society, 1981), 64–66, 69–70.

2. Ibid., 73, 79, 82, 88.

3. Sherry Monahan, *California Madams* (Helena, MT: Farcountry Press, 2019), 64.

4. Hadley Meares, "Hell's Half Acre: In the old red light district of Los Angeles, women worked in squalor while pimps and landlords grew rich," Curbed Los Angeles, Nov 17, 2017, https://la.curbed.com/2017/11/17/16654292/history-prostitution -los-angeles, accessed October 2, 2019.

5. AnneMarie Kooistra, "Angels for Sale: The History of Prostitution in Los Angeles, 1880–1940," Dissertation Presented to the Faculty of the Graduate School, University of Southern California, August, 2003, 24.

6. Meares, "Hell's Half Acre."

7. Wendy M. Nettles, "Neophytes, Shopkeepers and the Soiled Doves of San Louis Obispo," "The Copelands Project," prepared by Applied Earthworks, Inc., Fresno, CA, October 2006, 182.

8. Meares, "Hell's Half Acre."

9. Jay Moynahan, *Remedies from the Red Lights: Cures, Treatments and Medicines from the Sportin' Ladies of the Frontier West* (Spokane, WA: Chickadee Publishing, 2000), 25, 55.

10. *Los Angeles Herald*, December 5, 1896, 5:3; December 10, 1896, 5:1 and December 11, 1896, 3:1.

11. Meares, "Hell's Half Acre."

12. Ibid.

13. *Los Angeles Herald*, January 13, 1904, 8:1.

14. Meares, "Hell's Half Acre."

15. *Los Angeles Herald*, February 3, 1904, 5:4.

16. Meares, "Hell's Half Acre."
17. *Los Angeles Herald*, December 9, 1903, 3:2 and March 16, 1904, 12:2.
18. *Morenci* (Arizona) *Copper Era*, January 8, 1916, 7:5.
19. *Prescott* (Arizona) *Journal-Miner*, January 23, 1916, 1:6.
20. Ibid.
21. Jan MacKell Collins, *Good Time Girls of Arizona and New Mexico: A Red-Light History of the American Southwest* (Guilford, CT: Rowman & Littlefield Publishing Group, Inc., 2019), 33–34.

## CHAPTER 14: CORA PHILLIPS: THE 24-CARAT QUEEN

1. *Los Angeles Herald*, February 24, 1876, 3:2 and February 25, 1876, 4:5.
2. Ibid., February 27, 1876, 3:4.
3. Ibid., June 9, 1882, 3:3 and July 8 1882, 3:6.
4. Ibid., June 17, 1882, 2:4.
5. Ibid., July 8, 1882, 3:6.
6. Ibid., December 25, 1878, 3:4.
7. Ibid., July 6, 1882, 3:3.
8. "History of LA Madams," Naughty Los Angeles, https://naughtylosangeles.com /user/naughtyarticles.php?pkid=23&#.Xk78hShKhdg, accessed February 10, 2020.
9. AnneMarie Kooistra, "Angels for Sale: The History of Prostitution in Los Angeles, 1880–1940," Dissertation Presented to the Faculty of the Graduate School, University of Southern California, August 2003, 53–55.
10. *Los Angeles Herald*, September 20, 1888, 1:6.
11. Ibid., March 9, 1889, 4:4.
12. Los Angeles Theatres, https://losangelestheatres.blogspot.com/2019/03/cineo graph.html, accessed February 10, 2020.
13. *Los Angeles Herald*, September 28, 1890, 5:3.
14. Ibid., January 2, 1891, 4:3.
15. *Daily Alta California*, January 3, 1891, 8:4.
16. Los Angeles Theatres.
17. *Los Angeles Herald*, January 7, 1893, 3:4 and January 14, 1893, 8:4.
18. Ibid., October 19, 1895, 5:1.
19. Ibid., May 21, 1897, 6:6.
20. "Joseph Manning," findagrave.com.

## CHAPTER 15: SEX WITH THE STARS: HOLLYWOOD MADAMS

1. "History of Hollywood, California," United States History, https://u-s-history.com /pages/h3871.html, accessed February 20, 2020.

2. Jon Ponder, "Hacienda Park and the Origins of the Sunset Strip: Coronet Apartments, Villa of Vice?," wehoville.com, April 8, 2019, https://www.wehoville.com/2019/04/08/hacienda-park-and-the-origins-of-the-sunset-strip-coronet-apartments-villa-of-vice/, accessed March 1, 2020.

3. Ponder, "Hacienda Park and the Origins of the Sunset Strip"; J. H. Graham, "8588 Sunset Blvd," June 16, 2016, https://jhgraham.com/2016/06/16/8588-sunset-blvd/, accessed March 3, 2020.

4. *San Bernardino Sun*, April 26, 1940, 13:5.

5. Annie Murphy, "Ann Forrester: Seduction, Corruption, Deception and Protection—The Black Widow and the Vice Queen (Part 1)," Photo Friends, Los Angeles Public Library, November 28, 2017, http://photofriends.org/tag/ann-forrester/, accessed February 18, 2020.

6. Rasmussen, "History of Hollywood Madams Is Long, Lurid," *Los Angeles Times*, November 30, 1997, https://www.latimes.com/archives/la-xpm-1997-nov-30-me-59191-stroy.html.

7. *Long Beach Independent*, July 15, 1949, 28:3.

8. Ibid., July 20, 1948, 13:2.

9. Ibid., August 12, 1948, 6:1.

# SELECTED BIBLIOGRAPHY

---◆●◆---

## ARTICLES

Browne, J. Ross. "Down in the Cinnabar Mines," *Harper's New Monthly Magazine*, October 1865.

de Massey, Ernest. "Some Phases of French Society in San Francisco in the 'Fifties'," *California Historical Society Quarterly*, XXVIII, 1953.

Ferris, Joel E. "Hiram Gano Ferris of Illinois and California," *California Historical Society Quarterly*, XXVI, 1947.

Hennigan, Peter C. "Property War: Prostitution, Red-Light Districts, and the Transformation of Public Nuisance Law in the Progressive Era," *Yale Journal of Law & the Humanities*, Volume 16, Issue 1, Article 5, January 2004.

McClain, Laurene Wu. "Donaldina Cameron: A Reappraisal," *Pacific Historian*, fall 1983.

Simmons, Alexy. "Red Light Ladies: Settlement Patterns and Material Culture on the Mining Frontier," *Anthropology Northwest*, Department of Anthropology, Oregon State University, Number 4, 1989.

Weaver, J. G. "Madam Moustache, 'The Queen of the Green Cloth,' Noted Female Gamblers of the West," *Truth, the Western Weekly* (Salt Lake City, UT), March 28, 1908.

## BOOKS

Agee, James K. *Steward's Fork: A Sustainable Future for the Klamath Mountains*. Berkeley, CA: University of California Press, 2007.

Agnew, Jeremy. *Brides of the Multitude: Prostitution in the Old West.* Lake City, CO: Western Reflections Publishing Co., 2008.

Anderson, Ivy, and Angus, Devon, editors. *Alice: Memoirs of a Barbary Coast Prostitute.* Berkeley, CA: Heyday, 2016.

Asbury, Herbert. *The Barbary Coast: An Informal History of the San Francisco Underworld.* New York: Pocket Books Inc., 1957.

Bancroft, Hubert Howe. *The Works of Hubert Howe Bancroft,* Vol. XXXVI, *Popular Tribunals, Vol. 1.* San Francisco: The History Company, 1887.

Bancroft, Hubert Howe, *The Works of Hubert Howe Bancroft,* Vol. XXXVII. San Francisco, A. L. Bancroft & company, 1882–90.

Barnhart, Jacqueline Baker. *The Fair But Frail: Prostitution in San Francisco, 1849–1900.* Reno, NV: University of Nevada Press, 1986.

Best, Hillyer. *Julia Bulette and Other Red Light Ladies: An Altogether Stimulating Treatise on the Madams of the Far West.* Sparks, NV: Western Printing & Publishing Co., 1959.

Bledsoe, Anthony Jennings. *Indian Wars of the Northwest: A California Sketch.* San Francisco: Bacon & Company, 1885.

Botkin, B. A., ed. *A Treasury of Western Folklore.* New York: Crown Publishers Inc., 1951.

Broman, Mickey. *California Ghost Town Trails.* Baldwin Park, CA: Gem Guides Book Co., 1981, rev. 1985 Russ Leadabrand, ed.

Brown, Dee. *The Gentle Tamers: Women of the Old Wild West.* Lincoln, NE and London: University of Nebraska Press, 1958.

Buckbee, Edna Bryan. *The Saga of Old Tuolumne.* New York: The Press of the Pioneers, 1935.

Cain, Ella M. *The Story of Bodie.* USA: Pickle Partners Publishing, 2018.

Cairns, Kathleen A. *Proof of Guilt: Barbara Graham and the Politics of Executing Women in America.* Lincoln, NE: University of Nebraska Press, 2013.

Canfield, Chauncey L., ed., *Diary of a Forty-Niner*, reprint from 1881. Stanford: James Ladd Delkin, 1947.

Collins, Jan MacKell. *Good Time Girls of Arizona and New Mexico: A Red-Light History of the American Southwest*. Guilford, CT: Rowman & Littlefield Publishing Group, Inc., 2019.

Collins, Jan MacKell. *Good Time Girls of the Pacific Northwest: A Red-Light History of Washington, Oregon, and Alaska*. Guilford, CT: Rowman & Littlefield Publishing Group, Inc., 2020.

Collins, Jan MacKell. *Wild Women of Prescott, Arizona*. Charleston, SC: The History Press, 2015.

DeLong, Charles E. *Life and Confession of John Millian: (properly, Jean Marie A. Villain) Convicted as the Murderer of Julia Bulett, as Given by Him to His Attorney*. Virginia City, NV: Lammon, Gregory & Palmer, 1868.

Dillingham, William P. *Importing Women for Immoral Purposes: A partial report from the immigration commission on the importation and harboring of women for immoral purposes*. Washington DC: Government Printing Office, 1909.

Evans, Albert S. *A La California: Sketch of Life in the Golden State*. San Francisco: A. L. Bancroft & Co., 1873.

Fleming, E. J. *The Fixers: Eddie Mannix, Howard Strickling, and the MGM Publicity Machine*. Jefferson, NC: McFarland Publishing, 2015.

Flinchum, Robin. *Red Light Women of Death Valley*. Charleston, SC: The History Press, 2015.

Florin, Lambert. *Ghost Towns of the Pacific Frontier*. New York: Promontory Press, 1987.

Florin, Lambert. *Ghost Towns of the West*. New York: Superior Publishing/Promontory Press, 1971.

Francis, Lee. *Hollywood Madam*. Los Angeles, CA: All America Distributors Corp., Later Printing edition, 1986.

Gentry, Curt. *The Madams of San Francisco: An Irreverent History of the City by the Golden Gate*. New York: Ballantine Books, 1964.

Hallan, Pamela. *Dos Cientos Anos en San Juan Capistrano*. Irvine, CA: Walker Color Graphics: Lehmann Publishing Co., 1975.

Hereford, Robert A. *Old Man River: The Memories of Captain Louis Rosche, Pioneer Steamboatman*. Caldwell, ID: Caxton Printers, Ltd., 1942.

Hulbert, Archer Butler. *Forty-Niners*. Boston: Little, Brown and Company, 1931.

Kornweibel, Theodore, Jr. *"Investigate Everything": Federal Efforts to Ensure Black Loyalty During World War I*. Bloomington, IN: Indiana University Press, 2002.

Levy, JoAnn. *They Saw the Elephant: Women in the California Gold Rush*. Norman, OK: University of Oklahoma Press, 2013.

Lotchin, Roger W. *San Francisco 1846–1856: From Hamlet to City*. Lincoln, NE and London: University of Nebraska Press, 1974.

MacKell, Jan. *Brothels, Bordellos, and Bad Girls: Prostitution in Colorado 1860–1930*. Albuquerque, NM: University of New Mexico Press, 2003.

*Maxwell's Directory of San Diego City and County for 1887–88*. San Diego: Geo. W. Maxwell, Publisher, 1888.

McDonald, Douglas. *Bodie, Boom Town—Gold Town!: The Last of California's Old Time Mining Camps*. Las Vegas, NV: Nevada Publications, 1988.

Meyers, John. *Trinidad: Looking Back From My Front Porch*. Trinidad, CA: self-published, 2016.

Monahan, Sherry. *California Madams*. Helena, MT: Farcountry Press, 2019.

Moseley, Ann, Murphy, John J., and Thacker, Robert, editors. *Cather Studies, Volume 11: Willa Cather at the Modernist Crux*. Lincoln, NE: University of Nebraska Press, 2017.

Moynahan, Jay. *Photographs of the Red Light Ladies 1865–1920*. Spokane, WA: Chickadee Publishing, 2005.

Moynahan, Jay. *The Prairie Pioneer Prostitutes' Own Cookbook*. Spokane, WA: Chickadee Publishing, 2000.

Moynahan, Jay. *Red Light Revelations: A Glance into Sacramento's Bawdy Past of 1885*. Spokane, WA: Chickadee Publishing, 2001.

Moynahan, Jay. *Remedies from the Red Lights: Cures, Treatments and Medicines from the Sportin' Ladies of the Frontier West*. Spokane, WA: Chickadee Publishing, 2000.

Nash, Jay R. *Encyclopedia of Western Lawmen and Outlaws*. New York: Paragon House, 1992.

O'Meara, Walter. *Daughters of the Country: The Women of the Fur Traders and Mountain Men*. New York: Harcourt, Brace & World, Inc., 1968.

Paul, Rodman W. *The California Gold Discovery: Sources, Documents, Accounts, and Memoirs Relating to the Discovery of Gold at Sutter's Mill*. Georgetown, CA: The Talisman Press, 1966.

Pfaelzer, Jean. *Driven Out: The Forgotten War Against Chinese Americans*. Manhattan, NY: Random House Publishing Group, 2007.

Pryor, Alton. *Classic Tales in California History*. Roseville, CA: Stagecoach Publishing, 1999.

Quinn, Arthur. *The Rivals: William Gwin, David Broderick, and the Birth of California*. Lincoln, NE: University of Nebraska Press, 1997.

Roberts, Florence. *Fifteen Years with the Outcast*. Anderson, IN: Gospel Trumpet Company, 1912.

Robinson, W. W. *Los Angeles From the Days of the Pueblo: A Brief History and a Guide to the Plaza Area*. San Francisco: California Historical Society, 1981.

Rosen, Ruth. *The Lost Sisterhood: Prostitution in America, 1900–1918*. Baltimore, MD: Johns Hopkins University Press, 1983.

Rutter, Michael. *Upstairs Girls: Prostitution in the American West*. Helena, MT: Farcountry Press, 2005.

Seagraves, Anne. *Soiled Doves: Prostitution in the Old West*. Hayden, ID: Wesanne Publications, 1994.

Severson, Thor. *Sacramento: An Illustrated History: 1839 to 1874.* San Francisco, California Historical Society, 1973.

Shirley, Dame. *The Shirley Letters from California Mines in 1851–52: Being a Series of Twenty-three Letters from Dame Shirley (Mrs. Louise Amelia Knapp Smith Clappe) to Her Sister in Massachusetts and Now Reprinted from the Pioneer Magazine of 1854–55, with Synopses of the Letters, a Foreword, and Many Typographical and Other Corrections and Emendations by Thomas C. Russell; Together with "An Appreciation" by Mrs. M. V. T. Lawrence.* San Francisco: T. C. Russell, 1922.

Soule, Frank, Gihon, John H., and Nisbet, Jim. *The Annals of San Francisco: Containing a Summary of the History of California, and a Complete History of Its Great City: to which are Added, Biographical Memoirs of Some Prominent Citizens.* Cambridge, MA: Harvard University, 1855.

Sparks, Edith. *Capital Intentions: Female Proprietors in San Francisco, 1850–1920.* Chapel Hill, NC: University of North Carolina Press, 2011.

Sprague, Marguerite. *Bodie's Gold: Tall Tales and True History from a California Mining Town.* Reno, NV: University of Nevada Press, 2005.

Stanford, Sally. *The Lady of the House: California's Most Notorious Madam.* New York: Ballantine Books, 1972.

Wedertz, Frank S. *Bodie 1859–1900.* Bishop, CA: Chalfant Press, 1969.

Wiles, Gary, and Brown, Delores. *Femme Fatales, Gamblers, Yankees and Rebels in the Gold Fields [1859–1869].* Hemet, CA: Birth of America Books, 2005.

William, Gregory Paul. *The Story of Hollywood: An Illustrated History.* Los Angeles: BL Press LLC, 2005.

Williams, George III. *Rosa May: The Search for a Mining Camp Legend.* Riverside, CA: Tree by the River Publishing, 1982.

Wolsey, Serge G. *Call House Madam: The Story of the Career of Madam Beverly Davis as Told to Serge G. Wolsey*. New York: Paperback Library, 1963.

Zauner, Phyllis. *Those Spirited Women of the Early West*. Sonoma, CA: Zanel Publications, 1989.

## DOCUMENTS

Kooistra, AnneMarie. "Angels for Sale: The History of Prostitution in Los Angeles, 1880–1940," Dissertation Presented to the Faculty of the Graduate School, University of Southern California, August, 2003.

Nettles, Wendy M. "Neophytes, Shopkeepers and the Soiled Doves of San Louis Obispo," "The Copelands Project," prepared by Applied Earthworks, Inc., Fresno, CA, October 2006.

Ventura County, California Marriage Records.

Western State Marriage Index, Brigham Young University, Special Collections and Family History.

## INTERNET

Ancestry.com
   *California, County Birth, Marriage and Death Records, 1849–1880*
   *California Death Index, 1905–1939*
   *California Death Index, 1940–1997*
   *California, Marriage Index, 1960–1985*
   *California, Mortuary and Cemetery Records, 1801–1932*
   *California, Prison and Correctional Records, 1851–1950*
   *California, San Francisco Area Funeral Home Records, 1895–1985*
   *California, Select Marriages, 1850–1945*
   *California, Voter Registers, 1866–1898*
   *California, Wills and Probate Records, 1850–1953*
   *Historical Newspapers, Birth, Marriage, & Death Announcements, 1851–2003*
   *Philadelphia, Pennsylvania, Marriage Index, 1885–1951*

*US and Canada, Passenger and Immigration Lists Index,
1500s–1900s*
*US City Directories, 1822–1995*
*US Federal Census Mortality Schedules, 1850–1885*
*US Naturalization Record Indexes, 1791–1992*
*US Passport Applications, 1795–1925*
*US, World War I Draft Registration Cards, 1917–1918*

"An interview with Gerald F. 'Jerry' MacMullen, 1897–1981,
    September 5, 1971," San Diego History Center, Oral History
    Program, https://library.ucsd.edu/dc/object/bb74756107
    /_1_1.pdf.
"Annie May Wyant—'Diamond Jessie Hayman,'" July 2, 2016,
    Westward Ho, Ladies! http://womenwentwent.blogspot.com
    /2016/07/annie-may-wyant-diamond-jessie-hayman.html.
Banks, Leo. "Prescott prostitute found sorted [sic] life made fodder
    for film." *Prescott Daily Courier*, January 13, 2002, Sharlot Hall
    Museum Library and Archives, sharlot.org.
Baumler, Ellen. "Madam Mustache," Montana Moments, January 28,
    2013, http://ellenbaumler.blogspot.com/2013/01/madame
    -mustache.html.
Beebe, Lucius. "Panamint: Suburb of Hell," *American Heritage*
    magazine, December 1954, https://www.americanheritage.com
    /panamint-suburb-hell.
"Bodie's Dead: Rosa May," The Great Silence, December 14, 2010,
    http://the-great-silence.blogspot.com/2010/12/bodies-dead-rosa
    -may.html.
Bonagura, Marc. "The Tiger is Dead: Sally Stanford's Obituary"
    http://www.thetigerisdead.com/sallystanford.html.
"California Nuisance Abatement, Proposition 4 (1914)," Ballotpedia,
    https://ballotpedia.org/California_Nuisance_Abatement,
    _Proposition_4_(1914).

*California Statutes 1913*, Chapter 17, 20, https://clerk.assembly
.ca.gov/sites/clerk.assembly.ca.gov/files/archive/Statutes/1913
/1913.pdf#page=59.

"Cerro Gordo," Digital Desert: Mojave Desert, http://mojavedesert
.net/cerro-gordo/.

Chatwell, Nada. "Are You of This World?," Dana Point Historical
Society, October 31, 2012, http://www.danapointhistorical.org
/are-you-of-this-world/.

"City of Ferndale," https://ci.ferndale.ca.us/.

Crafts, Daniel Steven. "Barbary Coast," Found San Francisco, www
.foundsf.org/index.php?title=BARBARY_COAST.

"Culinary Historian Shares History of Beer and Baseball in Los
Angeles," Food GPS, https://foodgps.com/culinary-historian
-shares-history-of-beer-and-baseball-in-los-angeles/.

"Dance Halls and Other Establishments of Ill Repute," Rand Desert
Museum, http://randdesertmuseum.com/site/?p=8218.

"Downieville, California," Back Country Explorers, https://www
.backcountryexplorers.com/downieville-california.html.

Drexler, Paul. "'Bloody Babs' and the robbery gone wrong," *San
Francisco Examiner*, August 27, 2017, https://www.sfexaminer
.com/news/bloody-babs-and-the-robbery-gone-wrong/.

"Early History of the San Francisco Fire Department," The Virtual
Museum of the City of San Francisco, http://www.sfmuseum.net
/hist1/fire.html.

"Field Trips by Ellin Beltz," http://ebeltz.net/fieldtrips/mainstreetwalk
.html, accessed October 20, 2019.

Findagrave.com

Forty-Third Congressional Session, March 3, 1875, University of
Washington Bothell and Cascadia College, http://library.uwb.edu
/Static/USimmigration/18%20stat%20477.pdf.

Graham, J. H. "8588 Sunset Blvd," https://jhgraham.com/2016/06/16
/8588-sunset-blvd/.

"The Great 1906 San Francisco Earthquake," USGS, https:// earthquake.usgs.gov/earthquakes/events/1906calif/18april/.

"Historical Timeline of Los Angeles," Discover Los Angeles, https:// www.discoverlosangeles.com/things-to-do/historical-timeline-of -los-angeles.

"History of Hollywood, California," United States History, https://u-s -history.com/pages/h3871.html.

"History of LA Madams," Naughty Los Angeles, https://naughtylos angeles.com/user/naughtyarticles.php?pkid=23&#.Xk78hShKhdg.

"Hollywood," Encyclopaedia Britannica, https://www.britannica.com /place/Hollywood-California.

Los Angeles Theatres, https://losangelestheatres.blogspot.com/2019 /03/cineograph.html.

"The Love Story of Lottie Johl," Colorful Ladies of the Old West— Stories, fold3, https://www.fold3.com/page/2711-colorful-ladies -of-the-old-west/stories.

MacPhail, Elizabeth C. "Shady Ladies in the 'Stingaree District,' When the Red Lights Went Out in San Diego: The Little Known Story of San Diego's 'Restricted' District," The Journal of San Diego History, Spring 1974, Volume 20, Number 2, San Diego History Center, https://sandiegohistory.org/journal/1974/april/stingaree/.

McLean, Tessa. "Former madam's waterfront 'Valhalla' compound for sale in Sausalito for $11.8M", SFGATE, February 12, 2020, https://www.sfgate.com/sf-neighborhoods/article/waterfront -Valhalla-Estate-for-sale-sausalito-15047572.php.

Meares, Hadley. "Hell's Half Acre: In the old red light district of Los Angeles, women worked in squalor while pimps and landlords grew rich," Curbed Los Angeles, Nov 17, 2017, https://la.curbed .com/2017/11/17/16654292/history-prostitution-los-angeles.

Miller, Wayne F. "An Eye on the World: Reviewing a Lifetime in Photography," an oral history conducted in 2001, by Suzanne B. Riess, Regional Oral History Office, The Bancroft Library,

University of California, Berkeley, 2003, https://digitalassets.lib
.berkeley.edu/roho/ucb/text/MillerBook.pdf.

Murphy, Annie. "Ann Forrester: Seduction, Corruption, Deception and
Protection—The Black Widow and the Vice Queen (Part 1)," Photo
Friends, Los Angeles Public Library, November 28, 2017, http://
photofriends.org/tag/ann-forrester/.

"Old Sacramento Waterfront," https://www.oldsacramento.com
/history.

Peterson, Art. "Sally Stanford," Found San Francisco, http://www
.foundsf.org/index.php?title=Sally_Stanford.

Petrosova, Natasha. "Randsburg Mining District: Part II: Red
Mountain-The Sin City," August 25, 2016, Forgotten Destinations,
http://forgotten-destinations.blogspot.com/2016/08/randsburg
-mining-district-part-ii-red.html.

Ponder, Jon. "Hacienda Park and the Origins of the Sunset Strip:
Coronet Apartments, Villa of Vice?" wehoville.com, April 8, 2019,
https://www.wehoville.com/2019/04/08/hacienda-park-and-the
-origins-of-the-sunset-strip-coronet-apartments-villa-of-vice/.

"Quake Rattles Northern California," *Washington Post*, April 26, 1992,
https://www.washingtonpost.com/archive/politics/1992/04/26
/quake-rattles-northern-california/4b55d9f4-6446-4530-bd3f
-1f26166184b2/.

Rasmussen, Cecilia. "History of Hollywood Madams Is Long, Lurid,"
*Los Angeles Times*, November 30, 1997, https://www.latimes.com
/archives/la-xpm-1997-nov-30-me-59191-story.html.

"Rosa May Oalaque," Bodie, California, https://www.bodie.com
/history/cemetery/78-rosa-may-oalaque/.

"San Diego House," Old Town San Diego Guide, http://www.old
townsandiegoguide.com/history.html.

"San Francisco Earthquake, 1906," The Center of Legislative Archives,
National Archives, https://www.archives.gov/legislative/features/sf.

"The San Francisco Madam: An Adventure Story Starring Mayor Sally
Stanford," Sausalito.com, http://www.sausalito.com/story/The

-San-Francisco-Madam-An-Adventure-Story-Starring-Mayor-Sally
-Stanford/588743.

San Francisco Theater Scrapbook, Online Archive of California.
https://oac.cdlib.org/findaid/ark:/13030/c8zg6zfq/.

Sharpless, Megan. "Unity in Numbers: The Archaeology of the
Demimonde (1840–1917)," A Senior Thesis Submitted for
University of Wisconsin at LaCrosse, May 2008.

Sternberg, Thomas H., M.D., Ernest B. Howard, M.D., Leonard A.
Dewey, M.D., and Paul Padget, M.D., "Venereal Diseases." Office of
Medical History, US Army Medical Department, http://history
.amedd.army.mil/booksdocs/wwii/communicablediseasesV5
/chapter10.htm.

"The Story of Belle Cora," thebellecora.com.

University of California, Hastings College of the Law UC Hastings
Scholarship Repository, "1914 Voter Information Guide for 1914,
General Election," https://repository.uchastings.edu/cgi
/viewcontent.cgi?referer=&httpsredir=1&article=1081&context
=ca_ballot_props.

Vargo, Cecile Page. "Enterprising Women of the Western Mojave
Mining Camps: First Came the 'Ladies,'" Explore California
History, magazine for enthusiasts, February, 2004, http://explore
historicalif.com/ehc_legacy/feb2004.html.

"What is the Mann Act?" FindLaw, https://criminal.findlaw.com
/criminal-charges/what-is-the-mann-act.html.

"Who were her husbands?" Sally Stanford, Madam Mayor, http://
sallystanford.com/sally-faqs/husbands/

Wikipedia.org

## INTERVIEWS

Eleanor Smith, San Diego, circa 1970s.

Irene Smith, Pasadena, circa 1970s.

Ferndale Museum docents, Ferndale, California, interview by author,
February 5, 2017.

## MAPS

1886 Sanborn Fire Insurance Map from San Luis Obispo, San Luis Obispo County, California. Sanborn Map Company, https://www.loc.gov/item/sanborn00822_001/.

1887 Sanborn Fire Insurance Map from San Diego, San Diego County, California. Sanborn Map Company, March 1887.

1895 Sanborn Fire Insurance Map from Sacramento, Sacramento County, California. Sanborn Map Company, 1895.

## PERIODICALS

*The Journal of San Diego History*

Newspapers:

**Arizona**

| | |
|---|---|
| *Clifton Copper Era* | *Phoenix New Times* |
| *Morenci Copper Era* | *Prescott Journal-Miner* |

**California**

| | |
|---|---|
| *Bakersfield Californian* | *Long Beach Independent* |
| *Bodie Morning News* | *Los Angeles Chronical* |
| *Bodie Standard* | *Los Angeles Herald* |
| *Bodie Weekly Standard* | *Madera Tribune* |
| *Bridgeport Chronicle-Union* | *Marysville Daily Appeal* |
| *Calaveras Enterprise* | *Oakland Tribune* |
| *California Police Gazette* | *Sacramento Daily Bee* |
| *Coronado Mercury* | *Sacramento Daily Record* |
| *Daily Alta California* | *Sacramento Daily Union* |
| *Daily Bodie Standard* | *Sacramento Transcript* |
| *Grass Valley Daily Union* | *Sacramento Union* |
| *Hayward Daily Review* | *San Bernardino Sun* |
| *Inyo Independent* | *San Bernardino Weekly Sun* |
| *Lompoc Journal* | *San Diego Sun* |

*San Diego Union*
*San Francisco Bulletin*
*San Francisco Call*
*San Francisco Chronicle*
*San Francisco Examiner*
*San Francisco Marina Times*
*San Luis Obispo Daily Telegram*
*San Luis Obispo Morning Press*
*San Luis Obispo Morning Telegram*
*San Luis Obispo Morning Tribune*
*San Luis Obispo Semi-Weekly Breeze*

*San Luis Obispo Tribune*
*San Luis Obispo Weekly Press*
*San Pedro News Pilot*
*Santa Barbara Morning Press*
*Santa Barbara Weekly Press*
*Santa Cruz Evening News*
*Santa Cruz Sentinel*
*Senora Union Democrat*
*Shasta Courier*
*Stockton Independent*
*Van Nuys Valley News*
*Weekly Bodie Standard*

**Colorado**
*Greeley Daily Tribune*

**Montana**
*Butte Daily Miner*

*Butte Weekly Miner*

**Nevada**
*Gold Hill Daily News*

*Tonopah Daily Bonanza*

**New York**
*National Police Gazette*

**Oregon**
*Portland Oregon Journal*

**Utah**
*Truth, the Western Weekly (Salt Lake City)*

# INDEX

Italicized page numbers indicate photographs.

*Pilgrim* (ship), x

pimps

  arrests of, 91–92

  assaults on prostitutes, 181

  crib, 175, 177, 178

  expectations of, 174

  masquerading as boyfriends, 164

  pantaloon promenades, 90

  theft of prostitutes by, 90

Pinkham, W., 47

Placerville, 3–4, *4*

Plumas National Forest, 8

pneumonia epidemics, 43

poetry, 4, 37, 118

poisoning, 28, 82

poker, 58

Policeman's Ball, 151

politicians

  brothel ownership of, 109, 163

  corruption, 112, 175

  crib profits to, 112

  as customers, 123, 200

  ex-madams as, 170

  madam relations with, 102, 201, 202

  as madams' husbands, 186, 189–90, 190–91, 192

  protection payments to, 75, 199

Pomeroy, Grace, 193

Ponder, Jon, 197–98

Porter, Jean, 162–63

Portola, Gaspar de, 171

Poulton, J. P. C., 118–19

Powellson, James, *88*, 90

Powelson, Frank, 193

Powers, Ella, 180–82

Powers, Josie, 89

pregnancies, 162, 197

Presti, Ernest, 182

Preyssing, Bertha, 62

Preyssing, Henry, 62

Prohibition, 32, 44, 84, 153, 161, 162

promenades, 102

Prostitutes Ball, 105

prostitution, overview

  benefits of, xi, 105

  California history of, ix–xviii

  census occupation statistics on, xvi

  perceptions of, x, 15, 103

prostitution rings, 201–2

protection payoffs, 75, 199, 203

Purity League (Vice Suppression Committee), 67, 68, 69, 70

Puterbaugh, George, 70

Quartzburg, 6

raids

  advanced warnings of, 17, 79, 198

  anti-prostitution investigations and, 97–98

  on brothels, 17, 21, 52, 62, 96, 111, 166–67, 200

  Chinese child prostitutes rescued during, 125

  city corruption and forbidden, 112

  customer arrests during, 190

  escapes during, 79

  of Los Angeles cribs, 178

  police transfers due to, 144–45

mining camps advertising for, 3
respectable, xiii–xiv, 15–16, 103,
  105–6
saloon patronage bans, 29
scarcity of, xi, 2, 3
Wood, L. K., 46
Wood, Maud, 92
Woods, Ann, 47
Wood's Opera House,
  172
Wyant, Annie May (*aka* Jessie
  Hayman), 112–17, *114*,
  149
Wynne (judge), 15, 16

Xin Jin, 129

Yankedos, 99
Yankee Doodle Hall, 64
Yan-Wo, 119
Yates, Ella, 162
Yaw, Ellen Beach, 184
Yee Ah Tye, 133
Ye Olde Whore Shop, 111
Yorba, Miguel, 58–59
Young, Billy, 87–88
Young, Earl, 194

Zelleken, Virna, 78

# ABOUT THE AUTHOR

**Jan MacKell Collins** has been a published author, speaker, and presenter since 2003. Her focus has always been on Western history, with an emphasis on historical prostitution. Collins has published numerous articles on her subjects in such magazines as *True West*, *Montana Magazine*, *All About History*, and numerous regional periodicals. In 2016, she appeared on the television show *Adam Ruins Everything* as an "expert" in historical prostitution. Collins currently resides in Oregon, where she continues researching the history of prostitution.